Martin Brundle Scrapbook

Martin Brundle & Philip Porter

Design by Andrew Garman

Porter Press International

First published in July 2013

ISBN 978-1-907085-12-3
ISBN 978-1-907085-13-0 (de Luxe edition)

Published by
Porter Press International Ltd.

PO Box 2, Tenbury Wells,
WR15 8XX, UK.
Tel: +44 (0)1584 781588
Fax: +44 (0)1584 781630
sales@porterpress.co.uk
www.porterpress.co.uk

Designed by Grafx Resource
Printed by Butler, Tanner & Dennis

COPYRIGHT

Acknowledgements

We have had a lot of assistance and we have had some exceptional help. Books such as this are very much team work and we would like to thank a number of individuals and organisations for their tremendous support.

On the photographic side, I would like to thank all those named. We have tried hard to trace all the photographers but in some cases it has proved impossible. I would like to single out several names for special mention. For the behind-the-scenes shots of the television years, we are most grateful to Andrew Parr. Martine Walkinshaw very kindly unearthed shots involving her late husband, Tom, of TWR fame. Chris Rigg was able to kindly supply a great deal of material covering Martin's early years. Graham Brown went to great lengths to find Hot Rod photos. Derick Allsop was very helpful indeed with cuttings from his period of working together with Martin. At the Jaguar Heritage Trust, I would like to thank Mike O'Driscoll, Tony Duckhouse and Karam Ram.

Sutton Motorsport Images, in the person of Keith Sutton and his colleagues, have given us absolutely incredible support. We greatly appreciate their involvement and their stunning images enhance the book considerably.

We have a trio of distinguished painters in Alan Fearnley, Michael Turner and Graham Turner, who have kindly given permission for their wonderful work to be reproduced.

The Brundle family have all pulled together, as clearly they always have. Sincere thanks go to Alma, Robin, Helen, Charlie and Alex, and especially Liz.

I would like to thank all our interviewees, otherwise known as 'victims'. All have been most generous with their time and recollections. Our thanks go to the publishers of the various publications featured for permission to reproduce the cuttings and images, again acknowledged where possible.

In our office, our little team has been tremendous, as ever. My thanks to Hayley Zamur, Louise Gibbs, Annelise Airey and Sarah King, and our trainees Phil Powell and Suzy Burns. Special thanks go to Abigail Humphries for much help behind the scenes and for photographing half of Martin's possessions!

My wife, Julie, has been as supportive as ever. Mark Holman, in New Zealand, has kindly read and checked the proofs, and played a key role, once again.

Above all, enormous credit for creating this book should go to designer, Andy Garman. Luckily, Andy is an F1 enthusiast. Designing these books is a highly skilled task and Andy has not only done a great job, he has had the patience to hone and hone as we have found better photos or wanted to change this or tweak that in our aim for perfection. Massive thanks go to Andy.

Philip Porter

Introduction

Having interviewed Martin at length for the *Murray Walker Scrapbook* in 2008, I bumped into him somewhere in 2009 and asked him how he would feel about a *Martin Brundle Scrapbook*. He responded, "I am not sure I am old enough yet for a Scrapbook." The next few times our paths crossed in the intervening period, I would say to him, "Are you feeling old enough yet?" and he would reply, "I knew that question was coming." Finally, I wore him down!

I have fond memories of the first time we met, back at the first Goodwood Revival, in 1998. I was dressed in period clothing. Martin was about to go out in the Coombs D-type. I introduced myself. "Sorry," said Martin, "I didn't recognise you. It must be the silly hat!" "Likewise," I said, pointing at his helmet. "That's why I have my name on mine," he fired straight back. A splendid example of the Brundle wit.

As with all the books in our 'Original Scrapbook' series, this one has been very hard work for all concerned but extremely rewarding.

Martin has been an absolute pleasure to work with. Everyone says that, whatever he has tackled in life, he has always given it 100% and done it in a totally professional manner. This book has been no exception. We have pushed, under pressure as always, to go the extra mile, and then another mile, to do the very best job we possibly can.

Martin has thrown himself into this project with total commitment and enthusiasm. In spite of a hellishly full schedule, he has made the necessary time and helped to drive the book forward. Remarkably, he has always responded swiftly and turned everything round almost instantly. And we have had some fun. Refreshingly, Martin does not take himself too seriously. There is plenty of humour in the book and we have laughed a good deal while working hard together.

People may think that this concept of book is easy to create and really they are just thrown together. Nothing could be further from the truth. They are far more complex than a traditional book – lengthy interviewing with Martin and around 50 *victims*, transcribing, choosing the relevant nuggets, sorting logically and chronologically, sourcing images to supplement Martin's own archives, copying 1500 illustrations, selecting a final collection, obtaining permissions, captioning and so on, and presenting all this in a balanced and readable style. As ever, it has been a challenge, but an extremely enjoyable one.

I am most grateful to Martin for agreeing to this book and then putting in so much time and effort. I hope very much you will enjoy this remarkable story, a story of dedication, hard work, family support, overcoming adversity, strength of character, building partnerships, loyalty, great humour, modesty and tremendous ability.

Philip Porter

I've very much enjoyed helping create this book, and it has served to remind me just how fortunate I have been in my life. It's also forced us to search out our archives for pictures, cuttings and memorabilia, and I will treasure the end result in this convenient yet very comprehensive book. My memory has been jogged on many great moments too.

Racing teams and TV crews are very similar in many ways. They are a hard working and very focussed and professional group of individuals, constantly travelling the world facing tight deadlines. They include extremely creative designers, along with engineers and mechanics, or producers, editors, cameramen and sound crew. In turn, they are supported by highly efficient logistics, data and IT teams. All are guided confidently by team principals and executive producers.

Out front getting most of the acclaim are the drivers and presenters, and so this is a great opportunity for me to thank each and every team member I have had the pleasure of working with in the past 40 years.

Motorsport is notoriously expensive and I've been fortunate to have so many sponsors and financial backers without whom the racing would have faded away very quickly, meaning my TV career would never have happened.

My hard working mother and father sacrificed much for my racing career and I'm relieved that I have been able to justify their support. And at every turn my sister Helen and brother Robin have been among my most fervent supporters, never once jealous or bitter at my opportunities and good fortune.

My wife Liz has tolerated much stress and pressure through the years, at many points single-handedly bringing up our two amazing children, Charlie and Alex, while I was absent racing or making TV. At least this book confirms that I was quite busy, although that's a poor excuse.

I must also thank Philip Porter and his Porter Press team, along with Andy Garman, for the vast amount of creative and diligent hard work required to assemble so many words and images, and to speak with so many people.

I'm humbled and a little embarrassed by the very kind words which friends and colleagues have said about me in this book. I very much appreciate their sentiments but, rest assured, I'm not as nice, or as accomplished, as they would have you believe.

Martin Brundle

Cast List

James Allen – motor racing journalist and commentator

Derick Allsop – journalist, author and former motor racing correspondent of *The Daily Mail* and *The Independent*

Rubens Barrichello – former F1 driver, 326 GPs

Herbie Blash – formerly with Lotus and Brabham, FIA Observer and close colleague of Bernie Ecclestone

Mark Blundell – former F1, sportscars and CART driver, Le Mans winner, pundit with ITV, co-founder of 2MB

Ross Brawn – former TWR designer, Benetton, Ferrari and Honda F1 technical supremo, Brawn and Mercedes-Benz team principal, multiple World Constructors' Championships

Alex Brundle – son, born in 1990, racing driver

Alma Brundle – mother, married to John, partner in garage business

Charlie Brundle – daughter, born in 1988, works in motor industry as designer at Jaguar

Elizabeth (Liz) Brundle – wife, married to Martin in 1981, director of MB businesses

Robin Brundle – younger brother, former driver and business partner in garage, former MD of Aston Martin Racing and Lola Cars

Jenson Button – F1 driver, 2009 World Champion with Brawn

Arthur Coleman – garage mechanic who assisted with racing in early days

John Coombs – owner of Coombs of Guildford who entered saloons and E-types on behalf of Jaguar

David Coulthard – former F1 driver, managed by MB, co-commentator for BBC F1

David Croft – motor racing commentator

Helen Dickson – older sister, like father an entrepreneur, has thriving wedding dress business

Tony Dowe – set up TWR Inc. in 1987 which won 16 IMSA GTP races

Neil Duncanson – CEO of North One, producers of F1 coverage for ITV

Louise Goodman – journalist and former F1 PR, later ITV F1 pit lane reporter and presenter

Mike Greasley – former manager and journalist at *Motoring News*

Maurice Hamilton – motor racing correspondent for *The Observer* 1990-2010, author, F1 commentator

Johnny Herbert – F1 driver, Le Mans winner, pundit with Sky F1

Jools Holland – composer, pianist, bandleader, broadcaster and car enthusiast

Eddie Jordan – founded Eddie Jordan Racing in 1979, formed Jordan GP in 1991, analyst for BBC F1

Lord March – mastermind of the brilliant Goodwood Festival and Revival events

Alastair Macqueen – race engineer who worked with MB at Eddie Jordan Racing, TWR and Bentley

Sir Stirling Moss – arguably the greatest all-round racing driver of all time

Adrian Newey – arguably the greatest F1 designer, having won World Constructors' Championships with three teams

Jonathan Palmer – former F1 driver, CEO of MotorSport Vision

Win Percy – three-time British Touring Car Champion, long-term TWR driver

Dave Price – founded David Price Racing in 1976

Dave Redding – F1 engineer, MB's number one mechanic at Benetton, McLaren Team Manager since 2009

Chris Rigg – early sponsor and keen supporter

Nigel Roebuck – GP reporter for *Autosport* from 1977, *Motor Sport* Editor-in-Chief from 2007, one of the world's leading F1 journalists

Ayrton Senna – World Champion in 1988, 1990 and 1991, one the greatest of all time

Roger Silman – joined TWR to run sportscar racing programme, later Director of Operations for TWR

Sir Jackie Stewart – World Champion in 1969, 1971 and 1973, former President of the BRDC

Keith Sutton – top F1 photographer and founder of Sutton Motorsport Images, the leading F1 photographic agency

David Tremayne – long-term leading F1 journalist, motor racing author, winner of the Guild of Motoring Writers Journalist of the Year 1990, 2001 and 2004

Martin Turner – Sky Sports F1 Executive Producer

Martine Walkinshaw – widow of Tom Walkinshaw and Brundle family friend

Murray Walker – legendary motor racing commentator

Derek Warwick – former F1 driver, World Sports Car Champion, President of the BRDC

Mark Webber – F1 driver with Minardi, Jaguar, Williams and Red Bull

Barrie Williams – very long term, incredibly versatile and successful racer

Martin Whitmarsh – McLaren team principal, CEO of McLaren Group

Early Days
1959-1976

Martin Brundle was born on June 1, 1959. His parents, John and Alma, lived in the King's Lynn area of Norfolk. Martin's grandfather was a farmer and initially John had a smallholding in the Terrington Marshes, where Martin first lived. However, John had a love of anything mechanical and soon set up a small workshop at Terrington and gradually became involved in the motor trade. Martin has a sister, Helen, who is 18 months older, and a brother, Robin, who arrived three-and-a-half years after Martin.

By the early '60s, John Brundle had a garage in West Lynn and the family lived in a house alongside the premises. Father was a natural salesman and, with Alma looking after the office functions, they built a thriving and growing business. John dabbled in trials, rallies and autocross events, involving his family most weekends. Young Martin also had an affinity for devices with wheels and, if not at school, was usually to be found in the garage workshops. Here he learnt a great deal on the practical side and started driving, on private ground, at a very early age. A sharp young lad, he first sold a car at the age of eight!

Proving bright at junior school, he went to the local Grammar School where he would gain passes in 12 'O' level exams. Meanwhile, at 13 he had started grass-track racing with, initially, a Ford Anglia. With a good grounding in car control and competitive events, and plenty of successes against the adults, he graduated to Hot Rod racing at the age of 15. Once again car control was paramount and it was all good experience. At 16, he won the Grand Final against some of the biggest names in that world.

Martin Brundle

Tank Rider

"I was born in '59 and my very first ever experience of being on a motorbike was when I was about four, sitting on the tank of my dad's motorbike as he went into work. He was a smallholder but he had a passion: he spent more time fixing everybody else's tractors and implements than he did farming his own few acres.

"My dad used to feed the family, as you could back then, with fruit and so on, with just six acres. Incredible. He was a great, and very popular, man."

"My dad spoke fondly of his National Service days and, like me, loved anything with an engine."

Alma Brundle

Baptism

"He was about a year old when we took him to some kart racing. He had to come with us because John and I used to go racing at the airbase at Lakenheath. So most Sundays we used to go over there to race the kart. He was in a carrycot and we had a big old yellow J2 van and I took a little gas heater, and when we parked up for the day I would put this heater on to feed him and keep him warm."

Alma Brundle

Reluctant Farmer

"John's dad used to come round and look after the smallholding because John was always doing up somebody's car or tractor. He wasn't interested in agriculture. John's father was a farmer. It took him all his time to drive his car straight!"

"They still can't get my hands off the steering wheel today."

"I remember this being taken! Bizarrely, the photographer had a pet monkey on his shoulder which we are looking at."

Martin Brundle

First Accident

"We were at Butlin's on the bumper cars, and I was about four and I can still see the operator saying, 'You're going to hit the side,' every time I went round. 'You're going to hit the side, you're going to hit the side.' And sure enough, I hit the side. And the nut holding on the steering wheel had no protection and I suffered a nasty cut just above my eye. So I'd taken a chunk out of my head and that was my first ever drive."

Alma Brundle

An Early Casualty

"So we sat at the hospital most of that day. He had to have stitches and it took both Dad and me to hold him down while it was done. That was the first day of our holiday!"

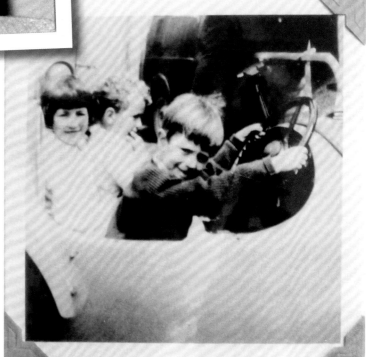

Martin Brundle

First Grand Prix

"I remember being woken up about 4am one morning when I was five or six. They said, 'You've got to get up. Your Uncle Keith's going to take you to the Grand Prix.' Brands Hatch was the first one, which meant a long run through Chelmsford, the Blackwall Tunnel; it was a bit of an epic journey.

"We went several times and I remember you could walk around the paddock. I remember standing in a polite queue at Jack Brabham's Zephyr, waiting for an autograph. And standing on the pit straight with Acker Bilk playing some jazz because literally everybody just went on the track afterwards and there was music and fun, mostly because it was probably going to take five hours to get out of the place. My Uncle Keith went to see Jim Clark win, those were his words, but there was Clark, Stewart and Hill."

"There were always cars in our lives from the very beginning."

"I don't think Mum and Dad enjoyed that soup!"

Martin Brundle

All Part Of The Service

"In those days a service on a car took pretty much all day and then you'd road test it at the end of the day. So one of our mechanics, Stan Rolfe, would let me sit on his lap, steering, and he would do the pedals. I was about four or five years old. So that would be my first on-road driving experience. You'd get locked up now. Can you imagine now a mechanic letting a five-year-old drive down a road? And in customers' cars! But it seemed fine at the time.

"And there was this road that went round the marsh - Terrington Marsh - fantastic road if it snowed. Dad and I used to go that way in his rally car to come home for lunch. It was nowhere near the right direction but we'd do a lap round the marsh in the snow because it was just incredible fun!"

A Bouncing Boy

"Every waking moment, we were subjected to something to do with racing because my father was a rally driver and did trials. He used to take the whole family. Robin would be a baby so he wasn't involved. It wouldn't be allowed to happen these days but Martin and I used to have to sit in the back of this Hillman Imp as Dad was trying to get the car up the side of the hill. My father would be saying, 'Jump up and down – we've got to try and keep the wheels on the ground.' We'd only be six or seven.

"We used to go every weekend to some form of motorsport – whether it would be rallies, autocross or trials. My poor mother: she was subjected to it as well. I used to go along – we didn't have any choice at that time. That's how Martin got interested in the racing at such an early age."

Robin Brundle

Your Daredevil

"When we were very young, we played together with all sorts of model cars and Scalextric - mostly cars, trucks, trains and Scalextric rather than anything else. We used to play together well at that. When we were very small, our parents had a garage at West Lynn. We were made a little wooden go-kart that we used to push one another in, up and down a big concrete slope at the garage, and we had great fun with that. One time we were trying to go further, higher, faster, as you always do with anything with wheels. It only had a wooden block [as a brake] on one wheel. Martin had his first stunt activity on this little go-kart! We got almost to the top of the concrete slope and I slipped. As the kart went backwards, he decided to pull on the handbrake which locked the one rear wheel. The whole thing literally went vertical in the air, pivoted on the one locked wheel and then crashed down again. Of course, we thought that was absolutely hilarious at the time. That is my first recollection of a daredevil moment."

"The scar above my left eye was witness to my incident on the bumper cars."

Robin Brundle

Model Mechanic

"Marty would always have a screwdriver in his hand and take the Scalextric cars apart and put them back together. Amazingly, they would always go back together and work perfectly. That was probably our first true bit of competition too, as back in those days with Scalextric, or a similar set-up, they had a certain type of track that enabled you to run two cars on the same lane, before digital. And we had a stock car set that had a little button on the back so if you caught your opponent up, and touched their exhaust it would spring them off the track!"

Alma Brundle

An Enquiring Mind

"We paid all this money for a Scalextric for him. I think he must have been six, because I said to John, 'Are you sure it's for him and not you?' It was Christmas morning and I thought, 'It's all quiet upstairs'. I went up and he'd taken every little car to pieces. They were all in little bits. You can imagine I was quite cross because it was not a cheap thing to buy. So I said, 'You just sit there until you put that all back together again'. And he did. He was very clever, even in those days with cars.

"He had them taken apart because he wanted to know how they worked. With everything, it was the same. He's always wanted to know how things worked."

Martin Brundle

Business Roots

"Dad started with a little place at Terrington, literally fixing motorbikes, then moved to West Lynn where he was selling cars. That's probably where he did best. We used to live alongside the garage, and he had a tuning business there as well because he used to rally. And then he moved to a big site over at Tottenhill, about five or six miles outside town. Probably a big mistake, really, because then he suddenly got overheads, and the business took off."

Alma Brundle

Fledgling Business

"We had a little workshop in Terrington St Clement. And we started off with one motorbike and then it went from there. We sold motorbikes and then this garage wasn't big enough, so we moved up to Fox's Lane in West Lynn and then we sold cars as well. Not many new ones, mostly second-hand. But that was a lovely time for selling cars because you didn't have any VAT to worry about and things like that, so it was much, much easier and people accepted their car on a handshake in those days."

"Maybe this is why I don't like using the train."

Martin Brundle

Robin Has An Off

"Robin and I both had Raleigh Choppers, which actually came from the same Tottenhill site that Dad would eventually own. Mine was a Chopper Mk 1 and Robin's was a Mini Chopper. I remember clearly skidding the back wheel around a lamppost. It took Robin, who was behind me, by surprise and he crashed. He was knocked out and a neighbour carried him home!"

Robin Brundle

Room-To-Room Track

"We had a playroom attached to our bedroom which in modern terms would be the loft space over the garage. We used to build the [Scalextric] track so that it would go from one room to the other. Our sister only got one doll to our 10m of track! But she was great at putting the cars back on the track."

"Motorsport seemed so pure back then."

Alma Brundle

Boys Will Be Boys

"He was happy when he was in the garage helping with everything. He'd come home, and I daren't let him any further than the kitchen and I used to stand him in the kitchen sink and wash him down. When he was about seven or eight, I got so fed-up with him forever coming in the house all grease and oil from head to toe that I had some little overalls made for him. He was always greasy!

"Our daughter's the eldest and we had the garage from just after the boys were born. Both boys were always happy in the garage, with the workmen there, with the cars.

"Helen's the eldest by 18 months, then Martin, and then there's three-and-a-half years to Robin. They got on extremely well and they still do. Best of friends. It's lovely."

Martin Brundle

A Favourite Tune

"Dad loved his rallying and we always had some sporty cars around, especially in the '60s. He always claimed we were East Anglia's leading sports car centre: he had a yard full of E-types and Aston Martins, and that sort of thing. When I went out to play in the back yard, that was the sales lot and just off to the right was the workshop where I would mess around. And we had a tuning company. So I would stand for hours with the guy polishing cylinder heads and just understanding it. I used to come up with a design for an engine or steam engine, or something like that, in my head and draw it out. So I had a mechanical interest that had a motor sport influence and bias immediately because Dad was rallying, doing rallycross, autocross, that sort of thing and in the tuning shop he'd have Mini Coopers left, right and centre that were all being tuned up."

Robin Brundle

First Car

"At West Lynn Marty and I had our first car, a little Austin A30. We had to wait for father or mother or someone from the garage to take us down to a local farmer's field. One of us would sit on the passenger seat and help to do the gears whilst the other was busy in the foot-well because we weren't big enough to do all at the same time. It was teamwork. That was our very first car. It was a very sad day when we lost the car in the winter as the anti-freeze wasn't strong enough and it popped the plugs out of the side of the block. I'm sure it was destined for the scrap heap anyway."

"My Dad would buy and sell absolutely anything."

Helen Dickson

As A Brother?

"He's always been a good brother. He was quite quiet – he doesn't really say a lot but what he does say is profound. He was a very nice brother to have. I haven't got any memories of us falling out. We had the usual brother and sister bickering though. On the whole he was quite easygoing. Being the eldest with two brothers, I took quite a bit of stick. They never let me drive the Scalextric cars. I used to have to sit on the corners and, every time the cars came off the track, I had to put the cars back on the track. And they never let me have a go with the controls. The corners were my job!"

NORFOLK EDUCATION COMMITTEE

Swimming Certificate

This is to Certify that:

Martin Brundle

of St. James' Junior Boys' School

has passed the following Test satisfactorily.

DISTANCE TEST

SWIM FREE STYLE 440 YARDS

July, 1969.

Chief Education Officer

Martin Brundle

Hairy Parkers

"All the cars had to be put in the showroom at night and so tightly you had to climb out of the windows. Robin and I used to do this during school holidays and customers of the Dray & Horses pub on the A10 opposite used to spectate. We did do the odd lap around the garage for fun and had a few accidents and incidents! I hit the workshop wall with a sideways Imp and backed a Jaguar XJ into the showroom wall. Robin did so many laps in a Reliant Robin the front wheel fell off!"

"It's funny how these certificates meant the world at the time."

Martin Brundle

Field Studies

"When I was seven, we had a black Austin A30 - it was obviously unsaleable. So that became our car, parked near our front garden. The mechanics would take us, literally 500m down the road, and we'd charge round the field all day. I could drive it at that point looking through the steering wheel. My younger brother, Robin, would kneel on the seat and I would do his pedals for him. We'd charge round the field all day long, just in an oval."

Alma Brundle

Valet Parking

"At the Tottenhill garage, when it was time each night to put all the cars inside, he would be driving these cars in. I used to just close my eyes and disappear because they were cars that were up for sale that he was belting around in!"

Helen Dickson

Young Chauffeur

"There was a field behind the garage and when Martin was about five, and I would be about seven, he used to drive old bangers around the field, even at that age. It was unbelievable really. I'd be sitting beside him and he'd be driving me. You just can't imagine that ever happening today – you'd be taken down to the Social Services!"

"I had no idea my Mum had kept these for nearly 50 years. Greaseproof but clearly not fireproof."

Please Pick Me Up

"We moved away from that garage to live in a house that didn't have cars just outside it. But even then, even when I was at school, I'd blag my way to the garage. I'd ring up: 'Who's delivering parts, who's delivering cars? Pick me up. I'm coming to the garage.'

"So it was ingrained in me – internal combustion engines were part of my life. And I'd be messing around in the garage all day."

The Footballer

"We did other things as well – we enjoyed kicking a football around in the back garden if we had friends around. We were lucky enough to have a third of an acre plot. There were two trees strategically placed, with a neighbour's long garden shed, with his fishing trophies and jaws of sharks on his shed wall, the perfect backdrop as a goal net for us. Every time someone scored a goal at some pace and height, it used to rattle the panels on the shed and knock his trophies off the wall. Inevitably, being the youngest, I was always the one standing in the garden when he came yelling over the garden fence. And Marty and the older friends would hide. Marty was quite handy with a football - he played for the local Grammar School team and enjoyed his football."

SHELL PETROL & OILS
GREEN SHIELD STAMPS

T. L. Stebbings

THE GARAGE GRIMSTON

PHONE HILLINGTON 251

VISIT

THE UNION JACK ROYDON

THE OLD ORIGINAL ENGLISH PUB
GOOD BEER WITH A CHEER

RASPBERRY BROS.

MAIN HONDA DEALERS

Also GOOD SELECTION OF USED CARS

TEXACO GARAGE, GRIMSTON

Tel: HILLINGTON 281

Ruane Carrstone

Sand and gravel supplied

A QUICK SERVICE

Tel: KING'S LYNN 840405

PRINTED BY SEABANK PRESS SPORLE

FANTASTIC BANGER RACING

AT
MILL HILL RACEWAY
CLIFF-EN-HOWE ROAD
POTT ROW, GRIMSTON
SUNDAY, SEPTEMBER 23rd 1973
2-30 p.m.

PROGRAMME OF EVENTS

Officials of the Meeting
Promoters: Mr C. W. Barlow
& Mr C. E. Panks
Clerk of Course: Victor Felgate
Scrutineer: Victor Felgate
Starting Marshal: R. Cartwright
Pit Marshal: F. Bensley

Public address supplied by P. Curston

Admission by Programme 40p
Children 15p   Nº 0638

"Fantastic banger racing - not on many Formula 1 drivers' CVs."

Burns Night!

"I think he was about 11 when he prepared his own car [for banger racing]. He pulled it all to pieces, took out the windows, just one seat… One night he came home and he'd got a massive burn on the top of his foot. We had to try and find a doctor at that time of night to get it sorted. He'd only been welding the doors up. He was actually capable of using the welding equipment but he'd set light to some underseal which eventually turned molten and dripped on to his foot while he was welding another part. He still has the scar today!"

Idols

"Jim Clark was his favourite. He was devastated when Jim Clark died. And Bobby Moore was his favourite footballer. Martin would meet him many years later at a Buckingham Palace garden party, not long before he died."

Brundle M.

FORM 4B Spring Term begins Tues 8th Jan. 1974 , ends Fri 5th Ap 1974
Age on 30th Sept. 14.3 Summer Term begins Tues 23rd. Ap 1974 , ends Fri 19th July 1974
Average age 14.6. Autumn Term begins Tues 3rd. Sept. 1974 , ends Fri 20th Dec. 1974

SUBJECT	AUTUMN TERM		SPRING TERM		SUMMER TERM	
	Place	Comment	Place	Comment	Place	Comment
English	17	Inconsistent. Much of his work has lacked detail. KBG	7	He is making a more consistent effort now. KBG	14	A borderline O L. to be more positive
History	10.	I don't think that work is one of his priorities JBS.	3	An excellent exam. He has actually... and is beginning to use it. JBS.	7.	Generally sound exam disappointing
Geography	8	Made a reasonable attempt this term	9	Moderate effort only	8	A better exam.
French	22	He must make a greater effort next term KBG	23	Progress is steady if too slow	17	Progress quite good
Mathematics Set I.	30/31	He needs to work much harder if he is to do well. MJH	26th	He needs to give much more time to his work. MJH	25th	...he could do very well MJH
Physics Spanish	14/15	Works well when he really concentrates, but far too often inattentive AM	9.	Exam quite good. Term work much better. AM	7.	Again did quite well in the exam. Has ability. AM
Chemistry	20/32	Not working as well as he might. Too easily distracted. SPC	11/32	Much improved SPC	5/35	A good term. Average exam SPC
Biology						
Latin						
Art						
Woodwork Tech Dy.	13/31	...standard of ... Good level work & progress. DM	12.	Capable in both subjects. Exam 93% + 63%	7.	Good... DM
P.E. & Games	15 x1	A useful reserve defender.		X country — fair effort only		Athletics — fair swimming somewhat better
House Master's Report		A useful member of the House		Prepared to do his best when required		✓
Form Master's Report	10.	He is clearly not making full use of his opportunities and he needs a changed attitude towards work & school. BHt.	5.	Certainly a better term. I hope he can maintain his improvement next term. BHt	5	A much better term. He is obviously making much more of his opportunities now. BHt.
Headmaster		He needs to work harder now that he has started on the certificate course.		Much improved. I hope it will not be necessary to apply pressure again.		A good term with one or two reservations.

Signed Brundle (Parent or Guardian)   Signed Brundle (Parent or Guardian)   Signed Brundle (Parent or Guardian)

Martin Brundle

Education

"I went to school around here, junior school at West Lynn, a bigger school at St James's in the Metropolis of Kings Lynn and then King Edward VII Grammar School. I would always advocate that Grammar Schools are a good thing if they were like that, because it was a great school. And then I went to technical college. I didn't go to university which actually I regret, having seen my two go through uni now, but frankly I couldn't have done that and had a racing career. And at 18 I was running all my dad's businesses anyway. So I had a reasonable education but it wasn't super high level or anything like that. It was interesting that I was chosen to do a reading at the school's Christmas Carol service, both at my junior and senior schools. I remember being thrust up there as a youngster."

Helen Dickson

A Smashing Routine

"He was banger racing in Pott Row – a little village near Kings Lynn. He used to work all week on an old banger and then go and smash it up on a Sunday, and then work the rest of the week and smash it up the following Sunday. He would be about 12 and I was a competitive swimmer so I was off out and about and didn't really get involved until the Sunday when we'd all troop off to watch him smash this car up going round and round in circles in Pott Row which was extremely scary. I couldn't understand for the life of me why he wanted to do it. I think he was Pott Row Champion at the age of 14. He was destined even then to be champion at everything."

Above and below: "My first major victory at a Hot Rod meeting was at Great Yarmouth stadium aged 16. I won over £50 and hopefully I spent some of it on a haircut!"

Helen Dickson

An Occasional Tippler

"One time my parents had a house party. Martin and I were to hand round the drinks and clear glasses away. Martin drank the dregs of each glass and he did suffer! Once we all went to Lloret de Mar on holiday. Martin and I would have been 12 and 14. We'd all go to bed after dinner. Martin used to sneak out of the bedroom and go to a bar, and he wasn't old enough to drink. Then he would sneak back into the room at about 5am a bit the worse for wear. My mother thought he'd gone down with a poorly tummy. I asked him, as he looked a bit peaky. He said, 'You should come to this bar; it's really good.' So, for the next four nights, I went with him. Poor mother, she had no idea."

Alma Brundle

Danger & Worry

"You're always worrying as a mum. But you get used to it. The first time he took his stock car, Dad wouldn't take him because he didn't like him doing this stock car thing. He felt it was too dangerous, and he wasn't very old. He wasn't old enough to go and get a licence for anything else. Bob Beckett, the man who did the servicing for the garage, had taken him down to Pott Row, not far from us, this first time, though Dad would later. So I thought, 'I'll just go and have a look'. As I drew up in the field, the car was on its roof and he was climbing out the side window. So I got straight back in the car and came home; left him to it!"

Great Yarmouth Stadium, Sunday, 20th July, 7.00 pm

No.	Name	Hometown
	HOT RODS	
	SILVER	
351	Barry Lee	Ilford
	RED GRADE	
44	Leslie Trussler	Guildford
99	Dave Bozzard	Redbourn
108	Bob Howe	Chiswick
112	Colin Thompson	Southall
205	Bruce Peacock	Soham
566	Micky Codling	Lewisham
	BLUE GRADE	
75	Jeff Cushing	Heston
20	Geoff Phillips	Colchester
37	Micky Elliott	Greenford
66	Lou Karmios	Chiswick
92	Sonny Howard	Ely
98	Nigel Murphy	Woodbridge
103	Graham Rolph	Peterborough
111	Ken Sheridan	Thetford
170	Terry Bell	Ely
171	Peter Stone	Chigwell
394	Roy Sheridan	Thetford
432	Noddy Robinson	Ipswich
	YELLOW GRADE	
193	Gordon Webster	Soham
	WHITE GRADE	
11	Gary Cooper	Farnborough
41	Paul Farnish	Stowmarket
47	Robert Turner	Bedfont
77	Tony Allison	London
82	Steve Cann	Harefield
117	Frank Ross	London
148	George Rolls	Romford
212	Adrian Whittaker	Chatteris
218	Martin Brundle	King's Lynn

No.	Name	Hometown
	BANGERS	
10	Terry Kirk	Rainham
11	Mick Bailey	Newmarket
12	John Baxter	Newmarket
14	Michael Baxter	Newmarket
51	Victor Price	Bacton
57	Martin Wallis	Ipswich
58	Jim Hammond	Norwich
63	Joseph Williamson	Norwich
66	Trevor Gosling	Colchester
68	Bill Scott	London
102	Malvin Morter	Norwich
108	David Abrahams	Norwich
109	Kevan Neve	Norwich
119	Dave Norton	Lowestoft
120	Gary Smith	Lowestoft
121	Reg Easey	Lowestoft
123	Graham Wright	Kessingland
125	Graham Overy	Red Lodge
133	Terry Witham	Woodbridge
164	Philip Morter	Norwich
169	Mark Wayne	Norwich
170	Charles Buckenham	Lowestoft
172	Derek Clover	Norwich
189	Mick Jacques	Gt. Yarmouth
251	David Scott	East Acton
317	Keith Overy	Red Lodge
196	Terry Clouting	Attleborough
171	Malcolm Fuller	Norwich
165	Graham Pettingill	
806		

Robin Brundle

Two In A Bed

"As small children, we got on well. We had to get on well when we moved to Gayton Road because we only had a double bed at that time so Martin and I shared a double bed, as we were growing up, for two years or so in the early days. We then progressed to bunk beds and older brother took priority in the top bunk."

Martin Brundle

Building Cars

"I'd go down the end of the used car lot and find a Ford Anglia or even better a Ford Anglia Estate because they had better gearing. Hopefully it was out of tax and probably almost scrap value. You'd mount the radiator in the rear window because that's where it wasn't going to get holed. Any number of tubes and pipes you could get hold of to plumb it back to the engine which was terrifying when you think about it. Put in a roll cage which was literally a tube just over your head. Put a new set of plugs and points in it. Arc weld the diff, so you've effectively got a locked diff, and go racing.

"I could do the engine, I could do the gearbox. The one thing I could never get my head round was the electrics. My mate, Steve Reddington, used to do the wiring.

"So by 12, I was building my own cars. And one of the reasons I was very lucky to get into professional motorsport was that we always had the garages. So, whilst we never had any money, we had facilities. And when I'd done all that, I'd go and tell my dad that I was going to use that car. It felt the right thing to do to tell him afterwards rather than before because he might say no before.

"It was grass track racing but there was also quite a lot of contact. It was banger racing really, a slightly posh form of banger racing. And Dad used to drop me off in the morning. He'd go and sell cars all day, I'd race and then he'd come and pick me up at the end of the day. We were winning quite a lot of races, to the point where they all thought I had some tuned up car or something, but I didn't. We just used to make sure they ran well. You learned car control, you learned to race close together, and frankly it's a very good grounding. I don't think too many of them come through banger racing now though!"

Alma Brundle

Burning The Midnight Oil

"He was a young man who more or less kept himself to himself. He was happy with his head in an engine rather than going out to play with friends. He had his little mates round after school when he was a wee bit smaller. But he was quite happy staying at the garage after the garage was closed. The guy that worked for us would bring him home. Some nights I used to be worried out of my life because it'd be two o'clock in the morning and he still wasn't home! He'd got to have his car done for a stock car meeting so they'd just keep going. It's amazing."

"Wimbledon Stadium on the shale - especially tricky when it rained. Great for honing car control skills."
(Fred Buss/Dean Cox Collection)

Martin Brundle

Offered A Drive

"My first ever drive, that somebody else provided for me, was at Pott Row, and this old boy who was a scrap dealer locally said, 'Will you drive my old Super Minx, boy?'

"'All right, I'll have a go.' It was a Hillman Super Minx 1500. It was in the bigger class but he reckoned it was a little bit special. I did all right but it was a bit of a handful – seemed to be bouncing a lot. Really this was the first time somebody had spotted me. I'd have been about 13. So, I was first spotted by a scrap dealer!

"Anyway, it transpired he'd filled the fuel tank up with concrete to give me more traction. He'd thought that would be just the ticket. That's why he thought it was going to be so special. He'd absolutely filled the main tank - it'd be about a 10 gallon tank or something - with concrete, which is why it bounced around a little bit!"

Martin Brundle

A Violent Reaction

"Dad got to Pott Row one day to pick me up, and there was some guy with a crow bar trying to hit me. Because the grand final of the day was the top runners from both the under 1500cc class and the over 1500s. So it would be my Anglia 105E and Rileys and what-have-you, up against Zephyrs and Zodiacs. Anyway I won it and somebody was quite upset about that. So as I'm going round with the flag out of the window, celebrating – they used to laugh at me because I'd look through the steering wheel, because I couldn't see over the steering wheel. I was tiny. I was probably 15 by then and he reversed round and wrote my car off as I'm going round on my victory parade – it was pretty rough stuff.

"So, when in later life Schumacher as my team mate would shove me a wheel somewhere, it seemed like nothing compared to a guy in a Zodiac trying to kill me and then try to come after me with a crow bar as soon as he got out of the car. Nothing really bothered me too much after that!"

"An unlikely rally car, which had completed the London-to-Mexico Rally - Dad could make it fly."

Arthur Coleman

Band Width

"The first real job I did for Marty at the garage was when he asked me about putting bands in the wheels to make them wider. I told him to cut the wheels with a hacksaw - you had to cut all the way around the rim and then you put the band in to make the wheels wider, and I would weld them up for him. You've got to be reasonably accurate when you're cutting it and you've got to hacksaw all the way round the rim. An eighth of an inch piece of steel is not very thick but once it's gone round the wheel you've got about three foot of it to cut."

Martin Brundle

Comedy Duo

"I remember seeing Jackie Stewart and Graham Hill on the BBC Sports Personality of the Year thing. They used to do a very funny sketch, talking about the year. I became a Graham Hill and Jackie Stewart fan from that.

"I think I used to love the little sketch because there was so little access to anything F1. Even in the James and Murray years, you'd wait up until 11.30 at night for 45-minutes of highlights, then get into bed after midnight and still have to be up for school assembly. It was so hard to see any motorsport on the TV. Occasionally there'd be some rallycross or something in the '60s when I would have heard Murray. I remember seeing Jenson Button's father at Lydden Hill in his Beetle."

Martin Brundle

Hot Rods

"Then I went to Spedeworth Hot Rod racing. Fibbed about my age. I was 15 by now, and we got a Hot Rod together. Did Wisbech, Yarmouth, Ipswich and Wimbledon.

"Apart from Wimbledon on shale, they were concrete or tarmac quarter mile short ovals, 30 cars on the track. Hot Rod was allegedly no contact, and so I got car control from that as well.

"The first Hot Rod race I did I had three slicks and one wet and two of my slicks were on some nice wide wheels. They were old, we would have had no idea of the age or the compound the slicks would have been. So the two slicks on the fancy wheels went on the crowd side, the wet went on the right rear, and the narrower wheel went on the right front, which was probably the right thing to do because it was a passenger most of the race – it was a right handed circuit. And that was it, that's what we went racing with – no spares. Absolutely crazy. When I think back, it's laughable frankly. But when I was 16 I went and won the final against all the stars like Barry Lee and George Polley."

"Now that's what you call under-steer!"
(www.oldstockcarpics.tk)

Norfolk County Council

The NORFOLK COLLEGE
of Arts and Technology, King's Lynn

To:

Mrs. A. Brundle,
54 Gayton Road,
KING'S LYNN.

FACULTY OF MANAGEMENT AND ARTS
FULL-TIME STUDENT PROGRESS REPORT

NAME	BRUNDLE Martin J.
CLASS No.	BD1
SESSION :	1975/76
PERIOD COVERED:	Sept. '75 - July '76
DEPARTMENT:	Business Studies
COURSE:	OND in Business Studies

SUBJECT/TUTOR	COMMENTS OF SUBJECT TUTORS	LATEST EXAM/TEST RESULT	INITIALS
Economics L. Burch M. Kampanopoulos	A good student who works in a quiet nature conscientious manner. Classwork 65% Homework 74% Has worked well.	66%	
ENGLISH G. M. Brown	Classwork: B Homework: B He has worked very well. His use of written English is generally confident and fluent.	59	
COMMERCE R. A. Simmons	Hard working + obviously interested. Should get 'O' without difficulty	83	
ACCOUNTS A. Williams	An excellent effort made throughout the year. Martin has acquired a sound understanding of basic accounting principles. Shows promise.	83	
Statistics	A very good year's work.	91	
LAW J. R. YATES	A very able student and achieved an excellent examination result	73	

An excellent year's work in all subjects. Martin is making excellent progress. In class he is polite and helpful and he has developed good relationships with staff and students alike. By conscientious application he is developing his own abilities to the full and making a positive contribution to the academic standards of the group and college. An excellent start.

A. Williams CLASS TUTOR

HEAD OF FACULTY

DATE 5.76

Mark I Havery BSc FIOB
PRINCIPAL

Martin Brundle

Spectator To Friends

"I never met Graham Hill but, to my utter amazement, people like Sir Jackie Stewart are close friends of mine now which I find extraordinary having stood on the bank at Copse and watched them. We used to take along boxes and bits of wood and anything you could to build your own grandstand out of."

Robin Brundle

Holiday Negotiations

"We'd always squabble for who had the middle back seat as it was raised slightly and you could see straight through the two front seats which gave you forward and peripheral vision which made it much more pleasant. Being tiny, sitting in the back of this thing for two and a half days to Spain was not much fun. He would negotiate his way to sit in the middle seat all the way in England on the basis that he would exchange it once we got to the other side and of course that was when it got hot, and he wanted to sit beside a window. A great negotiator even at that early age."

Arthur Coleman

No Flies

"He was a very sharp boy. A good salesman as well. He proceeded to sell me a couple of cars."

"I never did like that English teacher."

Robin Brundle

Driving On Left & Right

"We had a lot of fun on those holidays. When he was 17, father actually let him drive abroad, towing the caravan. I have to say that there was one time when the caravan got a real tank slapper on due to some cross winds and Marty's driving skills came to the fore to keep this caravan under control."

Great Yarmouth Raceway, Tuesday 3rd August, 8.00 pm

HOT RODS			SUPERSTOX		
GOLD			**RED GRADE**		
306	George Polley	Heathfield	636	Conrad Self	Dereham
			923	Kenny Cooke	Norwich
SILVER					
351	Barry Lee	Chigwell	**BLUE GRADE**		
			299	Pete Smith	Diss
RED GRADE			447	Pete Barrett	Downham Market
118	Lloyd Shelley	Chelmsford	470	Mike Baker	Halstead
170	Terry Bell	Soham	558	Dick Hall	Norwich
171	Peter Stone	Chigwell	562	Horry Barnes	Dereham
218	Martin Brundle	Kings Lynn	776	Tony Jones	North Walsham
304	Derek Fiske	Diss			
331	Phil Powell	Purley	**YELLOW GRADE**		
504	Terry Selby	Streatham	99	Wally Hall	Red Lodge
566	Micky Codling	Lewisham	126	Willy Barnes	Dereham
			156	Ray Goudy	Stowmarket
BLUE GRADE			238	Eddy Aldous	Diss
14	Colin Facey	Saffron Walden	272	Dick Doddington	Bungay
98	Nigel Murphy	Woodbridge	274	Geoff Hubbard	Long Stratton
388	Kevin Dutton	Barrow	303	Alan Parker	Norwich
			340	Stu Piper	Norwich
YELLOW GRADE			446	Rod Barrett	Kings Lynn
53	Mark Poole	Oxhey	525	Nigel Trench	Ipswich
193	Gordon Webster	Soham			
			WHITE GRADE		
WHITE GRADE			31	Mick Gilboy	Kings Lynn
62	Derek Perry	Stanford Le Hope	106	Dave Abrahams	Lowestoft
92	Sonny Howard	Ely	139	Mark Wayne	Norwich
199	Jack Hunter	Bury St. Edmunds	153	Keith Lane	Norwich
			167	Graham Lawes	Norwich
			242	Richard Shorten	Norwich
			329	Graham Skoyles	Gt. Yarmouth
			418	Eddy Eglen	Kings Lynn
			483	Geoff Warman	Eye
			498	Nigel Toole	Beccles
			585	Basil Tyte	Ipswich
			931	Jack Dain	Norwich

"Some legendary names on that entry list from the world of small oval racing."

Liz Brundle

Students Both

"We met at technical college in King's Lynn and we were both doing Business Studies – we were in the same class. He was 16 and we spent two years studying - friends the first year, then started going out the second year.

"I think he was quite shy when I first knew him, which actually now you can't really imagine. He is still quite a shy person actually, but nowadays because he speaks to millions, you wouldn't think so. There was something about him - he was clever and ambitious. There was a maturity, even though he was only 16, and an intelligence there, I think, beyond his years. He was good-looking, he had a nice smile, that sort of thing – and he had a racing car!"

Robin Brundle

Elizabeth

"He was always cagey about having a girlfriend, letting us know who it was and where he was going - until he met Elizabeth. We hadn't seen a girl on the scene, or we thought we hadn't, for quite some time. Then, suddenly, Marty arrives home to introduce Elizabeth. There stands a very tall, beautiful, blond-haired woman with nice long legs and knee-length boots that were fashionable at the time. And of course he went on to marry Elizabeth. Just as we thought perhaps he wasn't interested in girls, he pitches up with the best one in town!"

Martin Brundle

Fast But Late Food

"When I was 16, I had a moped and I used to come back from the garage at 3am to whatever food Mum had left for me – by then congealed – in the microwave."

Alma Brundle

Family Support

"He's worth it. They're all worth it. They're all lovely. You love your children and you want to do what you can for them. It certainly paid off where Martin is concerned. His dad helped him an awful lot. He knew so many people."

Robin Brundle

Take Away & Back

"The moped era – how we survived that I don't know! He had a Garelli moped. Chinese takeaways were just coming in when he was 16 and we had one in our town. Marty had volunteered to go down and fetch some for our supper - on his moped. They put the food into paper or cardboard-type carrier bags with silver foils where they folded the lids over but it wasn't sealed like they are today. He had about a mile to go. On the way back, one or two of the dishes spilled their juices and soaked the bottoms of the bags. So Marty had our Chinese food for the whole family and it was all spread for about 200 yards on the road. Using his initiative, he went back to the Chinese and explained the situation. The lady took pity on him, re-did it all again and put double bags on so he could get home."

"My first ever Hot Rod race at Wisbech Stadium."

"Selling cars was my professional life at that time."

JOHN BRUNDLE and his wife, Alma, directors of John Brundle (Motors) Ltd are seen here in the new showroom at Railway Road with their eldest son, Martin who is a trainee manager in the sales department of the family business. In the picture is a selection of used cars (TC 5178).

Liz Brundle

Interested In Cars?

"No, not at all. I had no idea at all about racing. I remember going to the garage fairly early on and talking to his dad and asking him, 'So when did you start racing?' asking him all these questions and being really interested in it. And then the first time I went racing would have been when he was still doing Hot Rod racing. So I only went to a couple because then he moved on to track racing.

"I thought it sounded really exciting; I just knew nothing about it. Obviously it was exciting, because he was very good at it, so when you went along he was usually winning the races, so that was good."

Alma Brundle

The Three Priorities

"That's all we lived for – our three children, the businesses and the racing."

Touring Cars & Formula Ford
1977-1981

By June, 1976 Martin had reached the magic age of 17 and, following two years successfully racing Hot Rods, it was time to think of something more ambitious. In 1973, the garage business, which by now had moved to much larger premises at Tottenhill, had taken on a Toyota franchise. In '76 the Samuri Racing team had been very successfully running a pair of Celica GTs for saloon car legends, Win Percy and Barrie 'Whizzo' Williams. When the cars were advertised for sale towards the end of the season, it was not surprising they caught the attention of the Brundles. Though stretching them financially, they managed to acquire the pair and the transporter.

Martin was now at the local technical college, honing his commercial knowledge with a business studies course. A fellow student was a very attractive girl, called Elizabeth. In the second year, they began going out together. In early 1977, young Martin did a few club events with the Celica to obtain his full licence for he was planning a season in the British Saloon Car Championship, no less. In a fairytale start, he qualified on pole for his first Championship race and led, until cruelly robbed by a puncture.

After a steady year, accumulating knowledge of the main British circuits, he finished up third in his class and seventh overall. A second year with the ageing car and limited budget yielded the same class result and an encouraging fifth overall. It was time to move up again and Martin then had two seasons in Formula Ford 2000 single-seaters. The results were good but not spectacular. However, fate took a turn in '79 when Brundle managed to obtain a drive in the current BMW County Championship. A close second and a win against some very big names began the pivotal relationship with Tom Walkinshaw, of TWR fame. Martin drove the BMWs alongside his FF2000 racers in 1979 and '80.

For 1981 Walkinshaw was to run the BP-sponsored Audi works team of saloon cars. No less a personage than Stirling Moss was signed to drive one car and a young fellow called Brundle was entrusted with the other seat. The cars were neither reliable nor competitive so it was a disappointing season. However, BP were impressed with Martin and that proved crucial. During the year, he had also married Liz, his long-term girlfriend and intensely loyal supporter.

SAMURI RACING
Offer for sale their R.A.C. Touring Car championship

(At Brands Hatch on 24th October)

GRP I TOYOTA CELICA GT

The most successful and reliable Group I car over the past 2 years, as driven by Win Percy & Whizzo Williams. 17 class wins, T.T. Class winner, holder of every 1600 class lap record, 2nd overall in 1975. Must be the fastest 1600cc car in Europe, and still favourite for outright championship honours. Would make ideal Tarmac Stage/Rally car. The whole car is in immaculate condition and ready to race. Complete set of spares, full sets of Wets, Inters, Slicks, everything in fact for a full season's racing. Also their
FORD D300 TRANSPORTER the famous ex Ford Motor Co. rally transporter. 5 speed, 2 speed axle, electric winch, 6 seater sleeper cab, purpose built with special engine, spares compartments. Excellent condition. M.O.T. Fast and economical.
All enquiries to BOB GATHERCOLE Tel. BEDFORD 854090.

Reproduced with the kind permission of Autosport

"I remember reading this advert at the bottom of the stairs before rushing up to show my Dad."

Martin Brundle

The Next Step

"We were running out of the ability to do much more in the Hot Rod races. Then, one morning, I opened up Autosport – we'd been Toyota dealers since '73 - and in the back was the transporter and the two Celicas that the Samuri Team had been racing in 1976, driven by Win Percy and Barrie 'Whizzo' Williams.

"So we went to Brands Hatch to see them, and I stood at Paddock Hill bend which is where I used to stand and watch the Grand Prix, and these 30-odd cars came past and frightened the life out of me. I said, 'I can't do that!' I was 16 at the time. And Whizzo, or Win, drove me around the paddock in one. And we ended up buying them. We 'hire-purchased' the lot of them. We hadn't got any money. So the transporter got hire-purchased as a breakdown truck, and the two Celicas got hire-purchased as demonstrators! That's the only way we could find the money."

Martin Brundle

Near Thing

"On the way home, Dad ran wide on an 'S' bend near Braintree and we came perilously close to crashing into a tree on a bank!"

MARTIN (17) ALL SET AS RACING DRIVER

"Keeping the sponsors happy. Mechanic Bob Beckett in the background. Martin Crannis (leaning on the bonnet) was, ironically, the next door neighbour whose shed was effectively our goal net."

Martin Brundle

Budget - Zero

"Dad rallycrossed one of the Celicas and I went circuit racing in the British Touring Car Championship in the other one. I think I finished seventh overall that year in the British Touring Car Championship. We spent £3000 in the whole year or something and we used to transport this thing all over the country. Had to get my licence first, so we went out and did a 10-lap Special Saloon race at Croft and a few small events like that. And that went quite well. I started off in the Championship by getting on pole and looking pretty good. But we had very little budget - we probably ran the same set of tyres all year. The good thing was that, because we had the Toyota dealership, I could get parts for it."

Barrie Williams

Whizzo Stuff

"He came to Silverstone and I had my white Celica GT - just an ordinary road car - and he had never been round a race circuit before. So I drove him round and round the Grand Prix track and then he drove me round, and he drove very well. It was all a bit different to grass track racing: it was a big area. And then we sent him out in the racer. He had a couple of spins - never been on slicks before. But then he settled down, and he started going really very well. He was really quite good. Anyway, he came in at the end of it all and went into a big confab with his dad, and I think the words were, 'Well son, what do you think of it?' And he said, 'It's fantastic, Dad. This is a proper racing car.'"

"These were great cars - they took real punishment."

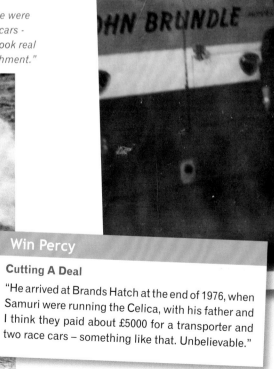

Win Percy

Cutting A Deal

"He arrived at Brands Hatch at the end of 1976, when Samuri were running the Celica, with his father and I think they paid about £5000 for a transporter and two race cars – something like that. Unbelievable."

"Celebrating victory at Silverstone with Bob and my brother Robin."

Liz Brundle

Racing Regime

"I went with him when they bought the touring cars. I was quite involved early on really. I used to do time-keeping at the track. We'd leave college on the Friday evening and we'd go to the garage, collect the transporter, head off up to Croft or somewhere up North. He used to deal with pretty well everything himself, apart from the mechanic Bob Beckett we had with us.

"Bob would come with us and help Martin fix the car. But Martin did a lot of it - prepared everything. We used to have the car on the transporter and tow a caravan behind. Martin and the mechanic were in the caravan and I used to sleep in the cabin at the front of the truck. It was great – had my own little room there. And we'd go off on Friday evening and come back Sunday night, having raced all weekend and then head off to college on Monday morning!"

Autosport - April 14, 1977

Oulton Park - British Touring Car Championship First Round, Race for Up To 1600cc Cars – Practice

"Sitting on pole for this race was 17-year-old Martin Brundle in the ex-Williams Samuri Toyota Celica. Brundle did 1m 16.2s in a car that still has a novice's cross on the back. In fact he has only done five races, Oulton was his sixth, and had only driven at Oulton once before in the wet in a Special Saloon race. He is an ex-Hot Rod driver and, hopefully, if his first appearance in the championship is anything to go by, should be very quick."

Eastern Daily Press

All set for Silverstone — Marty Brundle with car and back-up team. From the left: mechanic, Bob Beckett; sponsor, John Brundle; timekeeper, Elizabeth Anthony; and lap recorder, Robin Brundle.

"The canny spectators know that by putting their umbrellas up they can make the cars slide around." (Alan Cox)

Autosport - The Race

"...from fine starts, it was Lloyd, Brundle, Unett and Burrows into the first corner. At the end of lap two the first position was now in the hands of Brundle, but unfortunately this only lasted for two laps as on lap three he had a puncture in a rear tyre and spun four times going down Cascades and stopped."

Liz Brundle

Time Out

"It was quite unusual [for a student]. Martin used to get Wednesday afternoons off, which was sports afternoon, to go and work on his racing car – that was his excuse. I used to think it was an excuse but he said it was very definitely something he needed to do, while the rest of us had to go and play hockey or tennis or whatever."

Barrie Williams

Talent Apparent?

"Oh yes, yes. When he was driving me round Silverstone in my little road Celica, or when we put him in the racer, you knew what he was up to. He was a little aggressive, because that was the grass track bit, he would sort of chuck it into a corner, and he didn't need to do that: better to have it all smoothed out. But he was always willing to listen, which is half the battle. He listened to his peers all the time. He was always willing to listen and pick things up and capitalise."

Autosport, October 20, 1977

Seasonal Survey

"I still think that's a great looking racing car."

"...young Martin Brundle impressed many people with his mature drives in the ex-Williams car."

Liz Brundle

Single-minded & Determined

"Nothing stood in the way of racing. Nothing. I used to get quite frustrated at college, because there'd be a party or there'd be something on, and I'd ring his home and say, 'Is Martin going to come to such and such?' 'Oh, he's working on his racing car.' And it was either a question of go on my own, or go to the garage and watch him work on the racing car. So I used to go to the garage and I'd stand there and I'd pass this tool or that tool, while all I could see were his legs underneath the car, and he'd work there till the early hours of the morning."

2nd RACE, 1st WIN

"Luckily we only photograph the good moments in life."

Liz Brundle

No Worries

"I don't remember feeling worried at all at that stage. I suppose in my naïve mind at the time I thought that if you're in an enclosed car it looks as though you're more protected, and you're not travelling as fast, and he was good at his driving, so I don't remember feeling worried. I don't remember him crashing at any time either actually."

"A good shot of the Brundle family nose, enhanced by a malicious head-butt when playing volleyball at school."

Another Twist Of Fate

"I was Director and General Manager of a building company which was a subsidiary of a big builder in Norfolk. Together with another subsidiary, we bought a Mallock Clubmans car. We had a lot of fun with that. So, we decided to go up another stage and the following year we bought a FF2000. We had a good competent driver who drove it for a season. At the end of the season, Martin's father, John Brundle said, 'Ooh, Martin would love to have a go. He has never had a go in a single-seater.'

"We went to Snetterton for the final test of the season and at the end of the day, Martin got in the car, just to try it for three or four laps. He went quicker than it had ever been with its regular driver!

"So, Martin drove it for the next season. In 1979 he was in the old Reynard and for '80 we bought a new Reynard. To be honest, that new Reynard was bloody hopeless. I think he came fourth in the Championship – he should have been 24th with that car. The Royales were so much quicker that year."

Martin Brundle

Mum At The Wheel

"She did a bit of autocross and was quite handy in my dad's Escort Twin Cam. I remember her saying she was so nervous her knees were knocking!"

"Our garage mechanic Arthur Coleman looked after the single-seater."

"A varied collection of cars for a display at King's Lynn Speedway." (Arthur Coleman)

Arthur Coleman

Woops!

"When we first had the Reynard, we went testing at Snetterton for the day, myself and Martin. We'd done what we wanted to do and we were getting the car ready to put in the transporter to come home, and his mum arrived. 'I would like to see my son go around in this little car.' So OK, we got the car ready again, plonked Marty in it, his mum made comments like, 'Hmm, I don't like you sitting in that. Doesn't look like you can get out of that very easily.' Off he went. We were all standing in the pit lane at the old part of Snetterton. Marty came through Russell, as he'd been doing all day, and promptly lost it. So he did a lovely pirouette in front of his mum, and parked the nose into the Armco barrier. Mother went three parts ballistic, but she was OK after that. But she never did like him getting in the car, or him being strapped in, not even in Formula 1.

"That was the first time his mother had seen him in a single-seater!"

Arthur Coleman

Mechanic Recruited

"He'd done quite well in the saloon cars and then one day he asked me if I would I be interested in helping him with a single-seater. I was racing a kart myself at the time and said, 'Let's go and have a look at it.' So we went to Silverstone and, as soon as it came out of the lorry, I just said, 'Yes, I'm having a basin full of that, mate!' And that was what we raced for the next couple of years."

Arthur Coleman

Looking & Learning

"We agreed we would learn as we went on as neither of us knew anything about single-seaters. We learnt by looking at other people's cars and having sneaky looks at Formula 1 cars that used to be at the meetings when we were there and we learnt from them, what they were doing, how they did it."

"What stands out for me here are the thoroughly-annoying concertina showroom doors which were a pain to open."

Chris Rigg

Mine Host

"It was great fun going to events because John Brundle was extremely generous. He was a great character. He used to take a Winnebago type of motorhome to these events. The weather was often pretty awful and in the end virtually everybody would take shelter in the motorhome and he was permanently cooking steaks and things for everybody. They were great days."

Martin Brundle

Raising The Steaks

"Dad was legendary for his copious use of garlic salt!"

Above and left: "I love those calm moments on the grid just before a race."

Arthur Coleman

Keeping A Watch On Martin

"Liz was with him right from the very start and she was the timekeeper. She kept up with what was happening with the laps and she'd shout to us and let us know, 'Something's happened somewhere because his times have changed.' Most of the time Liz and I stood alongside each other while he was racing - I was hanging the board out and Liz was telling me what to put on it."

Martin Brundle

Revenue Sponsors

"I nearly broke the companies because the Formula Ford 2000 that Arthur Coleman ran with me cost about £25,000. The tax man came after us and we were very close to going broke because he wanted a chunk. In the end, he didn't take any. He had claimed it wasn't sponsorship - it was a benefit-in-kind, but as long as we didn't do it again, he'd turn a blind eye to it. We didn't have a lot of money. Mum and Dad were still building the business back then. Because I went racing, mum didn't go on holiday - ever, through that phase."

Martin Brundle

Life-Changer

"Soon after I began racing the FF2000 in '79, I did a really bizarre thing that changed my life."

"Pits and paddocks have definitely improved since the seventies."

"Probably the most important racing car in my life."

Arthur Coleman

Racing Accidents

"On the circuit we had two and neither of them was Marty's fault. He was tapped at the back end at Silverstone going into Woodcote which spun him onto the grass. His nose was sticking out on to the circuit. He's waiting for the cars to come past so he can continue and the last one run over the nose of the car. At Oulton Park at Deer's Leap, he got squeezed over to one side which was a naughty move really and put him out onto the grass, and took the front corner off. The only concern we had there was that it was the Saturday and we were racing at Silverstone on the Sunday so I had a little bit of work to do once we got to Silverstone that Saturday night. But those were the only two that we had. Otherwise, he steered clear of accidents and things."

"I'm showing Carter Builder boss Colin Gutteridge the workings of his single-seater."

Martin Brundle

The Breakthrough

"The BMW County Championship had just been launched and a guy called Tom Walkinshaw prepared a dozen BMWs to be identical racers. And our local Norfolk dealer had a car in it. And I wrote to Tom Walkinshaw, saying, 'I think I'm going to be a top driver. I've been driving in the British Touring Car Championship. Will you please give me a chance? I'd like to drive the Norfolk car in the Norfolk round.' They ran it like a gladiatorial, jousting championship. So it was Norfolk versus Suffolk versus... involving whichever of the dealers who wanted to participate.

"So I drove at Snetterton in this car and had this amazing race with Frank Sytner and Andy Rouse and Co., and beat a lot of very well-known drivers. I finished second to Sytner on the day and just beat Rouse. I had this incredible race."

"I was proud to represent my home county of Norfolk."
(Ros Barnes)

Brundle edges out Le Mans driver

LYNN'S young motor racing ace, Martin Brundle was hailed as one of the stars of the Gunnar Nilsson Memorial meeting at Donington Park last weekend.

He drove the best race of his career to bring the Norfolk-backed BMW home ahead of many of the big names in motor racing and win the Donington round of the BMW County Championship.

Only a month earlier Martin beat many more experienced drivers when he finished second before a home crowd at the Snetterton round in his first event in the car.

At Donington Martin qualified the Norfolk car — sponsored by Sorensons Motors, of Snettisham — into pole position alongside Le Mans driver, David Hobbs. He went into the lead at the first corner and stayed out in front for the whole race, in spite of a strong challenge from Frank Sytner, the championship leader.

Sorensons are now determined that Martin should continue to drive their car for the rest of the season when his schedule with the R G Carter Formula Ford 2000 allows. His next race with the BMW will be at his favourite circuit, Oulton

Park, on June 30.

Meanwhile, another local driver, David Sears, from Ashill, has added two more wins to his string of successes.

Driving his Anvil Oil-backed Royale Formula Ford 1600 he won the last two rounds of the P & O Championship at Snetterton and Mallory Park. This gives him a clear 23-point lead over his nearest rival in the championship at the halfway point in the season.

David is due to try his skill on the German Hockenheim circuit this weekend in a qualifying round for the European Formula

Autosport, May 24, 1979

"...best race seen at Snetterton for several years."

Arthur Coleman

Helping Hand

"At meetings, Martin was always saying, 'Well, what can I do? How can I help?' I always told him to go down the pit lane and see if you can get himself a drive in a Formula 3 single-seater. After that he'd come back and say, 'Right, I want something to do on the car.' 'All right, you can polish it.'"

Win Percy

Second Opinion

"When we had the BMW County Championship, Tom said to me one day, 'We need someone from Norfolk. That young Brundle has written to me. What do you think?' I said, 'He'd be wonderful.' I didn't do that particular race as any one driver was only allowed to do six rounds. I was representing Avon; I was the man from Avon! And Martin turned up, drove for Norfolk and nearly won the race. That impressed Tom straight away."

"It's easy to tell none of us were paying for the damage."

Arthur Coleman

Racing A Brace

"Quite often Marty would drive two cars over a weekend. He would be driving the Formula Ford 2000 which was his main car and then he would hop out of that and get into the BMW County car. So he was still doing his saloon car racing while he was single-seater racing."

"A ride on this classy machine was my reward for dominating at Donington."

Martin Brundle

No Fluke

"After the Snetterton race, it just all kicked off. So they put me in it again at Donington for the Gunnar Nilsson Trophy Memorial weekend. And I won the race against Hans Stuck, Alan Jones, David Hobbs... all these famous people. And it put me on the map overnight, basically. From nowhere I'd just suddenly turned up and beaten these guys."

The Rivals

Beaten That Day

Brett Riley, Frank Sytner, David Hobbs, Jeff Allam, Alan Jones, Andy Rouse, Jackie Oliver, Hans Stuck, Nigel Mansell and Stefan Johansson.

Chris Rigg

Game-Changer

"In a very amateur-ish sort of way, I was trying to get him some sponsorship and it was so great that he suddenly came up on the stage and beat the big boys."

Arthur Coleman

Kit Car!

"For 1980, we had a Reynard which we built from a kit. I think I did most of the work but Martin was there every night when we were working on it and he would come down after he'd finished his work in the office. So from around half six/seven, Martin was down there, quite often until midnight putting this car together."

"I must be pretty pleased with myself. It's not often I stick my hand out of the window."

"The Reynard SF80 was not one of our better decisions."

"Brundle Stars"

"The most exciting race of the day at last Sunday's Marlboro Formula 2 Trophy Meeting at Silverstone was undoubtedly the BMW County thrash, which held the crowd on tenterhooks as Martin Brundle and Nigel Mansell enjoyed a wheel-to-wheel battle throughout the 12 laps.

"Practice for the BMW race on Saturday afternoon indicated that their race might be a hard-fought affair and so it turned out to be. The whole field ran together for the first lap, Frank Sytner making the best start from the outside of the front row to lead into Copse, although he got elbowed out of the way before the end of the first lap and passed Woodcote in last position!

"Brundle and Mansell led the pack in the Norfolk and Gloucestershire cars respectively, with Jock Robertson right up there in third place until an incident at Becketts on the second lap saw his Lancashire car firmly embedded in the barriers.

"This served to give the two leaders a little breathing space and they continued to lap in very close company for the rest of the race, swapping places in spectacular style, although it was always Mansell who led past the start/finish line until the penultimate lap when a superhuman late-braking effort saw the Norfolk car scrabbling through in the lead. Having worked his way up from the fourth row of the grid, Philip Bullman gradually caught the leaders with his Avon car and the brake-locking antics of the two leaders at Woodcote on the penultimate lap enabled Philip to close right up: A real 'Silverstone-type' finish was on the cards!

"Mansell got back through at Becketts; it was Brundle again at Stowe and he swept through the flat-out Abbey curve just inches ahead of Mansell, keeping right on the edge of the track and ensuring that there was no room for Mansell to slip-stream past on the inside line into Woodcote. Undaunted, Mansell switched to the outside line and drew alongside in what should have been the braking area! At the last possible moment, both men stamped on the middle pedal, their brakes locked up and it seemed as if both cars would spin. Somehow, Brundle brought his car under control, bounced across the kerbs and slithered across the line to score a most magnificent victory, while Mansell spun in his efforts to avoid crossing the chicane's penalty-line."

"Year Two of the BMWs cemented my relationship with Tom Walkinshaw." (Alan Cox)

Martin Brundle

Door Handles At Dawn

"So we won the BMW Championship in 1980. You weren't allowed to drive every round, but we won the Championship for Norfolk and I won some great races. I had had a ding-dong battle with Mansell at Silverstone. We were literally door handle-to-door handle, and it was just who was going to be latest on the brakes and make the last corner. I did. He didn't. He spun off at Woodcote, the final corner. Again, this really put me on the map, to have such a ding-dong with Nigel at that time."

Brundle forces past Mansell in the thrilling finale to the BMW County race

Reproduced with the kind permission of Autosport

Martin's bonus

The Forward Day Centre for the mentally and physically handicapped in Lynn is to receive yet another cheque from Lynn based BMW dealers — Sorenson Motors Ltd bringing a total donation to date of £1,250.

This time the cheque is for £250 — the prize money for winning the seventh round of the 1980 BMW County Championship Charity race series which was held at Silverstone circuit.

Driven by Martin Brundle (21) who lives in Lynn the No 1 BMW 3231 sports saloon sponsored by Bowrings Ltd, in its red and black county colours completed the twelve lap 35.12 mile race in 22 minutes 45.38 seconds at an average speed of 92.77 mph.

ABOVE: Martin Brundle on the winners rostrum at Silverstone receives the cheque on behalf of the charity together with another for £150 which is his own prize money and the usual winner's bottle of champagne, from BMW (GB) Ltd Sales Director Paul Layzell.

Arthur Coleman

Good Guy

"As a person in those days he was a very likeable boy. He didn't jump up and down when things went wrong or when things weren't coming right. He was quite calm on that score and just accepted it. His 21st birthday was spent racing at Silverstone. I think we got something like a second or a third that day. I still have a lot of time for Martin. He was always polite to me. Never known him to be impolite to anyone else either."

Martin Brundle

Fate Mail

"It really scares me to think if I hadn't written that letter to some bloke I'd never met and, more incredibly, that he actually responded to it, gave me a very brief test at Donington in the car and I went well. The rest, as they say, is history."

"Formula Ford 2000 was a very strong championship back in the day." (John Gaisford)

Success for Martin has helped centre

LYNN motor racer Martin Brundle took his spoils of victory to the Town Hall on Tuesday after winning a championship which has boosted a local firm and helped a day centre for the handicapped.

Martin (21), who was presented to chairman of West Norfolk Council Mrs Edna Feary, won the BMW County Championship, driving a 323i model from Sorensons Motors. About £14,000 was donated to Lynn's Forward Day Centre from the prize money gained by Martin and other Norfolk drivers who competed in 12 races.

A national championship with charity in mind, the final race was clinched by Martin when he free-wheeled over the finishing line just 23 hundredths of a second in front of his rivals after his clutch broke.

The giant trophy Martin won will hopefully be on display at the Sorensons Garage on Hardwick Road and managing director Mr Peter Buck, who attended Tuesday's reception, praised the young driver. "For a 21-year-old to win a major championship like this is really saying something," he said.

Martin, who now aims to step up to Formula Three racing, beat grand prix champion Alan Jones during the championships which ended on September 4.

His father, Mr John Brundle, and brother, Robin (18), have also scored a triumph with Martin by winning a 2-litre class as a family in June at the Willhire 24-hour race at Snetterton, driving a Toyota Celica 2000 GT.

Martin Brundle

FF2000 Summary

"I won one race but to be honest I wasn't going that well. I think, a bit like my son, I was something of a late developer. A lot of the stuff I did early on didn't involve brakes or gear shifts or anything like that! Mud and slippery stuff rather than grippy tarmac and slicks. I ended up doing a couple of years in a Reynard in '79 and '80."

Martine Walkinshaw

Benefactor

"The very first holiday I went on with Tom was to California. He met me at the airport and before we left, he said, 'Wait, wait, wait. We cannot leave yet. Martin is racing in Formula Ford this weekend and he hasn't got the money for his start and I've got to pay for it.' So, that was the start of my holiday!"

Martin Brundle

The Willhire 24-Hours

"For this new event, we took a Celica off the forecourt - it was our demonstrator. VVG 1S was the registration number, Black Celica. Stuck a roll cage in it, taped up the lights, gave it a service, and I think we finished every time! We entered as The Brundle Family. I did it with Dad and Robin for two years but I was not available the third year. Dad wasn't a natural race driver, but he did all right. He was more for going sideways in a rally car or rallycross car. Rob was quick and I could drive forever.

"One thing I've always had is stamina. Sometimes, I've not had quite enough strength and that's something I struggled with in the early-to-mid-'90s with F1 cars because they were so physical to drive. But I've always had a huge amount of stamina so I could literally drive forever. I think the year we won Le Mans I did 12 or 13 hours. I did eight-and-a-half hours in 2012 with no problems and I was 53 years old. Stamina really paid off in places like Daytona.

"The Willhire was the first 24-hour event ever in the UK and it was club racing, but it was serious and it was hard work - filling up with Jerry cans, changing tyres every so often... And of course we started having a few reliability gremlins. We had another demonstrator on the forecourt and so we drove that over as our spares department, a green one. So we just robbed bits off that if we needed them through the night! Tremendous experience to do that as a family of three."

Chris Rigg

Willhire - Will Acquire

"They kept running out of brake pads so they nicked them off one or two cars in the public car park – they put a note on the windscreens. Both the owners were delighted to have been involved in some way!"

"Had great satisfaction racing with my Dad and my brother."

Liz Brundle

Engaged

"We became engaged on Martin's 21st birthday at Silverstone in 1980."

"Had great satisfaction racing with my Dad and my brother."

"After bangers and Hot Rods, the BMW racing seemed pretty elite!"

Autosport, March 19, 1981

Tricentrol RAC British Saloon Car Championship Preview

"The final pair of cars that makes up the TWR entourage is in the 1301-1600cc class, and are the BP Team Audi 80s driven by the oldest and the youngest drivers in the championship. Walkinshaw has inherited Stirling Moss from last season's team and introduced young Martin Brundle to [additionally] do the driving. By the end of last season the Audis has *(sic)* got over their teething troubles and actually won their last five races – though a little bit of luck helped them to that. Brundle could be the sensation of the championship."

Martin Brundle

Caught By The Catch-Fencing

"So in '81 Tom put me in the Audi team. I was testing it at Silverstone, and he had said, 'Just go along, take it easy,' that sort of thing. So I'm coming in and it was front-wheel-drive, and I'd never driven front-wheel-drive before. Coming into the pits, coasting in through the old Club, when Club was a proper corner, I lifted off - back end came out and I went down the catch-fencing. Bloody took the side out of the thing virtually. Made a right mess of it - catch fencing, the poles - terrible stuff - nearly killed me a couple of times.

"Tom turns up, massively underwhelmed, because there were some Audi GB people coming. Luckily, it was the other side of the car, when viewed from the pit wall, so they didn't see much of it as I was going round. And I broke the lap record that afternoon, thank goodness."

The Audi has already been clocked under the Silverstone and Mallory records.

BP back Audis for Moss and Brundle

After a 19 year gap BP and Stirling Moss are to join forces again . . . for BP is to sponsor the works Audis in their bid to win the British Saloon Car Championship, with Moss a team driver.

Joint sponsors with BP will be the Toleman Group through their Tamworth · based VW/Audi dealership Mayfair Garage.

The cars are to be prepared by Tom Walkinshaw Racing and Moss's young team-mate will be Martin Brundle, who has already put in practice times consistently under the class lap record at Silverstone and Mallory Park.

With Moss and Brundle behind the wheel the team is likely to have the oldest and youngest drivers in the series . . . Brundle was just two years old when Moss had the Goodwood accident that ruined his career.

Team BP Audi cars will run on Dunlop tyres and Lucas are providing extra sponsorship. A third car will appear later in the season for 'guest' drivers . . . the two names mentioned so far have been Tony Lanfranchi, who did such a good job for the team last year, and Rad Dougall who works for Toleman at Mayfair Garage.

Brundle, who has done most of the test work on the car in the close season and has a two-year contract with TWR said: "I have got the best drive in the championship. It's as simple as that. I

have a good relationship with Tom Walkinshaw and I think it's going to be a good year for the team."

Although the cars have been extensively rebuilt since last season they are mechanically virtually indentical to last year's specification. Later in the season a five speed gearbox is to be homologated.
● Last year's sponsorship deal with Akai came to end at the final race following noises from Audi in Germany suggesting that the Japanese connection should be dropped. The German car market is facing a Japanese invasion similar to ours.

BP celebrating past Moss victories.

Another success for
Stirling Moss and

BP Super!

Martin Brundle

Meeting A Gent

"I got the Audi drive and, because they needed a photo of the drivers in their overalls, the next thing is I'm at Silverstone, changing in the BRDC office gents' toilets with this guy called Stirling Moss, which I thought was surreal. I can picture it today, and I still think it's surreal. That was how I met Stirling for the first time."

"A quick kiss before leaving for the office."

"People never believe me when I tell them I was Stirling Moss's team mate." (Audi)

Martin Brundle

Pressure On Sterling

"I was really stupid that year because all I wanted to do was beat Stirling. It was the enthusiasm of youth, the arrogance of youth, whatever you like to call it. I just wanted to beat Stirling Moss. I thought that would be a good thing to do. I was 21, he was 51, and it was 1981. So instead of learning from him... Thankfully we're good friends today. He describes it as the worst decision he ever made in his career, I think. I remember us turning up at Mallory Park for the first test, and they'd spelt his name wrongly on the door – they'd spelt it Sterling as in pounds sterling! So that was one of my first experiences of Stirl. And Susie was there, of course."

Martin Brundle

The Joy Of Slicks

"Unsurprisingly, because it was on slicks, it was more my cup of tea than Stirling's. I was quicker than him until one magical day at Brands Hatch where it was wet. It was zero grip and he was gliding round the track. He just took off. It was the grip level he was used to, and off he went. We thought there was no grip but he thought, 'Ah, I remember it. This is how it always used to be!'"

Sir Stirling Moss

Rain Master

"I liked the wet far more than everybody else so it played right into my hands. I remember he was a young, keen, hungry driver."

Win Percy

Lessons In Life

"Martin is a very genuine person. And do you know what is nice about him? When he wrote his book about circuits, he mentioned about competing with Stirling in the same team. He admitted that he regrets trying to show Stirling how quick he was. We all had to do it because we're trying to prove that we can be good. I know Stirling has forgiven and forgotten. Lesson over. Maybe the team was unkind to Stirling. The guy was thrown into a front-wheel-drive car on slicks – everything he hadn't done in his racing career and he was expected to do well. And he was suddenly up against a young super-kid and he wasn't as quick - you wouldn't have expected it. I had one year of front-wheel-drive in '93 with Nissan and I hated it."

Barrie Williams

A Rival's Perspective

"He started doing the touring car championship properly then in the Audi and I was driving for Mitsubishi Colt, and I had some fantastic dices with Martin. I could trust him. He was one of those drivers you could go out and race against, and if you made a mad out-braking move and passed him up the inside, you knew he wasn't going to turn into you. You could see he was a finisher. He had a lot of mechanical problems with the Audi when doing very well. And we had Chris Hodgetts in amongst us, and Chris kept winning his class but Martin was always thereabouts. Now Stirling surprised us all and I think Martin learnt a lot from Stirling: how to conduct himself, etc. And Martin's driving was obviously superb."

"My claim to fame - I was the subject of a cartoon feature throughout 1981 in a comic."

Autosport, April 23, 1981

Tricentrol Championship, Oulton Park

"While Hodgetts [Toyota Celica], having smashed the lap record early on, was able to virtually cruise home to victory, life was a little fraught in Brundle's Audi. The throttle linkage stay had sheared leaving the throttle wide open. 'It was no problem,' said the young tiger. 'I would arrive at a corner and turn off the ignition and then once through I would turn it back on again... and I was catching the Toyota. I had a bit of drama once, though, when the key came out in my hand, still I could have continued like that to the end...' He didn't, as rounding one bend the throttle decided to close itself. Brundle trundled into the pits..."

"The black Toyota Celica came off the forecourt to become a racing car."

The speedy Brundles . . . John with sons Martin (left) and Robin.   Picture : PETER CASE

THE TOP GEAR FAMILY

Martin Brundle

No Longer Hands On

"I was racing at Oulton Park in the TWR Audi, and we had a throttle body problem, which we actually had most of the year, and I had to come into the pits during the race. Instinctively, I got out of the car and ran to the front, and got under the bonnet with the mechanic. After the race, Tom Walkinshaw took me to one side and very firmly said, 'Never do that again. Stay in the car and leave it to the mechanics.' But it was natural, I always did my own cars. So, I've come in the pits as a professional driver, got out, lifted the bonnet and helped them look for the problem - which is really silly, but that's what I'd done up until that point."

Sir Stirling Moss

As A Team Mate?

"He was clearly confident for his age and very quick. He had a good relationship with Tom Walkinshaw and that worked well for both of them. It was, though, a difficult year for all of us because the cars were unreliable and not quick enough. We were constantly beaten by the Toyota that year but Martin did a superb job in challenging circumstances. He certainly had a lot of ability. From my point of view, he was used to driving on slicks but I wasn't which made it rather difficult for me."

"My first works drive in the Audi was a little frustrating with recurrent mechanical problems all year." (LAT)

Liz Brundle

Settling Down

"We were married in 1981. We had known each other a long time before we got married. I was working away, with Marks & Spencer in personnel management. Once we left college, he went to run the garage business and I went off to M&S, did their management training scheme and travelled around the country to different stores. I'd come home at weekends, or he'd come up in the middle of the week and meet me. Then, I got posted too far away, and he said, 'I think perhaps we should get married now. I can't deal with the travelling!'"

Martin Brundle

Family Finances

"I've always been good with money since my early teens but in 1981, after we were first married, it was pretty tough-going financially. Liz's mum and dad loaned us some money which helped enormously."

"Mum and Dad looked pleased to see the back of me. I have yet to realise I have to pay my own living costs!"

"Courtesy of Howden Ganley and Tim Schenken, I had my first run in an F3 car with Tiga Race Cars."

Arthur Coleman

Seeing Potential

"I certainly said that he was going to be a world champion, and I thought he would make it in Formula 1."

Martin Brundle

Another Step

"BP were the Audi sponsors and for 1982 they wanted to take me to Formula 3."

Formula 3
1982-1983

The frustrating 1981 season's main benefit for Martin was an introduction to the giant BP company who had been involved in motorsport sponsorship for several decades. For 1982, they decided to sponsor the Dave Price racing team in the British Formula 3 Championship and they wanted Martin to drive the team's Ralt. This was a significant break for Brundle because a considerable budget was required for a full F3 season and would have been well beyond the Brundle family or enterprises. Indeed, the FF2000 seasons had put a considerable strain on the business. However, the pressure was now on to perform and justify BP's faith, and silence those who enviously claimed that Martin was merely a tin-top racer.

He began with a second and a third, and then had an accident when, having qualified on pole, he was punted off. Another accident followed and then a series of average results. The pressure was building, not helped by a few unlucky retirements. Then, with nothing to lose, it all turned around. He was on pole for five of the last six races, finished second in one and won two. His reward was to be chosen for the top Grovewood Award as young driver of the year.

The following season was to be a famous one. A young Brazilian, who would come to be known simply as Ayrton Senna, had been dominating the lesser formulae and was coming into F3 for 1983. His reputation was already such that he was the hot favourite. He had a name for taking no prisoners. BP decided that they had a better driver option to face this challenge and so dropped Martin.

Employing the £5000 that came with the Grovewood Award and modest sponsorship from elsewhere, including the splendid 'Racing for Britain' fund, he joined the Eddie Jordan team, an outfit similarly short of funds. For the first nine races, Senna proved the predictions to be spot-on. However, Martin was, by far, the best of the rest. But second was not first. Senna, sometimes asserting himself forcefully on track, had gained a psychological advantage, as well as a points one. Mid-season came a turning point for Martin once again. He won at the European round at Silverstone and Senna, spooked by someone leading him, crashed.

Interspersed with his busy F3 season, Martin also drove a Jaguar XJ-S for the TWR team, memorably winning brilliantly at a very wet Donington Park round of the European Touring Car Championship.

As to F3, Martin won eight of the last 12 races, finished second in two, third in another and was famously punted off by Senna at Oulton Park in another. By the final round, Brundle led his arch rival by a point. Sadly this was the race in which he finished third. However, the season was the making of them both.

Martin Brundle

Formula 3 Foretaste

"I'd actually had a taste of F3 when I did the televised final race of the season at Thruxton, the previous November. I drove a Ralt RT3/81 for Team Tiga, the team run by Howden Ganley and Tim Schenken, and finished sixth."

Reproduced with the kind permission of Autosport

Martin Brundle proved the VW engine's worth in his Team BP-Ralt at Thruxton.

Brundle: into F3 with BP and VW engines

"This was a great opportunity for me and elevated me to a new level."

Dave Price

Brundle Bundle

"I had sponsorship from BP that year [1982] and Les Thacker was running BP's motorsport programme then. Les had spotted Martin, more so than me. BP came to me actually and asked me if I wanted to run the F3 programme for them and the first year they wanted to put Martin Brundle in F3 so that's how that started."

Martin Brundle

Formula 3

"So then in '82 BP took me to F3 full-time. I finished second in my first F3 race of the season; I was going really well. I remember getting taken down to BP HQ in Victoria because Les Thacker thought I'd been a bit cocky afterwards, which I didn't remember. I remember being extremely happy because I'd felt a little bit under pressure to be honest because this was way beyond my sort of experience really, to be in the British Formula 3 Championship up against some good kids at the time. And there were a lot of people saying, 'Why has he got the BP backing, why has he got a Ralt, why is he with Dave Price? He's a tin-top driver,' and all that sort of thing. So I'd felt a little bit of pressure up against more elite drivers.

"In spite of finishing second, I got such a b********g about something, and I didn't really understand it. So I came home in a huff really. I'd gone down there expecting a bit of a pat on the back and to talk about some other things, so came home in a bit of huff and got nicked for speeding!

"Then I had an accident or two. It got messy and I made mistakes."

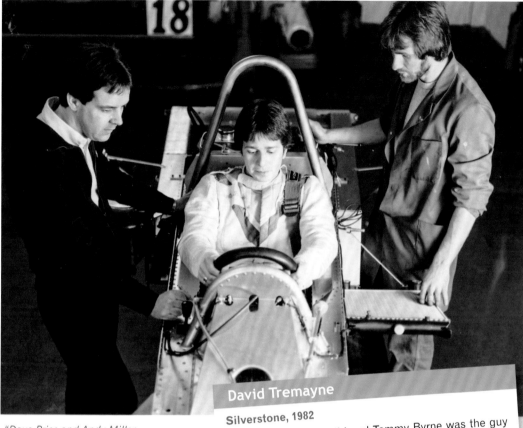

"Dave Price and Andy Miller certainly gave me some tough love in 1982."

"Pricey keeping the sponsors happy. I took the can for some early driving errors."

Martin Brundle

Tough School

"Pricey was ruthless with me. Broke me into bits. Prepared me well for life in F1, though."

Dave Price

Country Lad

"He was a country boy then. He was quite new to our world and the guys used to take the piss out of him mercilessly because of his lovely Norfolk accent, because we were all from London. So he used to get plenty of stick – and from me as well. So I think Martin would openly tell you that driving for me was never easy. You're always told where your faults are, that's for sure.

"Martin was a bit green behind the ears then. He'd been working for his dad in the garage and we were all a bit more worldly than him. We'd all been doing it a bit longer. My mechanics at the time were quite seasoned, ex-F1 guys as well. You don't get too many chances to survive. We had plenty of banter but Martin took it really well. I liked working with Martin."

David Tremayne

Silverstone, 1982

"He was a little bit wild and Tommy Byrne was the guy at the time grabbing all the headlines because he was winning a lot. With Martin you could see potential there for sure – he'd had a real big scrap with a couple of guys – Dave Scott in the first race at Silverstone. Martin was second and he saw Les Thacker the next day at BP, expecting a pat on the head, and was threatened with the sack, 'You can't drive like that. You've got to get better results.' You could see the potential – he was quick. It was just a matter of making it gel. And later in the year he began to get the results."

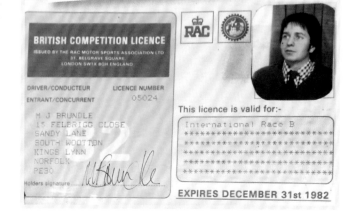

David Tremayne

Shy Guy

"My first proper memory of talking to him was at Mallory Park in '82. It's funny because Mark Blundell was exactly the same: getting anything out of Martin back then was like getting blood out of a stone. He was incredibly shy, so reserved. It turned out later of course that he was under massive pressure to justify the job and it was the plum seat - it was a fully-sponsored seat in F3 which was rare. At that time, all you saw was this kid whom you didn't really get much out of."

"If I was commentating on this action, I would say that I didn't trouble the corner apex." (Alan Cox)

"People still confuse us today. Derek is the one on the right!"

Dave Price

1982 Season

"It went really well. Martin seemed to take a little bit of time to get himself into the groove with F3. We had a few moments along the way and a couple of big accidents. We had a very big accident at Dijon, the week before Monaco. He'd qualified it on the front row but there was a massive shunt at the start of the race. They never really got to the bottom of that [cause]. All I know is that the car was sat on the floor with all four wheels missing. And that meant he missed Monaco which was the biggest shame really. That was always the big F3 race of the year in those times."

DEREK WARWICK, left, giving some tips to BP's Formula Three driver Martin Brundle. Four years ago, Warwick and Nelson Piquet, current world champion, were team mates in Formula Three. With BP's flair for spotting talent, could there be two world champions of the future pictured here?

Martin Brundle

Punishment

"The accident remains a mystery to me to this day, I made contact with a backmarker at the end of practice so something may have broken. I certainly wasn't very popular, being on the front of the French F3 grid! As a penalty for crashing the car, Pricey made me drive the team van all weekend in Monaco with 5.30am starts which really rubbed salt in my painful wounds. Wouldn't make that mistake again! I was ready to quit but Liz talked me out of it."

"Last minute advice on the grid from Les Thacker (to my left) and Dave Price."

Autosport, October 14, 1982, Brands Hatch Practice

"It was Martin Brundle who again set the pace, his Dave Price Racing/Team BP Ralt-VW being fastest in the morning and then clipping a further 0.21s from this time to make sure he started from his third successive pole position. 'We haven't done a thing to the car all day,' he said after qualifying. 'The car's going like a dream and the only problem I had was when the zip broke on my overalls!'"

Dave Price

Coming Good

"Later in the year he really got his act together. We made some improvements to the car as well. We made some fairly big changes to the car and Martin seemed to get to grips with it; we probably all got to grips with it at the same time. Martin won two of the last [four] races and he had a good finish to the season. It was a bit of a rough ride at the beginning. And I have to say that I used to have to cover his arse a lot with BP because they were getting a bit impatient with him in '82 over the results. He was under a lot of pressure but I always got on really well with Martin, and still do. So I was keen for him not to be shoved out and replaced. I couldn't see that there was anyone better anyway that fitted the British driver bill."

Martin Brundle

Cheers!

"After the great start, I crashed the car several times - my head went basically. And all of a sudden I was that tin-top driver who wasn't good enough to get the BP money. I hit rock bottom with nothing to lose and there's two ways to go then: there's carrying on and disappearing. Or you bounce back, you come back at them.

"My sister and husband lived a couple of miles from Oulton Park and I stayed with them. And the night before the race, we went out and, for some reason, I had a pint of local ale, which was really strong. I got up the next morning and felt slightly woozy with this stuff. I hadn't been much of a drinker and it was really strong - might even have been two pints for all I know. It was enough to make me think, 'Whoa, what are you doing?'

"I'd kind of hit rock bottom and I had nothing to lose, so I was quite relaxed. Stuck it on pole. Won the race by half a lap. Never looked back. Absolutely never looked back from that moment. I was on pole for the remaining three races, retired from one, was second in another and won the last one."

"Just like today, tyre pressures were critical." (Chris Rigg)

"What a great-looking racing car. Dave Price cars were always immaculate."

Dave Price

Feedback

"It was all a bit different then. There was no telemetry then but Martin was competent enough to tell us what we needed to know. We'd been doing F3 since '77 so we knew what an F3 car needed. And we were running a team in France at the same time. In '82 we won the French F3 championship with a French driver so we were running one in England and one in France. So we knew where we were which put a bit more pressure on Martin at the start of the year because our French team was winning races from the first race. But he came good in the end. I never lost faith in him, that's for sure."

Chris Rigg

Remembering Friends

"As soon as he got to Formula 3, he was completely out of my league. But he still used to invite me along. He invited me to the Grovewood Awards which he had no need to do. He's a genuine bloke."

"My ex-team mate and hero congratulates me on the Grovewood Award."

Martin Brundle

Recognition

'Then I won the top 1982 Grovewood Award for young up and coming UK and British Commonwealth drivers and £5000. And I just took off, and the confidence I got was quite extraordinary, and then I began to feel, 'Wow, I can really do this.''

Daily Telegraph

Martin Brundle, winner of the top Grovewood Award, and (right) David Hunt, who received a special commendation.

Motor Racing

Major award for Brundle

By TREVOR WILLIAMSON

Martin Brundle, 23, from King's Lynn, Norfolk, was last night given the top Grovewood award of £5,000 at the Royal Lancaster Hotel, London, as the motor racing driver to show most promise during 1982.

Brundle was racing Formula Three cars during the year and in a Ralt RT 3 collected two victories, three seconds, two thirds and three fourths on his way to finishing fourth in the Marlboro Formula Three championship.

He, to, plans to continue in the class taking in some foreign circuits before moving up to the bigger engined car.

Second was London driver Bailey 21, from Blackheath, who collected £2,500. He had a sparkling year on the track with 13 wins in 21 outings in his Lola and he ultimately wants to drive in Formula One.

Other awards saw Calvin Fish, 21, of Gt Ellingham, Norfolk take £1,500 and John Penfold, 22, of Lee Green, S. London received £500 and a special commendation.

"Close action, as always in F3."

"Dickie Davis telling me that I am (temporarily) £5000 better off. Embarrassingly, he had caught me earlier looking over his shoulder at the results."

Martin Brundle

Out With BP, In With EJ

"So then the following year Senna was coming to F3 and a guy called Calvin Fish had beaten him in Formula Ford 2000, and Les Thacker, the BP guy who'd given me the b********g at the beginning of 1982, felt pretty sure that he'd need fellow Norfolk boy Calvin to beat Ayrton Senna, and not me. We were supposed to be going to the European F3 Championship, then budget got cut and, all of a sudden, it was all over. So I got dropped. And I remember sitting in Pricey's office and he said, 'I'm going to send you to see a guy.' So he rang this guy up and said, 'I'm sending you a driver, 'e ain't got no bleeding money, but he's got a little bit, so see what you can do with him.' The bloke he rang was Eddie Jordan.

"So I went straight up to Eddie Jordan's semi-detached in Silverstone village, and he'd got no money either from what I could work out. But what I did have was the Grovewood Award money. I also painted Eddie's friend's Toyota truck in our paint shop over at Tottenhill. And we had a Citroen Familiale Estate on the forecourt we couldn't give away - it was a seven-seater thing. So the company gave the team this Citroen Estate as the crew car. I actually painted the Toyota truck myself, I rubbed it down and painted it, and gave Eddie the five grand, and we set sail. I'm so lucky that EJ took that gamble with me."

Martin Brundle

Tom's Investment

"Tom Walkinshaw lent us 10 grand which he never got back, but he got it back in kind when I later won a lot of races for him. He was a bit miffed with me for leaving touring cars, for leaving him. Tom always wanted to be a single-seater driver and he knew I wanted to be. Tom ended up being like a second father to me over the years."

"An early test day at Snetterton in 1983 with Dad and Robin in support. Yet another helmet colour."

"Celebrating victory at Eddie Jordan's Silverstone factory with Liz and Alastair Macqueen looking on." (Sutton Motorsport Images)

Martin Brundle

Support From Many Quarters

"Then we got some support from *Racing for Britain*, where the fans used to pay a quid here and there and that was topped-up by RfB sponsor Sieger Offshore. I was very grateful to Steve Sydenham, of RfB, and the fans because, without their support, it would have all been over early in the season. Patrick Howitt, of Howitt Printing, was an important backer through those years and Tim Clowes Insurance helped too. Support also came from a firm called Care 4 Cases, who used to make cases for musical instruments in transit. We had backing from GPA Helmets, which was Tom's contribution, and Shell. Most importantly, Team Toyota Europe provided their works Novamotor engines. And Eddie blagged a rent free unit off Silverstone circuits! We just blagged our way through the year."

"This is the racing driver's equivalent of the fisherman's story about the one that got away. My hands are temporarily F3 cars." (Sutton Motorsport Images)

Chris Rigg

Tight Line

"In his second F3 year, Martin was on a very limited budget and Eddie was very good because Martin hadn't got the budget to do anything like a season. It was almost on a race-by-race basis. We were getting little bits of money from *Racing For Britain* and people like that. Senna did have a proper budget."

"I am clearly pretending I don't know the man beside me. Believe it or not, that is Eddie Jordan." (Sutton Motorsport Images)

Autosport, April 7, 1983, Thruxton

Strong Arm Tactics

"Brundle also found his way past the Brazilian at the start but Senna da Silva fought back, muscling his way back into second place from the outside line into Campbell."

Autosport, May 5, 1983, Donington Park

Taming Big Cats

"The TWR/Motul Jaguar team could hardly have wished for a better venue for their first European Touring Car Championship victory of the season. In front of a fiercely patriotic home crowd, and in appalling conditions, Martin Brundle guided home the sleek XJ-S Coupé that he shared with John Fitzpatrick and Enzo Calderari to a magnificent victory in Sunday's Donington 500Kms.

"When Brundle took over behind the wheel, with 65 laps to go, he was more than one lap behind the Dieter Quester/Hans Heyer BMW 635CSi, but he never put a foot wrong as he gradually eroded the leader's advantage before taking the lead for good with a dozen laps still to run."

"This Jaguar XJ-S took some taming, wet or dry." (Jaguar Heritage Archive)

Martin Brundle

Leaping Into Jaguar

"During my busy F3 season, I also drove three times for Tom Walkinshaw's TWR team which was running Jaguar XJ-Ss in the European Touring Car Championship."

Win Percy

A Crucial Win

"He saved Tom's neck a little bit there."

"It was the glamorous race tracks that first attracted Liz." (Chris Rigg)

Ayrton Senna

Interview, Autosport, May 26

"I am fighting against experienced and good drivers, especially Martin – he is very, very good – and Davy (Jones). They both drive consistently and I am sure that if I make the slightest mistake they will be right there."

Martin Brundle

Browbeaten

"Senna won the first nine races and I was pretty destroyed by the fact that everyone thought Senna was going to win, that his reputation preceded him and obviously it's very easy to see why now."

"I won my first ever race with Jaguar at Donington. Part of the track was water-logged and we literally floated through the Craner Curves. At the bottom of the hill, we were on the water for so long, the engine sometimes stalled. Even I thought I drove well that day." (Jaguar Heritage Archive)

Martin Brundle

Turning Point

"I did some European rounds. I had bad luck at Monaco, but won Donington and Österreichring later on. Before that, a very critical thing happened and it was at Silverstone. Senna had won the first nine races and Silverstone was a combined European/British round. For the European series, you ran the soft Yokohamas and if you wanted to run to the British Championship rules, you ran the less grippy Avons. We needed the British points, so I'm trundling round on Avons, and Senna, who didn't need the British points, went European. It was all looking a mess and I stopped, talked to Eddie and said, 'Let's go European.'

"So mid-event, we go European and we put a set of Yokohamas on it. I go out and stick it on pole. And that was the first time I beat him, Senna. He was second on the grid and Johnny Dumfries was third. And I cleared off, led the race. Senna crashed trying to stay with me. And I won the race comfortably in the end. And, that was it. Psychologically - and it's something I would do later on again, when I was at Benetton against Schumacher – psychologically, I'd just turned a corner. For two reasons. One, I knew I could beat him, and two, *he* knew I could beat him."

Liz Brundle

Making A Stand

"As we got further into this season, I said, 'It's no good, Martin, you're going to have to crash with him. You're going to have to stand your ground, otherwise he's always going to beat you.' Whether he took my advice or not I don't know, but he did stand his ground against Ayrton, and that's why they ended up in several heaps. And Ayrton couldn't deal with it. When he was winning, he was fine, but if somebody was beating him, it seemed to me that he couldn't handle it. And then we'd got him beaten."

"I could often beat Ayrton off the startline. For this race, I borrowed a team mate's crash helmet for some reason." (Sutton Motorsport Images)

David Tremayne

The Double Act

"That year was fantastic. Martin was fast. Very often it was Ayrton and Martin in a class of their own. Then we had the Marlboro British round combined with the European round and you could run different tyres. On the Yokohamas, Martin and Tommy Byrne were first and second and Ayrton was nowhere. That was the first time Martin turned the tables on him. That gave him massive confidence. From then on, in the British series, there was so little to choose between the two of them."

"Amazingly, I would drive this car again, in perfect condition, in May 2013." (Sutton Motorsport Images)

Martin Brundle

Advantage Brundle

"We then went through this amazing phase where, with that confidence, I just started grabbing pole. I was always a better starter than him, just leading off the line. Generally just got my act together, my head together. And he crashed. He crashed into me – we had two or three very famous incidents. He got his licence endorsed twice for dangerous driving running into me, which he thought was very unfair, and it was a trait I saw in Senna later on, when he had the whole Prost incident in F1. So many traits of Ayrton I saw in that first year of F3 I would see later on: the world was unfair, the world was against him, and the Brits were against him, everybody was against him as far as he was concerned."

Martin Brundle

Gang Warfare

"In June, I was back in the Jaguar and had my first race win with 'the boss', which was at the Österreichring, sharing an XJ-S. It was pretty much war between BMW and Jaguar. We were leading comfortably but I kept coming across a slow works BMW which would try to run me off the road at high speed. I know the driver's name but I'll keep that to myself. Scary times."

Chris Rigg

No More Bullying

"I think it was the first five races, at the first corner – they were always on the front row of the grid together – Senna just took the line and drove across him – not necessarily unfairly but harshly. And Martin just couldn't afford to have an accident. It almost became a psychological thing. When he got to Snetterton, Martin said, 'I've got to do something about this. It's getting ridiculous. I've got to put some doubt in Senna's mind. So, this time, I'm going to hold my line and, even if we are on a collision course, I'm just going to stick to it.' They collided on the back straight. There was a big hoo-hah and an enquiry afterwards with the stewards. Fortunately, he did have an independent witness who saw it all."

Martin Brundle

My Piece Of Tarmac

"We had a few run-ins really. At Snetterton, I left him half a car's width to come past me down the back straight. He elected to try and take it half way down. We touched. I saw the rivets on the underneath of his car and he kept his foot in to try and T-bone me at the end of the straight and missed me, and I went on to win the race."

"Celebrating victory at my home track of Snetterton after Ayrton touched me and then crashed out." (Sutton Motorsport Images)

"Celebrating another victory at Oulton Park, one of my favourite circuits." (Sutton Motorsport Images)

"This is a typical Tom Walkinshaw expression. I wish he was still around to contribute to this book." (Martine Walkinshaw)

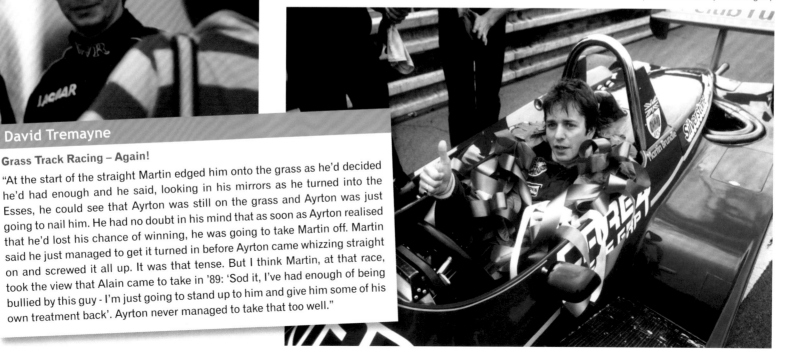

David Tremayne

Grass Track Racing – Again!

"At the start of the straight Martin edged him onto the grass as he'd decided he'd had enough and he said, looking in his mirrors as he turned into the Esses, he could see that Ayrton was still on the grass and Ayrton was just going to nail him. He had no doubt in his mind that as soon as Ayrton realised that he'd lost his chance of winning, he was going to take Martin off. Martin said he just managed to get it turned in before Ayrton came whizzing straight on and screwed it all up. It was that tense. But I think Martin, at that race, took the view that Alain came to take in '89: 'Sod it, I've had enough of being bullied by this guy - I'm just going to stand up to him and give him some of his own treatment back'. Ayrton never managed to take that too well."

"An important trophy - it was the first time I beat Senna, and it changed my life." (Abigail Humphries)

"There was plenty of support in 1983. I doubt Ayrton understood the British humour." (Sutton Motorsport Images)

"Left to right, me, Davy Jones and one Ayrton Senna."

Autosport, July 21, 1983, Silverstone, British GP meeting

"The Brazilian and the Englishman have proved themselves to be very closely matched indeed in recent races and such was again the case this time out...

"The gap between the two leaders remained fairly constant for the first half of the race, both of them driving very near the limit. It was interesting to note, though, that Ayrton was liberally using the very edges of the road and even the kerbing, notably at the chicane, whereas Martin seemed rather more smooth and, if anything, slightly more within himself."

Autosport, July 28, 1983, Donington Park

Honours Reversed

"In a mirror image of their duel at the recent Marlboro British Grand Prix meeting, Brundle and Ayrton Senna da Silva circulated in tandem, but a superb start was enough to earn a slight advantage for the Englishman. It was one he had no intention of throwing away. 'I've had enough of playing second fiddle,' said an elated Martin later, 'and I think I showed today that I'm every bit as good as he is. That's probably the best race I've ever driven in my life.'"

David Tremayne

No Chance

"Donington was, arguably, one of the best races I've ever seen. Martin was in front. It was a 25-lapper from memory. If Ayrton had been in front with Martin chasing, yeah, it would have been interesting. But it was Martin in front and he stayed in front of Ayrton Senna for every lap round Donington Park. It was electric because it was, 'Where is Ayrton going to try it' and he never got the chance. It was a superb drive by Martin."

"Eddie Jordan Racing preparation was immaculate. It never once broke down." (Ros Barnes)

"Early morning sun for yet another day in combat with Senna." (Ros Barnes)

Alastair Macqueen

Importance Of Experience

"Certainly in the European races, our advantage over Dick Bennetts and Ayrton was the fact that we'd run James Weaver the year before on Yokohamas and won European races. We took that knowledge into the European arena but for the British arena we certainly didn't hold all the trump cards because Dick Bennetts had won the Championship for the previous two years. We had the upper hand in the European races but neither the set-up or knowledge of Avon tyres that Dick had in the British races."

Liz Brundle

Eddie

"Eddie was extremely good at motivating drivers. He was always there on the grid in 1983, encouraging Martin, telling him that he was better than the rest and that he could beat Senna. Martin responded well to that."

"Under-powered F3 cars were all about corner apex speed and momentum." (Sutton Motorsport Images)

Martin Brundle

Success, Tragedy & Drama

"When I sometimes read that I had a technical advantage over Senna, it makes me very unhappy because we were blagging it and, in August, our truck went over the edge of a cliff. I had won the European F3 race against Berger and others in Austria. Eddie and I then drove to the airport in Vienna. I got back to our dealerships and Eddie was calling me and I couldn't understand what he was talking about - something about our truck and a problem, and had I heard anything? Apparently, our truck had run out of brakes down a little mountain road and gone over a ravine - all the cars and the truck were wrecked, and Rob Bowden got killed, my number one mechanic. This was one of the darkest days of my career. Rob was a lovely guy and had been so helpful and supportive to me.

"So we had to rebuild that team during the season and get it all back together again. Tim Clowes of the insurance company helped us out massively. Ralt helped. Everyone helped us out and we got the bloody team back together again. Then we were found to have a skirt a quarter of an inch too low and Dick Bennetts, who ran Senna, was not happy and it was scheduled to be the subject of an enquiry after the season had ended."

David Tremayne

Head Butted

"One of my principal memories of that year was the fight they had at Oulton Park. Ayrton just couldn't stand being behind anyone and it was a fantastic race. Then Ayrton tried that celebrated passing move with him ending up parked on Martin's head and everyone realised that it was getting a bit tense between the two of them then because this was for the Championship and Ayrton didn't do losing too well back then - if ever."

"From pole position, I beat Senna into Turn One, which he tried to remedy in a clumsy way." (Sutton Motorsport Images)

"It was a desperate lunge from Ayrton which triggered a big accident."

Martin Brundle

Fair Means Or...

"That was an outrageous move, at Oulton Park, an outrageous move. I was leading and he couldn't get through so he just drove into the side of me going through a right-hander. He not only took me off, but landed on top of my car and nearly took my head off.

"He had his licence endorsed that day and was fined £200. He started to get very upset. Once again, he thought the world was against him. I remember sitting in the steward's office with him two or three times. And he's going, 'Oh, you know it's not fair, the British this and that...' He convinced himself that it wasn't him. In spite of this behaviour, I still had enormous admiration for his skill, speed and determination, even if I couldn't show it."

Eddie Jordan

Highs & Lows

"We had just won what I thought was a major thing. As a support race to a GP, we were all caught up in the F1 bug. Both our drivers were on the podium – Alan Berg finished third and Martin won it. Gerhard Berger was second and I still believe my close friendship with Gerhard started there because we had such fun. I was elated. But that elation obviously turned to horror, to pain and to misery for Rob Bowden's wife.

"We had a fatality on the way home and it was not just the death of Rob but your car - the Championship-leading car - all the cars and spares. I felt we had been hit by an earthquake. Having said that, everyone in the team came together. It was an emotional time. I remember dropping a little tear because I couldn't believe that so many people could want to be part of the resurgence of what you were doing and what we, as a young team, were doing. I think we got a lot of goodwill out of that."

David Tremayne

More Than Winning

"When Rob Bowden was killed, Martin's on-track performances were quite instrumental in pulling the team back together because Eddie was almost on the verge of giving up. So Martin played a key role in pulling them all together and maintaining their challenge against Ayrton."

"I can remember his car pushing my head to one side."

"His sidepod was resting on my shoulder and they had to lift his car slightly so that I could get out." (Top right: Sutton Motorsport Images)

Liz Brundle

Spotted

"In Austria, I remember standing just in front of Sir Jackie Stewart and Ken Tyrrell. And they didn't know who I was. Jackie said to Ken, 'Watch this young British lad, he's going to be good!' And Martin won the race way ahead of Gerhard Berger, who was, of course, the local hero. And I told Martin later, 'Oooh, you know, they were talking about you.'"

Martin Brundle

Playing Mind Games

"To play mind games with people you need a fundamentally strong starting point. You need some strength somewhere, to be giving that kind of treatment. Senna did it in F3. I saw many traits in Senna in F3 that I later saw in him in F1. His speed, of course. But his being prepared to have an accident to make a point, to establish some kind of pecking order: 'OK mate, make your decision, I'm coming through now, make the decision, do you want to have an accident today, or are you going to let me through?' This was a dominance he had in qualifying: 'Get out of my way. It's Ayrton crossing the line just before the flag drops, last lap, banzai, pole position. Don't be the one that spoils it.' And that's psychological stuff."

"Winning the F3 race in Austria was in front of the F1 teams, being the support race for the Grand Prix, and so especially important." (Sutton Motorsport Images)

"A few hours later celebration turned to tragedy with the whole team in the bottom of a ravine."

Race team in mountain death crash

Martin Brundle: stunned by the tragedy

TRIUMPH turned to tragedy for Lynn racing driver Martin Brundle yesterday when his back-up team was involved in a fatal crash in the Austrian Alps.

The Brundles learned that a truck driver and ... ...ed more than 200 feet into ...

Liz Brundle

Learning Process

"When the transporter went over the cliff and his mechanic was killed, that was a very difficult time. Difficult in terms of the press wanting you to say, 'Oh, my career's been spoilt by the fact that my mechanic has been killed,' but that doesn't enter your head at the time. You're concerned about the family and the situation. So it was a learning curve as far as handling the press as well."

Eddie Jordan

Back From The Brink

"I had a lot of problems at home. I still could have gone back to the bank. I was a member of the Institute of Bankers so I was reasonably qualified to take a good position. I didn't want to subject [my wife] Marie to any more suffering because we were living in a one-bedroomed house with a loo outside and it wasn't really the way I felt I should be looking after my wife. My own life was in a turmoil. I owed a lot of money because not all the money was coming through for the race team. So I was struggling with so many things that it was becoming almost unbearable. But, as it turns out in life, I became quite good at juggling things like that. I was never afraid about money and debt, providing there was always a realistic opportunity that I would be able to make the repayment. And I think probably having been a banker and I understood cost accountancy, it helped me be calm in a situation. A lot of things fell into place for me too – I was enormously lucky and I often say to this day, 'I am the luckiest man on earth.' I had a massive ego and I wanted to show these people in F1 that there was this little F3 team. We could travel to Austria. A lot of the other teams didn't do that. Martin won and I think it did him a lot of good and certainly did us a lot of good."

Martin Brundle

Period Quote

"Even if I win every race and get fastest lap, I cannot catch him [Senna] on points if he finishes second every time, but it appears he cannot accept finishing second, so hopefully I've still got a chance."

"I know that face - I'm worried about something." (Sutton Motorsport Images)

"Ayrton on his way to becoming one of the greatest global sporting icons. I didn't realise it at the time."

Liz Brundle

The Power Of Money

"It got to the final race, and Martin was ahead, and it looked like he was going to win the Championship, and Ayrton went to Italy, I believe, and got himself a new engine. We didn't have the money. Each race as we were going along, it was, 'Have we got enough money for the next meeting?' And somehow they managed to get through the year, but of course Ayrton had a lot of sponsorship and was able to go and get a new engine."

Win Percy

Jaguar Interlude

"In touring cars, I did Zolder with him. We drove the XJ-S there together. As a touring car driver and sports car driver, he was outstanding."

Alastair Macqueen

Engine Matters

"It was a new engine but it wasn't built, I believe, to the latest belt-driven specification which really had very little, if any, performance advantage but Ayrton certainly went down to Pedrazzani's. Whether he transported his own engine back to England or watched it being built, or met the people at Pedrazzani, I don't know but I'm pretty sure he did go down there."

"Look at all the coolers and ducts, literally hanging off the car. This car moved around a lot. I ignored 70% of what it did and urgently attended to the other 30%."

Eddie Jordan

Junior School

"Those engines had a certain horsepower and they were all very equal. They were all controlled by the venturi which, for those who don't know, is the amount of air that can go through the engine at any one time. The great thing about F3 - it was about a young driver being aggressive, being quick, setting a car up for the first time on slicks and on wings. People often used to say that F1 is F3, except faster. If you look at so many careers, they've all come through the F3 'academy'."

Martin Brundle

So Near, Yet...

"And we ended up going to the last race of the Championship - I think I'd won eight races – I was one point ahead. But I'd damaged my engine at Donington, detonated the F3 engine, and we'd run out of money. Senna won the race and I didn't. So he won the Championship.

"Ron Tauranac, of Ralt, introduced two new parts in anticipation of the following season. He gave the revised sidepods to Senna and I had the new suspension. I only finished third in this final race, the car was ailing and, frankly, I didn't drive well under pressure either."

NOEL HUDSON MEETS RACING DRIVER MARTIN BRUNDLE

Local racer could soon join world's elite drivers

"It is extraordinary the amount of cigarette advertising there used to be in sport. This is Silverstone."

Eddie Jordan

Straight Talking

"There was no question that we had anything better than Senna. In fact, it was quite the opposite. In my view, we probably got shafted in some respects by Ron Tauranac – inadvertently, because I don't think he was that kind of person. But there was new technology coming out and new aero stuff - wings and bodywork, which Senna got for the last race at Thruxton and which had a huge effect on the car. In that particular case, we weren't able to keep up with him. He had the down-force but he had the straight-line speed which was the difference. Was it taken away from us? We had a great fight. Senna was an outstanding driver and a great character for our sport. I am very proud of what we achieved and of the number of times we beat him."

Alastair Macqueen

Significant Facts

"The performance of the engine was definitely down. Thruxton being such an open circuit and the cars being bereft of power, relative to almost anything else, the odd horsepower gone missing in the engine was very much a deficit for him at Thruxton but funds weren't available to do anything about it at the time.

"The new sidepods around the fast Thruxton circuit were a big benefit in terms of performance. The push-rod suspension, frankly, wasn't. It was as good as the rocker suspension and probably had some benefits in some respects but they were not performance benefits."

BRUNDLE F3 BID IN THE BALANCE

Martin Brundle has title in his grasp

Murray Walker

First Memories

"I was first conscious of Martin in 1983, because at that time I was doing not only Formula 1 for the BBC, which I started in 1978, but I was also doing Formula 3, touring cars, trucks, motorbikes and anything that God sent, and 1983 was the year that Martin and Senna had a colossal battle for the British Formula 3 Championship which Senna ultimately won, but which Martin was absolutely brilliant at. They took it right down to the wire."

Martin makes his point!

EVERY WEDNESDAY
Price 30p

5th October 1983　　1376

Alastair Macqueen

Senna, The Catalyst

"I think that season was the making of Martin. From being a relatively quiet, timid person, Senna brought him out of his shell and made him the competitor he has become and, subsequently, the person he has become. I think it was a very pivotal season. He was a person honed in competition."

"I now lead the Championship and it is written all over Senna's face and body language." (Courtesy of Motorsport News)

"It was always rewarding to have achievements recognised by the BRDC." (Abigail Humphries)

"Aryton drinking my victory Champagne at Donington but he would have the last laugh."

Murray Walker

Measurement By Comparison

"The British Formula 3 Championship now is not what it was. At that time, it was the most important Formula 3 championship of the lot, and there were Formula 3 championships in a lot of countries. So that was the one to win. And Martin, by virtue of the fact that he was doing as well as he did - and particularly that he was doing it as well as he did against somebody like Senna, who was obviously going to be a superstar of the future - indicated that Martin was very good indeed."

Eddie Jordan

Vintage Year

"We had such a good time and I believe Martin learned a lot from Senna and of course we didn't want to believe how good he was at the time and we weren't sure that he would go and win world championships. Very few team owners in F1 have ever considered taking a rookie out of F3. It was only the very, very best of them that ever made that step. So I think it was an epic year. Has there ever been – maybe I'm biased - as exciting an F3 season as 1983?"

BARC CHAMPIONSHIP FINALS RACEDAY

THRUXTON 83

SUNDAY, OCTOBER 23
◄Marlboro► THRUXTON ◄Marlboro►
OFFICIAL PROGRAMME 65p

"At the end of the season, Ayrton and I became team mates with Teddy Yip, along with Roberto Guerrero, at Macau."
(Sutton Motorsport Images)

Nigel Roebuck

Reflected Glory

"I first became aware of him in '83. People were talking about Senna being the second Messiah so it registered that this English kid was giving him a run for his money and more than once just plain beat him fair and square. So that marked him out as someone with a lot of potential."

Martin Brundle

Love And War

"I have a picture in my gym where Senna's shaking my hand on the podium at Thruxton where he's congratulating me for losing the Championship, presumably! And he said very nice things about me, about how he thought I was the best British driver to emerge since Jim Clark, he said all sorts of things.

"Looking back, 1983 was one of the best years of my life. We had so much success, but not forgetting the tragic loss of Rob. Eddie did an amazing job to eke out enough money to do the British championship and several European rounds from such a low starting point. He would crouch beside my cockpit on the grid and convince me I could beat Senna. And on many occasions I did.

"Without Senna I would have dominated the Championship and possibly waltzed into a better F1 opportunity. But with him, we attracted so much attention that it was guaranteed that we would both leapfrog straight into the big league. I was very privileged to have known and raced wheel-to-wheel with the great man over 11 years."

Eddie Jordan

Playing The Game

"Sure, I would have loved to have won the Championship as it would have meant that we were moving on but it really felt like we were winning a championship. We'd won all those races in Europe, we won on Yokohama tyres, we won on Avon tyres - an amazing year and the fact that we actually fought to the last race, for me, says everything. And just to be in the competition on this occasion - I'd never normally say this - was nearly better than winning. And when I reflect, it makes me think about why I wanted to continue in motor racing and it gave me such joy because it brought me real success for the first time."

Brundle gets his Super Licence

WEST Norfolk racing driver Martin Brundle is a step nearer joining the elite band of Formula 1 competitors.

The 24-year-old Formula 3 star was told yesterday afternoon that he has been granted a prestigious Super Licence, which makes him eligible to compete in F1 races.

A number of Grand Prix teams have already shown an interest in Martin, who is judged to be the most promising British driver on the circuits this season.

His father, John, said that the Super Licence takes Martin a step nearer to realising his ambition to race Formula 1.

"I understand there are only around 36 other drivers who hold the Super Licence," he said.

Formula One - Part 1
1984-1987

The reward for both Senna and Brundle in late '83 was a test with McLaren, and also for Martin with the Tyrrell Formula 1 team. Martin was then taken by Tyrrell to the Rio F1 pre-season tests but it took until just before the first race for Ken Tyrrell, suffering from a lack of sponsorship, to confirm that Martin Brundle was now an F1 driver. At this stage, all the front-running teams had turbo-charged engines but Tyrrell, unable to either secure a deal or afford to pay for such power units, soldiered on with the normally-aspirated and under-powered Cosworths that had dominated GP racing for so long. It all started magically ... and ended disastrously. At the first race, in Brazil, Martin finished fifth which impressed a lot of people. At Detroit, in June, he finished an amazing second and very nearly won.

Then, at the next race, in Dallas, he crashed very heavily in practice, badly damaging both feet and particularly one ankle. The local doctors wanted to amputate. Thanks to Prof Sid Watkins, and the surgeons of Harley Street, he gradually recovered. But he was out for the rest of the season. Then, for highly questionable reasons, Tyrrell was thrown out of the Championship and Martin's results erased from the records. It was a tough start.

Returning to Tyrrell for 1985, he and team mate Stefan Bellof struggled on with their aging, under-powered Tyrrells until mid-season when the team obtained first one and then, finally, two Renault turbo engines. Tragically, Bellof was killed, within sight of Martin, in a sportcar race at Spa in September. Martin was driving TWR's new Jaguar XJR-6, which he had débuted most impressively at Mosport the previous month.

The 1986 season with Tyrrell, where Martin spent the final 12 months of his three-year contract, was little better. He retired seven times out of 16 races. Two fifths and a fourth in the final race were the only highlights.

For 1987 Martin moved to Zakspeed but, in hindsight, it was a mistake. The car was neither competitive nor reliable. Three outings in the TWR XJR-8 resulted in retirements at Silverstone and Le Mans but a win at Spa. It was time to do something radical.

"The first time I would ever slide into a Formula 1 car. What a team with whom to have a first taste of F1."
(Chris Rigg)

Martin Brundle

McLaren F1 Test - October '83

"Back in those days, Marlboro sponsored F3 and a prize if you won the Championship was a test for McLaren. They decided to run three of us – Senna, Stefan Bellof and myself at Silverstone, which I just thought was great. John Watson set the car up and all us young hot shoes beat that time quite quickly. In fairness, that was later in the day and the track was better. We were all pretty much even and somehow Senna negotiated another go in the car and beat our times.

"I'll never forget standing on the pit wall as he came past, blue smoke coming out the back but he kept his foot in. He got out of the car - and I was standing beside Ron Dennis who had his stopwatch out and was timing him - and Senna climbed up onto the pit wall and said to Ron Dennis, 'What was my time? What was my time? It was my best lap but then it had an engine problem, coming out of Woodcote.' The engine already had a problem, and he'd kept his foot in till he passed the McLaren pit just before Copse. Ron slams his clipboard shut, and says, 'I find it very difficult to press the stopwatch when my car's pouring blue smoke out the back.' Turned round and cleared off. But still Senna got another go in the car, much to our chagrin, that day. But all three of us ended up in F1 the following year."

Martin Brundle

F1 Beckons

"What 1983 did, of course, was put us on the radar of the FI teams. Toleman had decided they were going to take whoever won the F3 Championship, but I think they wanted Senna anyway. Ken Tyrrell had decided to give the best British driver in the Formula 3 Championship a test, which was only going to be one person."

"Next up was a Tyrrell test. Ken Tyrrell is interested to know what I think of his 011." (Chris Rigg)

Chris Rigg

Contrasting Styles

"I attended both test sessions and it was fascinating to compare the teams. McLaren were all very disciplined – even kept changing the drivers' names on the car, depending on who was driving because that was their disciplined way of doing things. By contrast, Tyrrell were very laid back!"

Chris Rigg

The F1 Tests

"Regarding the McLaren test, Martin was a little unfortunate because Senna had already had a test drive in a Formula 1 car [with Williams] before Martin. So Senna had had some experience of driving a F1 car. Although Martin went quickly, he was not sparkling. He was determined not to put it off in the Armco or anything. But when it came to the Tyrrell test, he was absolutely on a fantastic pace. He'd had a bit more experience and knew what to expect, and was a little bit more confident he could handle it."

"Departing driver, Danny Sullivan (behind car) generously came to give me advice before I try the 012." (Chris Rigg)

Martin Brundle

Tyrrell Test -November '83

"I'll never forget: it was at Silverstone, it was one of those lovely days in November when you can get really crispy, cold, perfect days. It could so easily have been icy, it could have been raining, could have been anything. I went out in the 011 which Tyrrell had first raced in '81 and had been superseded during '83 by the 012. I set a time in the morning in the old 011 that would have put me on the second row of the grid in the Grand Prix that year. By lunchtime - I didn't even know it was in the truck - this Tyrrell 012 is coming out, and I'm going to get a go in that. So Ken was pretty pleased and I smashed the lap record in that."

Martin Brundle

Rio Test

"So the next thing is I get invited by Tyrrell to a test in Rio. I'd never been to anywhere like that in my life. Weird place, great though. I did the test in Rio and it was so hot. There was a pivotal moment when I was going down the back straight on a new set of qualifiers and you weren't going to get too many sets of qualifiers. Coming up behind me was Derek Warwick in his Renault turbo. It was an anti-clockwise circuit with a really fast left-hander at the end of the main straight. And I had to block Derek at that final corner so as not to compromise my qualifying-style lap. I did a really good lap time but, at that time, I still hadn't got the drive."

"I have no idea why I look so unhappy in this photograph with Ken Tyrrell."

"The test in Rio was super-hot. It looks like my neck muscles are already fading." (Sutton Motorsport Images)

Jonathan Palmer

Two Contenders, One Seat

"Martin really came into my world over the winter of 1983/4, when we were both trying to get into F1. There was a drive at Tyrrell that we were both trying for. I'd just won the F2 Championship and had been British F3 Champion two years earlier – Martin had just finished second in the F3 Championship. So, as far as I was concerned, I had the better credentials, as I kept telling Ken Tyrrell! Martin, though, had impressed Jackie Stewart, who was telling Ken that Martin was the driver he should take – and given that Jackie was a Tyrrell team triple F1 World Champion, he clearly had a lot of influence! Ken was always better at asking questions than giving answers and, despite me asking many times over the winter if he'd done a deal with Martin, he always denied it. However, after a while, I knew I was going to have to do a deal elsewhere. Fortunately John McDonald was eager to have me at RAM, so I ended up there and Martin, of course, at Tyrrell."

Brundle's biggest Brazilian break!

David Tremayne

Agony Uncle

"We all knew there was good chance that Uncle Ken would take Martin in '84 but he also had the offer of the works Ralt F2 seat. I remember, late January/early February in '84, phone rang and it was Martin. He's quite cool on the outside but he thinks things through a huge amount. He was threshing on this dilemma. It was a bit like being Marje Proops, back in those days with the F3 drivers. You were like an agony aunt/father confessor. You don't get that in F1 because everyone thinks they know everything by the time they get there.

"We were on the phone for about an hour-and-a-half: did I really think there was a chance with Ken because he was under a lot of pressure from Ron Tauranac to sign the Ralt deal. We hashed and dished it for ages. I must have said, 'I think Ken's serious.' You could tell Ken had taken a shine to Martin. I guess Martin talked to lots of people and then decided to give up on the possibility of a F2 seat, knowing that door would close the minute he said he didn't want it. So he was threshing on the horns of a dilemma for quite a few weeks before Ken finally managed to sort out the deal. But it was an interesting insight into the kind of guy Martin was – he wasn't afraid to ask for advice."

Martin Brundle

Derek Warwick

"Derek was very good to me when I first went to Rio for the test in '84 despite me having to cut him up down the back straight. I got there and he said, 'Right, come on, let me show you around the race track.' And wherever we went in those early days of '84, Derek would show me the track. It was very generous to me because, at the end of the day, I was another British driver coming along and he had no reason to do that but he did. Great guy Derek, doing a wonderful job at Silverstone and the BRDC. I have a huge amount of time for him."

Maurice Hamilton

The Big Stage Now

"The first time I really met him was quite memorable. Ken Tyrrell was having a British press lunch in a London hotel for all the Fleet Street guys and we didn't know who was going to be driving for him in 1984. Ken said, 'I'm sure you guys would like to know. You've heard all the rumours. Well I'm about to show you.' He got up and he went to these double doors and threw them open. And standing there was this shy, timid, terrified-looking, young Formula 3 driver Martin Brundle!"

"It was crazy how the cockpit sides didn't even reach my shoulders in those days and there is barely a headrest." (Sutton Motorsport Images)

NEW Tyrrell F1 signing Martin Brundle was busy at Silverstone last week, putting a Tom Walkinshaw Racing Group A Jaguar XJ-S through its paces, in preparation for a limited programme of events in the car, alongside his F1 commitments, this year. Team manager of TWR's Jaguar programme, Paul Davies, reported that it was basically just a shakedown exercise, although he was paying particular attention to some new dampers. Although Brundle did the bulk of the driving, Win Percy was on hand to give the car a quick whirl, although he was to spend most of the day driving his other 1984 charge, the Team Toyota GB Celica Supra (see separate story).

Martin Brundle

Tyrrell Decision

"Ken was very impressed that I was prepared to block the works Renault turbo to finish my quick lap at Rio - he liked that sort of thing. But still I hadn't got the job. And it was about February. And then I got a call from Ken to go and see him. I was living just on the edge of King's Lynn. To Ockham and back was six or seven hours in the car in those days. I went down and I sat in Ken's office, and he said, 'Well, I've got bad news for you, I'm afraid: I haven't got any sponsorship.' I'd told him I had £150,000 of sponsorship to put in, but actually had nothing at all. I don't know why I said that but I did - I just thought I'd find it, somehow I'd find it, but I didn't have it. So I'd promised him £150,000 and he said, 'So I haven't got any sponsorship, and I know you don't have the £150,000,' - didn't even have £150, let alone £150,000 - and he said, 'But I'm going to sign you anyway.'

"I remember sitting in his office; I can see it now. I wanted to jump up and down and scream and shout, but I just sat there going, 'That's good, thank you. I'm really looking forward to this.' And I just played it really cool and calm and got out. And then I did scream and shout when I got in the car to come home!"

Martin Brundle

Wrong Type Of Points

"I had been nicked for speeding on the way to this reveal and knew that meant I would have 12 points and a driving ban. I was worried silly that evening that I would lose my race licence too."

"I loved the Touring Car racing but it seems strange, looking back, that I diluted my F1 focus." (Jaguar Heritage Archive)

Martin Brundle

The Tyrrell Years

"So Ken took a chance on me really and put me in the car and I ended up with him for three seasons. We had some ups and downs; we had some success. He was always short of money and he was always at war with Bernie, and that sort of thing. We scored a lot of points here and there. Lovely man. Ken and Nora ended up being great friends of ours until we lost them both. Super man. Absolute quality guy. I don't think I've met a more quality bloke in Formula 1 than Ken Tyrrell."

Roger Silman

Herding Cats

"I joined TWR in January 1984 with a view to the Jaguar sportscar programme that Tom was confident was going to come his way. To fill in that first year, I helped out with the XJ-S. So the first time I saw Martin was when he came along to Enna. He was immediately the fastest of the regular drivers who at the time were Tom, Hans Heyer, Win Percy and Chuck Nicholson. Anyway Martin was immediately impressive, comfortably the fastest and really confident in what he was doing, which I found a surprise as often people that come from single-seaters don't like sports cars or saloons. They often can't cope with being shut into a car."

Martin Brundle

Keeping The Day Job

"I talked to Michael Schumacher about this. He was the same; he had no concept in the early stages of being a professional racing driver and nor did I. I came across this guy called Senna in Formula 3 and jumped in an F1 car, went pretty well and all of a sudden, I'm a Grand Prix driver. But, I'd come back from Rio and go straight to the garage, into the sales centre, and for the first few races I was still in the garage selling Toyotas. I was on so little money from Tyrrell, I had to do that. It was £30,000, minus taxes and all my expenses getting around the world and all my insurances, in my first year at Tyrrell."

"The infamous victory for Jaguar at Enna. Tom's face, on the left, underlines that this wasn't in the plan." (Sutton Motorsport Images)

Above and left: "Finally, some sponsorship for Tyrrell. The 012 was a great F1 car, pure and simple. This was Monaco." (Sutton Motorsport Images)

Liz Brundle

Breaking News

"It was only just before the season started that Ken offered Martin a drive. I was working at the time in the local newspaper office, having left M&S when we got married. Of course, the newspaper also wanted prior knowledge so they could break the story. And the others in the office were curious and every day they were saying to me, 'Has Martin got a Formula 1 drive yet?' It was a difficult time because Martin had turned down other drives and at this stage we didn't know if he was going to be an F1 driver or a Toyota salesman in 1984. Then, when I finally knew he had the drive, I couldn't say anything because it hadn't been officially announced. So, every day I said, 'We haven't heard anything yet.' Then it became public knowledge and, a few weeks later, we both went off to Rio - like rabbits in the headlights, I think."

David Tremayne

Head Not In Gear

"I remember seeing it and thinking, 'Holy shit,' because it was a horrible one. He got back to the pits, got into the spare car and was about to go out and Ken stopped him when Martin said, 'Just remind me which way the circuit goes at the end of the pit road.' He had no idea with that bang on the head what he was doing."

"Quite how I did not lose my life, or at least my right arm, in this crash, I will never know. Bottom left - check out how unyielding the barriers are and how close the spectators are." (LAT)

Liz Brundle

Anxiety & Frustration

"At Monaco I was standing in the pits. I'd heard there'd been an accident but in those days we didn't have the screens or anything like that so we couldn't see anything. A photographer came up to me and said, 'I've got all the pictures.' I said, 'Well, that's great, but could you tell me, is my husband alive or dead? Is he OK?' 'But I've got all the pictures...' 'GREAT...' And then Martin came running back but he didn't race for the rest of the weekend. That was the weekend that Stefan Bellof finished third in the Tyrrell. We were watching, and Martin was saying, 'That could have been me.' So that was difficult."

Brundle survives high speed crash in Monaco

Liz Brundle

Familial Support

"We were young and we hadn't travelled much but Ken and Nora Tyrrell were brilliant, because they were like surrogate parents to us. It was a great team: really family-orientated and they looked after us. But Ken was demanding of Martin, too. Expected a lot from him and if he thought Martin was getting a little bit big for his boots, he'd soon pull him down a peg or two."

Nigel Roebuck

Skid Lid

"I've never forgotten when, at Monaco, he lost the brakes on the Tyrrell in qualifying and I was standing right there at Tabac. I can still see it clearly now. He came past me, still going at a fair lick with the car on its side and Martin's helmet dragging along the road. That was a big shunt. And of course he got back to the pits and wanted to get back in the spare car."

Jonathan Palmer

Heated Rivalry

"Given the background, we were never going to be best of buddies at the start of 1984, our first seasons in F1, and it didn't take long before a paddock spat occurred! Although normally-aspirated, the Tyrrells were reasonably quick – too quick as it turned out! – and much nicer to drive than my lumbering RAM with its unreliable, difficult-to-drive and not-even-very-powerful Hart engine. At Imola, Martin came up to lap me in the race and was frustrated not to be able to get past – I was still quicker down the straights. He ranted on in the paddock about me holding him up but I told him I was just getting on with my own race. My team owner John MacDonald added his own colourful support too - which couldn't be repeated in a book! Anyway we got over that and I guess it promoted a bit of mutual respect."

"Ken Tyrrell was always very expressive, talking here to Stefan Bellof, Maurice Philippe, the Tyrrell designer, and myself." (Sutton Motorsport Images)

"Detroit '84, with Bellof in close company." (Sutton Motorsport Images)

Martine Walkinshaw

The Close Relationship

"Although Tom was still driving then, he was probably thinking that at some stage he would back away from the driving seat and Martin would be a good successor. Of all the drivers, Martin was the only one who had the potential to go all the way to Formula 1. I think Tom saw that all along with Martin. It was always a good relationship. I don't think they ever had any time when they fell out with each other."

Win Percy

A Touch Of The Nelsons!

"In '84, he had a few drives with us. At Enna-Pergusa, I was sharing an XJ-S with Chuck [Nicholson], Tom was with Hans Heyer and Martin was co-driving with Enzo Calderari. That year we were supposed to be supporting Tom [for the European Touring Car Championship]. Martin qualified on pole and blasted off into the distance. Tom was next and then me. Anyway, I sat on Tom's tail, Tom handed over to Hans and I handed over to Chuck. Martin had to come in for an unscheduled stop because he had hit a swarm of flies at the far end of the Enna lake. So the guys cleaned the screen, added fuel and sent him out again.

"At the last petrol guzzle, Enzo got in and goes off, still in the lead. Enzo's father is on the pit wall with his signalling board but, every time Enzo went past, he turned the board round. So Enzo had no instructions whatsoever and he goes on and wins the race. Tom was miffed. 'What about my Championship? You've ruined the whole year...!' Luckily, he did win the Championship anyway."

Maurice Hamilton

Mega Martin

"I thought Detroit was a fantastic race. Martin drove, I reckon, one of his best races ever there. In those days, the press didn't have the facilities that we've got now where we have computer screens, TV pictures and everything. Back then, the best way to follow a race was to stand outside and keep a lap chart by the track side. So I stood by the final chicane and you could see the cars coming in very quickly, and how they were coming out and onto the straight. On that little Tyrrell, Martin was just mega there. He really was amazing because he could throw it around, and he was right up with Piquet at the end. He should have won it, but the mechanics were standing on the track, and really he'd have mowed them down if he had tried to have a go at Piquet. But it was a brilliant drive."

Martin Brundle

Boy Racer

"I finished second at Detroit with a really strong drive through the field. I overtook de Angelis, who was third, in the final chicane a few laps before the end and I caught Piquet, who was leading. I was literally a couple of metres behind Piquet as he crossed the line. I had to drive around all the Brabham mechanics, including Charlie Whiting, as they were all on the race track because they were allowed to do that back in those days.

"Ken thought I shouldn't have pulled some of the moves, which confused me a little bit, and he said, 'Jackie said you were risking too much when you passed de Angelis,' and I was quite upset about that. So we went out to dinner, and I'd just finished second, by just a few metres, behind the reigning World Champion and I was pretty pleased with life at that point. Ken had spotted that I was getting over-confident, and he decided, as only Ken could, to give me one of his 'froth' jobs, as Jackie Stewart would call it, that night which confused the hell out of me."

"The Detroit circuit ran around the famous Renaissance Center where we used to stay, 80 floors up." (Sutton Motorsport Images)

"I didn't keep the Championship points but I still have the trophy." (Abigail Humphries)

Martin Brundle

For The Defence

"I remember saying to Ken, 'Yeah, but I knew he'd lost second gear. Did Jackie know he'd lost second gear? Did you know he'd lost second gear?' I'd followed him and he was quite clearly jumping a gear, and he was slow. Even though de Angelis had the Lotus Renault turbo and I only had the normally-aspirated Cosworth, he would come out of a corner and then he'd just lose momentum, and I could hear the thing was flat, and I knew he'd lost a gear, so I nipped past him when his engine went flat which was absolutely fine, and I finished second."

Martin Brundle

Footloose

"Then I'm in hospital and there was a blackout of any coverage. I heard the race through the hospital window going on, but I never saw it because back in those days Bernie used to stop it being shown locally so that people had to go and see the race.

"I remember this nurse - big, big, lovely lady - she used to come in every hour or so, and she'd say, 'Can you feel this?' And she was sticking a pin in my big toe, because it had all swollen up and they were worried I'd got gangrene. I worked out what she was trying to do - see whether I'd got any feeling in my toes or not, which I hadn't. I began to say I could feel it, I could feel it. At one stage, Sid Watkins stopped them taking my foot off."

"My first F1 podium - back then it was a low-loader truck on which we stood and waved at our mechanics and friends." (Sutton Motorsport Images)

Brundle split second away from prix win

Martin Brundle

Disaster In Dallas

"Fortnight after Detroit, I smashed my legs up. It wasn't really my fault; I got a puncture. The track was, basically, around a park in Dallas, completely lined with concrete walls. It just took the front off my car and ripped my legs to bits.

"I'll never forget it. They took me out of the car and I tried to walk away, because I didn't want to believe anything had happened. I'd never broken a bone before, and I've never broken a bone since. Tried to walk away and fell over because my leg wasn't attached to my foot, basically. My foot was off. Just a tube of skin holding it in place. The air conditioning in the ambulance was broken so I kept passing out. They stuck me in this medical centre that hadn't got enough space to turn a stretcher round so they got my foot caught. Got in there and they said, 'There's nothing we can do for him in here,' so they took me back out and put me in the ambulance. So I passed out again. Then they took me to hospital because basically I was smashed to bits."

Chris Rigg

Circuit Breaker

"I am absolutely convinced he would have got pole at the next race, the United States GP at Dallas. He was aware that that circuit was breaking up and he went straight out to do a lap before it deteriorated too far but he hit the Armco at the end of one of the chicanes. His tactics, though, were absolutely right."

"In Detroit '84, the garage area was a livestock auction ring - and it smelt like it." (Chris Rigg)

"It was a touch warmer than Norfolk in Detroit. Those gym sessions were paying off." (Chris Rigg)

Martin Brundle

Reassembled

"Sid dragged me out of there, and we flew home – I was drugged up to hell. I was in a wheelchair and we had to get two first class seats and lay them down. Sid came with me on the BA flight home. He got me to a Harley Street clinic where a surgeon put my foot back on my leg. He talked to all his medical mates around the world and they came up with a way of doing it. They were going to cut my foot off which would have been a bit of a hindrance at that point because you still needed a clutch pedal. I spent a month in the clinic in London.

"So that cost me because, first of all it compromised some of my fitness preparation, but also when it was beneficial to brake with your left foot, later on in my career, I simply couldn't do it."

Martin Brundle

Press Revelation

"I will never forget that one night I got a call from Barrie Gill, who was writing for a newspaper, and he says, 'Hello mate.' It's half-ten at night; I don't know how he got through to me - I was in a private room in the Harley Street Clinic. 'Have you got any comments about being disqualified from the Championship and losing all your points?'

"What really upset me was that Barrie Gill told me. Ken hadn't got round to telling me. Ken hadn't thought to tell me that he'd been thrown out of the Championship. Heard it from a journalist! So I'm in the Clinic, I've got my damaged legs up in the air, I'm feeling terrible, my career's in tatters and then I've got this guy on the phone asking me how I feel about losing all my points and my podium.

"So I don't actually exist in the 1984 Championship in some people's minds. But I've still got the trophy from Detroit."

Liz Brundle

Bad News

"He was taken to hospital and Norah Tyrrell came to find me at the hotel - it was the first session I'd missed all year. I used to go to every racing session, and even in Formula 3. If I didn't go to the track, he used to crash and I used to think it was because I wasn't there. So for Formula 1, I went to every one. But in Dallas it was 104°F, the track was a little bit basic at the time and he said to me, 'Don't bother coming in today, it's Friday, it's unofficial practice, it's not important, why don't you stay by the pool?' So I stayed by the pool with Rhonda Warwick, Derek's wife, and Norah Tyrrell came back and found me, and said, 'He's gone to hospital. I think he's hurt his legs. We need to go to the hospital.'"

"I always loved, and thrived on, street circuits like Detroit." (Chris Rigg)

Martin Brundle

Turbulent Times

"So Tyrrell got banned; I was on crutches for three months. My fantastic start to F1, where I'd outshone Senna to start with - I was really on a roll. I hit F1 and I thought, 'This just feels right, I can do this, this feels easy to me - despite not having a turbo.' Then Ken got banned for ballast, and he also got banned because he wouldn't agree to something so they had to get him out of the Championship. So my career kind of went off the rails almost before it started."

"I had a lot of fun with Stefan Bellof who was a great character with a unique and memorable laugh." (Chris Rigg)

Martin Brundle

Disqualification

"We got thrown out for supposedly having fuel in an auxiliary tank, which was laughable because, being a Cosworth, it only had about 480–500 horsepower, so we didn't need to fill the fuel tank we'd got. We never ever filled our fuel tank up to do a Grand Prix - just didn't have the power. We had this water injection system, and somehow or other the team had obviously used a fuel churn or something to put the water in and so they found a trace, or allegedly found a trace, of fuel in a water tank and they said we had auxiliary fuel tanks, which we absolutely didn't have and nor did we need them."

"I look slightly wrecked and I am clearly deep in thought." (Sutton Motorsport Images)

Robin Brundle

Determination & Commitment

"There were only two occasions in his career that I've known him to be down and one was when he damaged his feet and he had a period of time when he had to move about his house on his bottom, sliding down the stairs because he had both legs in plaster. He wanted to be back in the car, but had all the pressures of getting back into F1 when you've had an accident - he had to work very, very hard on his psychological strengths. I don't mean that he was in danger of going mad, but that to perform at the highest level in any sport you have to be 100% fit, mentally and physically, all the time. He had to work at getting back from 90% to 100% with that bit of doubt as to whether he could get back at the right level. Once he'd got his feet working again, he very quickly was back on the fitness programme."

Press Man As Press Man

"It was part of my job, as a Fleet Street journalist, to know the British drivers so I got to know Martin quite well. We just struck up a good relationship and we started talking about press relations and all that kind of stuff. We struck an agreement that I would help him with his press relations and put out PR stuff. We did a deal with Le Coq Sportif and got him kitted out with gear from LCS and I remember when he had his big crash in Dallas in '84, he had all these pins and screws through his feet. When he had them out, I thought, 'Here's a great chance to do a plug for LCS. So we set up a picture of Martin holding his screws but we managed to show that he had Le Coq trainers on. So we got pictures in *The Daily Mail* (my paper), *The Express* and *The Sun*. I remember dear old Ken - he used to lean into you with that big horsey grin of his - saying, 'You don't do that.' But that's the whole point: papers understand papers and what they want.

"We got Martin on *A Question of Sport* and things like that, in the early days when he was a fledgling F1 driver. All that kind of stuff helped to try and push his personality and his name in the papers. That was the basis of our relationship – but we were mates anyway."

Martin Brundle

Water Hoarding

"We were missing hundreds of horsepower, having the normally-aspirated Cosworth as opposed to the turbo cars. Ken realised you can weigh a car at the beginning of the race and at the end, but not during the race. So there were times when it was underweight in the race. The water would be topped up during a pit-stop. He was stretching the rules as a lot of people have done. But the main reason he got thrown out is they wanted him to sign an agreement about turbo engines for which they needed unanimity. Ken, being an obstinate old so-and-so, wouldn't agree because it didn't suit him. So the only way to get it signed off was to disqualify Tyrrell from the Championship, so he no longer had a vote. They then unanimously passed what they had to do, and let him back into the Championship a few months later. So he was interpreting the rules in a very extreme and risky manner, but that was nothing to do with the reason he got thrown out of the Championship."

"I still could not resist doing something to the car, even then. Brian Lisles looking on."
(Chris Rigg)

Sponsorship safe, say Dow

Crash blow to Brundle fans

Brundle before the crash.

Lynn News & Advertiser

Overshadowed Again

"I remember being in the Departure Lounge at Dallas, sitting very near Martin. He was in a wheelchair, having shattered his ankles. It was a mixed year, because he had just finished in second place in Detroit. People always think of Senna's arrival in F1 in '84 but Martin's was pretty eventful too."

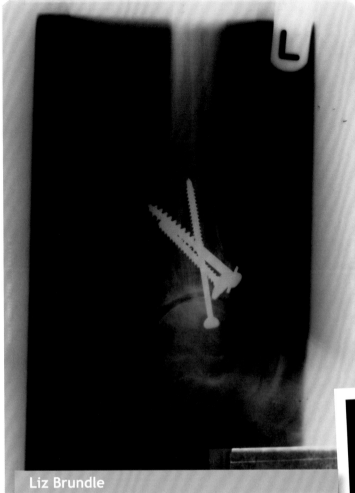

"These strategically placed screws in my left ankle saved my career. They remained in place for a year."

Martin Brundle

Nearly The Trucking Winner

"We were having Renault engines the year after and somebody from Renault came up with the idea that I could drive at the first British Truck Grand Prix, at Donington. It was an extraordinary event because 100,000 people turned up – people who didn't normally go to race tracks. People were leaving their trailers on an M1 park and coming in in their rigs, and fans had their legs dangling over the side of the walls around Donington and the whole thing was nearly out of control. Barry Sheene was in it, Steve Parrish and all sorts of interesting people.

"I decided to drive it because I'd got nothing else on at the time. The only thing I had got on was a cast on my left leg! I turned up in a plaster cast and crutch and I saw the guys running this truck looking at me a bit like, 'So, what's he going to do then?' But I could press a clutch - the good thing about trucks, even back then, is everything is air-assisted, everything was light. And then I'm leading the Grand Final, and I'm about to become the first British Grand Prix winner in a truck and, thankfully, the brakes failed three laps from the end and I didn't finish! At the time, I was trying like hell to win, but afterwards I thought, 'Martin, here you are, you're a Tyrrell works driver, you didn't want to be British Truck Champion, to be honest.' So luckily I didn't win that one!"

From the victory rostrum to the operating theatre

Liz Brundle

The Recovery Position

"He was in The Harley Street Clinic and I stayed with some friends in London and went in every day. The first week he didn't even know where he was; he can't remember anything from that week. The surgeon was very smart because he knew that the minute Martin was out, he was going to be in a racing car. So he used to tell him that he would be out the next week, and then the next week he'd say, 'Oh, sorry, you need to stay in another week.' And Martin was getting incredibly frustrated, but eventually, after a month, he came out, just before his brother got married actually. He was Best Man but he was on crutches and he looked dreadful - he'd lost a lot of weight. In the pictures the crutches are behind him so nobody knew. And then the first race he did was a truck race - the first truck race in the UK - because the pedals are really easy in trucks. So he was up there with his crutches, climbed into the cab and took it from there."

David Tremayne

Earned His Stripes

"He had that wonderful race in Detroit in '84 against Nelson. We all know Bellof was bloody quick and everybody remembers Bellof being the guy that was chasing Ayrton and catching him at Monaco, but the thing that impressed me most about Martin was that he held his head up against Bellof all the time they were racing. You'd never say that Bellof had him cowed. One might be quick one day, but the other one would be quick the next. That impressed me hugely. I remember going to see Martin in hospital in Dallas after he'd done his ankles. He was pretty mashed up. Two years later Johnny [Herbert] went through something similar. Both those guys were compromised ever after. I think their accidents with their ankles [being damaged] prevented both of them realising their full potential. But I think overall in '84 Martin did a superb job against so much adversity and then of course they were thrown out at the end of the year for the alleged water business, which was ridiculous. That was just to get a score settled against Ken Tyrrell. What Martin did in '84 showed that he certainly deserved to be a GP driver."

"I have had a very varied career but this truck was the most extreme thing I have raced."

Brundle blow as ban stays

Jonathan Palmer

Making The Grade

"It was a tough year for us both, me struggling with a dog of a car that did much to undermine my confidence and Martin having the dramas of a nasty leg-breaking shunt at Dallas and then season disqualification for Tyrrell. We both moved on from that, me moving to Zakspeed in 1985 and Martin with the Renault turbo-powered Tyrrell. So, we both made F1 stick."

Martin Brundle

The '85 Season

"It was a curious season, 1985, because we started with two normally-aspirated cars until I was given the sole Renault turbo-powered Tyrrell 014 car for the French and British Grands Prix. Then Bellof had the turbo for his home race, the German GP, and the Austrian round while I reverted to the 012 with its venerable Ford Cosworth power unit, now in DFY form. For the Dutch GP, we finally had two turbo cars and then Bellof was tragically killed in a sports car race at Spa. The reason we only had the one turbo for the first half of the season was twofold: cost and availability."

"Liz and Jill Palmer preparing to race each other in karts."

"Keeping cool and hydrated in Rio with Nigel Mansell and Stefan Johansson. I have obviously decided to dress like the Brazilian flag." (Sutton Motorsport Images)

Herbie Blash

Back In Business

"I think the thing that impressed me most with Martin in the early days before I really got to know him was the accident that he had with the Tyrrell in Monaco. That was a big accident. I've seen drivers that have had accidents like that and have lost the edge. Of course Martin didn't – he was a very brave and very courageous guy to come back so quickly after that accident."

Liz Brundle

Mirror, Mirror

"For the first half of the '85 season, we still had the normally-aspirated car and were again up against the turbos. I remember everybody signed an agreement to say that the normally-aspirated car could race, apart from Ron Dennis, who said they would get in the way of his cars. So Ken put some truck mirrors on the Tyrrell and pushed it down the pit lane and sat it in front of the McLaren garage to just pass the message back to Ron."

David Tremayne

Season Of Frustration

"It was just one of those awful years because the normally-aspirated cars weren't any good and the turbo Tyrrell was such a horrible car. It's a classic example that just putting a more powerful engine in something doesn't make it better if it isn't any good to start with. It was just a fairly unsanitary car. But Martin again drove the balls off it."

Sutton Motorsport Images

Martin Brundle

Short On Funds

"I think they were pretty difficult times. The blue '85 car just had Tyrrell written down the side of it. We did have some sponsors on it with a London-based financial organisation – the Porchester Group. Remember, we'd been slung out of the '84 championship so Ken was probably not getting a lot of money out of Bernie and not getting much sponsorship."

"How lucky was I to have advice from Ken Tyrrell and Jackie Stewart." (Sutton Motorsport Images)

Martin Brundle

XJR-6 First Test

"Tom asked me to drive the new Jaguar sports racer at Mosport. So, initially, we went to Snetterton, Mike Thackwell and myself. It looked beautiful – a carbon chassis. I'll never forget Mike Thackwell was sitting on the side of it in the door well with me sitting inside it. As I'm wiggling the steering wheel, the steering rack broke – the ramifications of that are quite massive. Of course, if that breaks out on track when you're pulling 3G or 4G, then you'll have the most almighty accident."

Derick Allsop

The Real World

"He was obviously always quite bright, in a very street-wise sense and I think that perhaps came from the fact that he flogged cars; he's a man of the world. He wasn't one of these drivers today who are pampered almost from nappies, from karting and all the rest of it. He had to make his own way and that was very apparent even back in those days. He was fiercely ambitious or he wouldn't have got half as far as he did, had he not been. But I found him engaging as well. You didn't sense that this was a manufactured young driver. He was an earthy type of character and because he didn't have a silver spoon in his mouth that made him more and more endearing."

"The Brit pack of Warwick, Mansell and Brundle - I'm no doubt thinking, 'I want your job.'" (Sutton Motorsport Images)

"Michael Turner depicts me leading my first ever sportscar race, against the mighty works Porsches."

"The Jaguar sport racers were so purposeful and elegant."

Martin Brundle

Not Short Of Power

"I think, with great irony, that at the British GP, I ended up starting at the back of the grid because my car failed to start on the grid. I have a memory of starting behind Bellof with the turbo. His normally aspirated engine would have had 520 horsepower and the turbo would have had 800/900 in qualifying trim and 750 in the race – so you had 50% more power. It was basically the '84 car with a turbo strapped to the back of it. And it was a bit of a beast, to be honest."

Roger Silman

Jaguar XJR-6 Début

"I don't think I'll ever forget that first lap of Martin's at Mosport. Porsche had been looking down their noses at us – they'd been doing sportscars for years. They were surprised by the speed of the car but of course the car Tony [Southgate] gave us was totally different from their concept. When Martin jumped out of third place on the grid to lead, then went on to lead for nine laps, it was out of this world. It was absolutely tremendous. He was brilliant."

Martin Brundle

Incredible Mosport

"I was third on the grid with Stuck and Ickx on the front row. As the flag dropped, the Porsches bogged down a bit with turbo lag. Being a normally-aspirated V12 with instant torque available, I just drove between them and led the race. They were trying to pass me for nine laps and then all of a sudden it was, 'OK, you've had your fun.' They just turned up the boost and poured past me down the back straight. Mosport was a slightly terrifying racetrack. Winkelhock had an accident. Then we had a bearing failure at the same corner, funnily enough. I'll never forget coming into the pits and Tom got down to fixing it, Tom Walkinshaw, working on the front axle replacing some bits and pieces."

Martin Brundle

Erroneous Prediction

"I drove the 012 Tyrrell at the Nürburgring, the German GP, flat out and I remember crossing the line in 10th and thinking what an amazing drive it was and nobody would ever recognise it or know it, but that was the end of an era. There would never be a normally-aspirated car in F1 again. I think the Cosworth DFY produced about 520hp by then and I remember absolutely thrashing this car the whole race, coming out of the last corner four-wheel drifting, really having fun. I was the only one doing that really. We were revving to a bit under 11,000 revs; Ken explained to me over dinner that he'd been told that with pumping losses and the laws of physics, normally-aspirated engines had reached their peak. So I remember crossing the line and thinking, 'That's it, that's the end of an era, because it will all be turbos in future.' It wasn't the end of an era, of course!"

"The normally-aspirated Jaguar leapt into life at the start as the Porsche turbos waited to spool up."

Martin Brundle

Fun, Games & Tragedy

"Mike Thackwell was a sensitive soul and a brilliant race driver. We got stopped for speeding the night before the Mosport race by a Canadian Mountie. We were in a big old Jaguar XJ12 and we were having a bit of fun coming back from the restaurant and coming home sideways! The Mountie's solution was that I sat in the back and Mike drove home. So, we got away with that one. Then, on the Monday, we went off to the Niagara Falls and we heard over the radio that Winkelhock had died which was really sad. Very funny guy. The night before the race, we had sat at the next table to Surer and Winkelhock having dinner. That was pretty tragic, to say the least."

"The right front wheel bearing would eventually fail at Mosport, causing a long pit stop."

Martin Brundle on ...

Stefan Bellof

"Stefan Bellof was incredible at Tyrrell. In fact, Bellof was just crazy. He was just so brave and so fast. I saw him pull some moves. He'd be overtaking me and I'd be trying to follow him through the pack, because we were always nose-to-tail in the Tyrrells, the pair of us. He was either on my tail or I was on his tail. Then he'd pull a couple of moves and I'd be like, 'Come on Martin, get on with it, get on with it, he's getting away, he's getting away!' Next thing is, he'd be three cars behind me because he'd gone off somewhere. He was absolutely crazy. And I watched him die, sadly. I was about to jump in the Jaguar in the pit lane, the old pit lane at Spa, and watched him go in. And that was horrible, absolutely horrible. I rang Ken to say, 'Stefan's dead,' and I didn't even get a chance to say anything. I said, 'Hello Ken, it's Martin,' and Ken went, 'I know,' and put the phone down. Ken didn't want us to do sports car racing because he thought it was dangerous. I was in a carbon Jaguar but Stefan was in the aluminium Porsche 956."

"I liked the safety of the Jaguar's carbon chassis but head protection was limited to one small headrest." (Martine Walkinshaw)

"Driver and car at rest. Drivers would not be allowed near the car without team gear these days." (Martine Walkinshaw)

Jonathan Palmer

Legacy

"In 1985, it was my turn to smash myself up, this time in the Porsche 956 at Spa, breaking my leg badly. Injuries and fatalities then were not unusual, particularly in the Group C sportscars that we both raced, and we've both ended up with minor disabilities that few will know niggle us most days.

"That, the general motorsport struggle, and mainly the fact that we were both pretty straightforward determined guys, brought us together as very close friends, and we would regularly holiday together with our wives, mainly en route between the Japanese and Australian GPs – Fiji and Dunk Island were great fun!"

Roger Silman

Bellof's Fatal Accident

"At that time, the pits were after the hairpin so we watched the accident from the pit road so it was very distressing and unpleasant, as it often was in those days. Remember this was Martin's team-mate in the Tyrrell but Martin was totally professional, and I felt that he withdrew into himself. I always thought he had a lot of inner strength - very quiet but he continued to get on with it. I admired him for that. It showed a very strong person. And then Tyrrell stopped him racing sportscars, so that was the end of that."

AUTOSPORT

AUGUST 15 1985 80

JAGUAR'S COMEBACK

MOSPORT GROUP C REPORT ◆ THREE WAY F3 TITLE FIGHT
KART GP ◆ BMW M635 TEST ◆ LOVELL'S RALLY BID

Reproduced with the kind permission of Autosport

Robin Brundle

Feet First

"His bravery. The accidents. As a brother, one is absolutely fearful. I used to dread the start of every race. In those early days, by the time the back of the grid got to where the front end started, they'd be doing over 100mph. With the feet in front of the axle line, if you hit the back end of a car that was stationary on the grid at 100mph, you would either be killed or lose your feet or legs. So, once the first corner had gone, I could relax and get into strategy."

Martin Brundle

On My Metal

"After Bellof was killed in August, I had a series of team mates and it was difficult. I wasn't really physically strong enough and the cars were fearsomely difficult to drive. I'd had three months on crutches and had a winter of getting myself back to fitness but my left leg and ankle were still pretty damn painful at that point. I'd still got about a foot of metal in my ankle. There were three pins, 4in or 5in long. I think there was always - especially with a turbo strapped to your back – that element of, 'If I have another big shunt and it bends the metal in my leg, what am I going to do then?' They did warn me that was a dangerous situation. So, after having such a great start in '84, it was a pretty dismal year."

"A podium finish in Mosport was thoroughly satisfying until we heard about the death of Manfred Winkelhock."
(Martine Walkinshaw)

Martin Brundle

Dangers

"The tracks were dangerous. I experienced the catch-fencing in my early days, and that was shocking stuff. There were walls that were too close to you and I never thought twice about them. Never even looked at it. Because you don't when you're that age. You're invincible, aren't you? Until suddenly you realise - you're not. I didn't see too much death. I saw Bellof die in the sports car. He was in the Porsche which was why I never wanted to drive a 956 or a 962. My first two sports car races: the first one Winkelhock died and I saw that, saw him going into the wall. The second one Bellof died, and I stood watching that, just as I was about to get in my Jaguar. The day before that Palmer had a big shunt in the Richard Lloyd Porsche and that was a honeycomb one where the car bent so much the gear lever hit him in the eye socket!

"I'd now been in sports car racing for two weeks effectively and one of my friends is in a really bad way and another guy I know well is dead, and that is the Saturday. Ken was desperately trying to stop me and Stefan from driving sports cars. After seeing the Bellof accident, initially I didn't want to get back in the car. I went back to our little caravan and thought about it for a few minutes and decided to get back in, on the basis of, well that's what you do. That's what I did for a living and we're halfway through a race. It was pretty brutal back in those days - a guy clearly dead and yet we finished the race."

Martin Brundle on ...

Niki Lauda

"Direct, intelligent, selfish, determined, networks at the very highest levels, worldly and wise. I'll never forget passing him at Monza. I was in the Tyrrell and he was in a McLaren, and I nailed him into the second chicane. And I was very pleased with myself. As we went down the pit straight to enter the second lap of the race, he just cruised past me with his McLaren TAG Turbo. He'd got a lot more speed than I'd got. I was just very pleased with myself for having passed Niki Lauda! He looked across at me – we were doing about 220, I would think - and put his hand up, as if to say, 'What are you doing? We've got a long way to go. What about your brakes? Your tyres?' And that sort of thing. Inevitably, halfway through the race, my car had broken down, I'd walk or get a lift back to the pits on the bike, look at the monitor... Who's leading the race? Niki Lauda!"

"Finally, the Renault turbos arrive. Bellof, Tyrrell, Brundle and Renault's Denis Chevrier look on." (Sutton Motorsport Images)

"This typifies 1980s style F1 - six tyres in view, all of them sliding sideways." (Sutton Motorsport Images)

Martin Brundle

Selfish Wins

MB: "If people are trying to score points off you outside the car, you just bat it away to be honest. It's almost water off a duck's back. I haven't met too many people who are pro-actively devious. I think all the great champions are very selfish people, and with that territory comes a little bit of getting your elbows out, creating the unfair advantage, which is frankly what it's all about. I don't see that as a negative, I see that as a positive to aspire to - now I look back! You've got to be selfish."

PP: "It's not the traditional British sporting way."

MB: "Of course it's not, but you've got to be totally selfish. They used to give each other their cars. Stirling gave away a world championship... and still would argue with me all day long on that. What I'm telling you is how you needed to be in recent years and today. To get on, you've got to fight your corner so hard and just get all the unfair advantages."

"The '85 car was basically the Tyrrell 012 with a monstrous turbo bolted to the back." (Sutton Motorsport Images)

Johnny Herbert

Two Things At Once

"He was a racer but also a thinker. I know if he looks back to F3 with Ayrton, there were certain things he wished he had done. Ayrton was canny and was able to do certain things which stopped Martin going for the Championship. I think Martin regrets being too much of a gentleman but that's what he was. He was hard but he was fair – I like hard and fair; I don't like anybody who is dirty. Racers are racers and I think Martin was a racer but also very intelligent. That is actually very different and very rare, even in the age that Martin was in, to have someone who could think about it while he was doing it. Even in the modern day there are drivers out there who still can't do both. So that would help him especially in races. He could feel where he was, and feel what he needed to do, be it go faster or slower, to give himself a better chance. In those days you had to look after the tyres a lot more with the Goodyears and especially with the sports cars where you have to feel the car much more and react to it, which Martin was able to do."

Good luck Martin

MARTIN at the wheel of the new Tyrrell Renault turbo, still with its distinctive royal blue livery, at a recent Silverstone test session.

MARTIN BRUNDLE will fulfil one of his racing ambitions on Sunday when he lines up for the British Grand Prix.

He drives for the first time in his "home" Grand Prix after missing last year's race because of injury.

Martin will be in the new Tyrrell Renault turbo, and although it will only be the car's second outing in a race and his test programme has been limited, he is optimistic he can go well.

This is the second season in the big time for Martin, who lives at South Wootton with his wife Liz.

IMPACT

He is determined to make an impact in front of the 80,000 fans who will be at the Silverstone circuit and the millions more watching on TV all over the world.

Can Martin be amongst the top finishers? We hope so. He has the skill and the courage and now, hopefully a car to match his talent.

We wish Martin every success in the Silverstone GP, the eighth round of this year's

Martin Brundle

Power Mad

"You've got a certain amount of power surfeit over grip and you just manage it. In qualifying in Australia with the '85 turbo Tyrrell, I remember it spinning its wheels down the main Brabham Straight in top gear in qualifying trim. It had so much power and so little grip."

Dave Price

F3 Macau GP

"Martin did come back to drive for me again when he was doing F1. He did Macau for me in '85. Martin came back to do a guest slot for me and got wiped out on the grid because the clutch failed on the line and some Japanese guy came flying through from the back of the grid and took the whole of the side out of it. We had some exciting times!"

"Uncle Ken with his two protégés."

"Surely the worst sponsorship application to any F1 car." (Sutton Motorsport Images)

Martin Brundle

The Turbo Era

"You used to fight the cars. I often say it, and people laugh, but I'm only half joking, that your main job all afternoon was to stop the car from crashing! Those turbo cars – it's jumping, hitting the ground, sparking, flames coming out of the turbo... You are hanging on to it, you're absolutely stopping the car from crashing, whilst maintaining as much forward speed as you can. And that was all you were doing."

"Cresting Eau Rouge in the glorious Jaguar, just a few metres past where Bellof would die that day."

Martin Brundle

In Hiding!

"I never tried to break my Tyrrell contract, but it had a November 30 option, which was very late. I went to the Caribbean one year at that time, hoping Ken couldn't find me because I wanted to go to Lotus. A message, taking up the option, was delivered to me - on the beach – on the last day!"

Liz Brundle

Man Of His Word

"I think it was frustrating; it was frustrating for both of us. For him because he couldn't get the results that he probably deserved, and for me watching it because I so wanted him to do well. Obviously, it was great that Ken gave him the chance, but then he was tied into a contract with Ken for three years. It was said that Ayrton broke his contract but Martin didn't. Martin didn't want to, really. But had he broken it, he might have had a chance of a higher level drive."

David Tremayne

Third Year Lucky

"In '86 he had a decent car and was able to get some good results with the Tyrrell."

"And now for something completely different - being interviewed by Stirling during the making of a TV show around driving, seen here with my team mate Lennie Bennett."

Derick Allsop

The Shape Of Things To Come

"Martin and Murray came and had lunch with me when I did a pre-season piece in 1986. They were a great combination those two, bouncing ideas off each other. It made for a really good piece."

Martin Brundle

Turbo Max

"The 1986 car was better but it was the most fearsome year with the turbos - the following year they restricted the boost to 2.5 bar. In '86 we had this incredible situation where you'd go out for practice on a Saturday morning with 800hp and a few hours later you'd get back into it for qualifying. They'd closed the waste gates, changed the inter-coolers and compressors and you'd have 1250hp and a set of qualifying tyres - so more than 50% more power. You'd creep out of the pits because you couldn't bring the qualifiers in until the last two or three corners of the out-lap. And then you'd let this thing go down the pit straight and it was just incredible, especially at somewhere like Monaco. It was like some kind of video game – some kind of warp speed off a sci-fi movie. The thing just took off with that amount of power. It wasn't power that you could prepare for or test; you had an engine that would overheat by the end of that first lap. It was not something you'd go round merrily trying. You'd start the lap with cold brakes, cold front tyres and hot rear tyres with all of this incredible power going through them. By mid-lap the whole thing was coming together but still at warp-speed and still spinning your wheels in top gear. By the end of the lap, your rear tyres were completely finished because they had been trying to transmit 1250hp and you didn't really have any more downforce or any more mechanical grip - you just had 50% more power and it wasn't very driveable power. They were just quite extraordinary times and I'm so pleased I experienced them."

James Allen

Timing Is Everything

"I did an interview with Briatore for F1 Racing magazine and we talked about Martin. He said he was just unlucky with his timing because actually, if he'd come along a few years later, he would have been in a top team and stayed in a top team throughout his Formula 1 career. He was just unlucky that he was around at a time when there was Piquet, Mansell, Senna, Prost, Lauda, Rosberg..."

"My Liz looks much better in my overalls than I do."

Martin Brundle on ...

Nelson Piquet

"Cheeky and crafty, fast and networked brilliantly. In wheel-to-wheel combat, as hard as nails. A very worthy Champion."

"The 1986 Tyrrell was far and away the best car I drove for them." (Sutton Motorsport Images)

"I commissioned this Michael Turner painting as a farewell gift to Ken and Norah Tyrrell."

Helen Dickson

Cool About Fan Club

"Martin remained very modest. In the early days, we used to say to him that he needed a fan club. People have always been interested but he could never see that side of it. He couldn't understand why people would be interested in him. He was too modest really. He wouldn't start a fan club and he didn't want us to start up one for him. He didn't have any interest in taking the limelight. He has got a huge following and there's many a time when we've had free drinks or got into areas that we wouldn't normally – without Martin's influence, it wouldn't have happened. Martin always had a little giggle about it. He's never let fame go to his head. He's never changed."

Robin Brundle

Pulling Together

"I have always enjoyed supporting him and followed him, been there to enjoy his successes and to try to support him where it hasn't gone quite as well, even down to training. Some people are absolutely natural athletes and have to do very little work to stay fit. Marty's been an athlete, but he wasn't a super athlete. So, to keep his super fitness and strength, he really had to work hard at it. He had a trainer and physio - called Tom Ryan - from the early days, and a gym at home and there were local sandpits. He would do 45 minutes-to-an-hour in the gym and then run in the sand dunes for another 40 minutes, and then come back and do another hour in the gym – that would be three or four times a week plus other lighter exercises in the gym on the off-days. I would do most of that programme with him. It would be common for him to push himself so hard that he was physically sick. I'm fortunate in that I am generally quite fit but couldn't keep up with him – it was bloomin' hard. But I was there to push him on and I thoroughly enjoyed that time."

James Allen

Poultry Games

"It was a fearsome machine to drive around the streets of Monaco. Towards the end of the race, Patrick Tambay would land on the top of my head." (Sutton Motorsport Images)

"He lived in an aggressive time, days when Prost and Senna were taking each other off, Mansell and Senna were wheel-to-wheel down the pit straight in Spain. These were the days when drivers felt safer in the cars and so they started playing games of chicken with each other. It was a very, very tough time."

"It is easy to see I was happy with life in 1986." (Sutton Motorsport Images)

Martin Brundle

Unreliability

"The cars were horribly unreliable back then. Problems with engines, brakes, clutch and transmission seemed to be the accepted norm when going GP racing. Then, in this period, you're into turbos, inter-coolers and radiators that were under extremely high pressure and so it goes on."

Martin Brundle

Dubious Characters

"Corruption's too strong a word for what I've experienced, but clearly, some men's egos get out of control. When people come into Formula 1, you spot quite quickly whether they're passing through, or they're in for the long haul. It's very easy to tell actually: the way they handle themselves, the things they do. So we've seen our fair share of gangsters with shiny surfaces and apparently good businessmen, but some of them are just winging it because they've got nothing to lose, or they're hiding something else that's going on. That's less and less now. You'd see a lot of very small teams strangely funded. When I first got into F1, there were 13 Italian drivers, because I think it was - five million goes to the team, three million goes to a Swiss bank account. It just seemed to be the accepted norm back in those days."

"The Monaco swimming pool section was a real challenge before they sanitised it with run-off areas." (Sutton Motorsport Images)

"Planting the throttle at La Source and aiming at Eau Rouge was a glorious experience in the turbo era with 1250 brake horsepower under my right foot." (Sutton Motorsport Images)

Martin Brundle

Putting Everything On The Black!

"It was the most outrageous time. Senna was at his finest. Qualifying was everything. I remember being clocked at 183mph going over the top of the hill into Casino Square at Monaco. You'd be staring in your mirrors, trying not to fire up your qualifiers. Others would be in the middle of their incredible qualifying laps. It was just such a volatile environment but brilliant all the same."

Brand's Hatch breakthrough

Shell Oils BRITISH GRAND PRIX **Shell Oils BRITISH GRAND PRIX**

Brundle grabs 5th at British GP

A BRANDS Hatch breakthrough for Martin Brundle and the Data General Tyrrell team.

That was the bonus of Sunday's spectacular British Grand Prix when Lynn driver Martin Brundle took 5th place and his team-mate the Frenchman Phillipe Streiff was 6th.

In a dramatic last lap, they both overtook the Brabham BMW of Derek Warwick who ran out of petrol.

Brundle's two World Championship points were the first he has scored since fishing 5th in the opening race of the season at Rio in March.

Brundle found the race physically exhausting. "I felt sick three or four times in the course of it," he said afterwards, "but the pleasure at picking up points here has helped me forget that.

"I had bad problems with understeer in the first half of the race, but once I changed tyres — and it was a pretty good stop — that was cured and it was relatively plain sailing.

"I think this is the first time since I joined the team we've had both cars in the points and I'm just thrilled for Phillipe and myself.

Brundle did reveal one glaring error when he was being lapped by Mansell and Piquet, the race leaders. "I was doing my best to be good to them while at the same time maintaining my own place behind Patrick Tambay. I pulled off their line, but they didn't come past and I had to keep coming back on it.

"The upshot was I missed third gear at one stage and lost several seconds."

Streiff revealed that 25 laps from the end he realised his steering wheel was coming off. He could only effect repairs on the straight which took three or four laps and let Dumfries close the gap.

"At the end I turned everything down to conserve fuel and fought all the way to keep him at bay," said the Frenchman.

There were no fuel problems for Brundle, however, a further demonstration of the excellent race he had driven.

LET'S go." Martin Brundle signals to his pits crew he's ready to start a practice lap.

Lynn News & Advertiser

Johnny Herbert

A Different Route

"He had got a lot of talent, came from a different background, didn't come through the normal karting route which, even in those days, people like Alain and Ayrton had done, as had Andrea de Cesaris, Riccardo Patrese to name a few."

Mike Greasley

Managing Martin

"I was working for a sports management company that specialised in representing rally drivers and I was their man looking after World Championship rally drivers - no racing drivers at all at that point. I was at a Lancia pre-RAC Rally test day where the media were invited to take part in scary rides alongside star drivers and I was minding my own business when this young racing driver came up and said, 'I hear you're pretty good with rally drivers. Do you know anything about F1?' 'A little bit. Why?' 'My name's Martin Brundle and I'm looking for a new manager. Would you be interested?' So that was it! I put it to the company and they said, 'Yes, yes.' So that's how we got involved."

"I shared this car with Eddie Cheever although I never actually got to race it." (Jaguar Heritage Archive)

Nigel Roebuck

Sorting The Men From The Boys

"I was talking to Berger recently about the turbo era. He said, 'When I look back at it now, I can't believe the specification of the cars we were racing in those days.' When he was at Benetton in '86 and they had the BMW engine, Berger said, at the Österreichring with qualifying boost, 'I had a genuine 1500 brake horsepower.' About twice what they have now. No surprise that that was Jenks's [Denis Jenkinson – the doyen of motor racing journalists] favourite era of F1. And Martin was part of it.

"When Martin drove the F1 Ferrari last year [2012 for Sky], he said that he loved everything about it but, 'Oh dear, these 2.4 V8s wouldn't pull the skin of a rice pudding!' You imagine what that would do to you or me - 750bhp: gutless in comparison with a V10 and completely gutless compared with a turbo. And also to think that this is 25 years ago and they were racing with so much more power than now! And the cars were nothing like as strong as they are now; nobody had a HANS device; tracks were much less forgiving..."

"Total commitment at Monza was only rewarded with tenth place." (Sutton Motorsport Images)

Martin Brundle

Easy Money

"I drove an XJR-6 once in '86 for Tom. Funny story around that – we were moving house that weekend and Tom rang me up and said, 'I need you in Jerez; I'm fed up with my drivers.' I said, 'I can't, I'm moving house.' He said, 'I need you down here – I'll pay you some money.' It suited us at the time because that money was very helpful for the house move. So I left Liz to it and I went down there. There were three Silk Cut Jaguars and they ran into each other on the first corner – Warwick, Cheever and Brancatelli. Derek and Eddie were team mates in F1, and in the Jags, but were always at each other's throats. Anyway, Eddie was coming through the field nicely – it was a 360kms race – and I'm standing in the pit-lane, helmet on, overalls on, and on the in-lap the drive-shaft broke and the car never made it back to the pits. So Tom paid me but I never ever sat in the car in the race!"

Maurice Hamilton

Press Relations

"He was certainly one of the first that I can remember who thought about having a lunch for the British press before the season and we all went to that, which was a very good idea. He was then telling us why he'd chosen Zakspeed and all the rest of it. I remember thinking that was clever, typical Martin. He was very good at promoting himself but in a nice way, not over the top. Some drivers would be - I won't mention any names - a bit in your face whereas Martin was Martin. He was aware of the influence of the press to a certain degree, and he was very approachable and very easy to get on with."

Martin Brundle

Promises, Promises

"I made a bad decision in '87. I wanted to stay in F1 but Ken had run out of money. I got smooched into going and driving the Zakspeed for the German team. Inevitably in the winter, every team has always got 25% more power and 50% more downforce than they had the previous summer. 'It's going to be so many seconds a lap quicker,' is the normal style of a chat over the winter. So, I drove for Erich. They had a good little car - they had no money really - but they had a good little car."

"Zakspeed had a very close relationship with the Nürburgring and they put on a race for the wives and girlfriends."

"This is actually my wife, Liz, demonstrating the art of over-steer."

Mike Greasley

Media Monitor

"The first deal that I really got involved with was not exactly one that is to be remembered. It was Zakspeed in 1987. I remember him saying, 'I'm really interested in somebody to look after my back'. I remember those words very well. I suppose I became more of an advisor than what you would strictly call a manager because I was a journalist then and a lot of the F1 rat pack were mates of mine and I used to travel a lot with them. I knew them all intimately.

"So he thought that, with me being involved with that lot, I could keep an ear to the ground and see which way the wind was blowing. A smart idea really. Those guys were certainly opinion-formers and, if they thought you were doing all right, then they said so. So Martin saw those things as being important and I was happy to get involved on that basis. And the company was certainly happy to be involved – it increased its profile in the world of sport, having an F1 driver on its list. We became friends and still are friends. My wife and I are godparents to Martin's children."

"Monaco '87 with my ever-supportive wife Liz and my adorable mum, Alma."

Martin Brundle

Beer Testing

"We went testing with the Zakspeed at Nürburgring every other week because we could because they had a deal there, but we never had anything to test. So I pounded round there, day-after-day, but with nothing to test. Then I'd go out to dinner with Erich. He was a really nice guy but he didn't speak a word of English and I didn't speak a word of German! So we'd go out to dinner, then we'd go to the Pistenklause at the Nürburgring and have a beer, and it'd be midnight and I was staying at his house. 'Erich, I'm testing tomorrow, I have to go.' 'Schlafe, Schlafe.' They were very quiet meals! Erich liked his drivers to go to the Pistenklause and have a few beers with him, even when you were in the middle of testing."

"Driving Silverstone with the Le Mans-spec bodywork. It would arrive at Stowe Corner at a terrifyingly high speed." (Philip Porter)

Martin Brundle

Unique Points

"Zakpseed in '87 was a nice little family team. They had a new car at Imola and it looked much nicer but actually it was just a dressed up version of the old model. I remember Christian Danner, my team mate, who still had the older car, saying to me in practice, 'Are you going as fast as you can?' 'Yes, I am.' He said, 'Right, I'm closing in on you and I think we can go faster with the old car,' which was shocking but it was true. I finished fifth and scored Zakspeed's first, and last, points – ever!"

"Zakspeed was a great little team - we tried our best." (LAT)

"That's a forlorn look I have there. I am not happy about something. The '87 season is not inspiring me."

Jonathan Palmer

All Change

"At the end of 1986, by strange irony, the positions of winter 1983/4 were reversed – I ended up moving from Zakspeed to Tyrrell, driving a normally-aspirated car, and Martin moved to my old Zakspeed team! Have to say it was quite satisfying to get the better deal – I won the Jim Clark Cup [championship for non-turbo cars] and scored three times as many points as Martin, who broke down most of the time!"

"My first Le Mans. It is interesting to see how rapidly the cars have developed in just two years." (Philip Porter)

"I loved driving at Le Mans, the challenge of the track and super-high speeds. I knew I would be going back."
(Sutton Motorsport Images)

SPORTSMAIL SPECIAL　The 24-hour showdown

Driving force

Roger Silman

Flying At Le Mans

"He was very serious in his approach, didn't leave anything unexplored. I think it's normal now, but in 1987 I wouldn't say it was normal. This was the year that Win Percy had his huge accident. It's a very difficult time in sportscars, especially at Le Mans, when you experience something like that. Darkness in the middle of the night only makes it worse. There are so many stories that spread and not necessarily based on fact at all. And it's a long time before you get the car back and see for yourself what went on. So, as a driver with that hanging over your head, it's not easy. Mulsanne was a very dangerous place anyway and for Win to have had such a huge accident there – he only got away with it because nothing stopped the car in a short distance and it just went on for so long. For Martin and the others, they just continued to drive until we got the car back and had some idea of what had happened to Win's car."

Above and right: "With at least 28 scheduled pit stops, team work was everything at Le Mans." (Top - Philip Porter, right - Sutton Motorsport Images)

Martin Brundle on ...

Alain Prost

"Just quietly got on with it really. I never once saw him do a qualifying lap. He must have done, around me somewhere, because he was often on pole or at the front of the grid. Whenever you saw him on track, if you were backing off and he came through, he never looked like he was on a qualifying lap or a hot lap. He just had such elegance and economy of driving. He could be political. I had a few encounters and observed him in drivers' GPDA meetings. Very complete really – just hard-working, and supremely skilful, which you saw when he did ice-racing. You've got to be a man manager to run a Grand Prix team. Jackie Stewart managed to somehow do it, but I don't think he's the most selfish person in the world by a long way. But Lauda and Prost and Co., weren't good at running businesses because they would be focussed on themselves, not everybody else."

"Tom was like a second father to me.
When he spoke, I listened."

Martin Brundle

Percy's Flying Circus

"We were leading the race at Le Mans and going very well in the '87 car and then I came across this piece of bodywork that was blackened and then a piece that was white and purple, and it looked like a plane crash. Eventually I came across this blackened-looking tub. This was in the night and it was on its side with nothing really attached to the tub, it seemed. I radioed in, 'Has one of our cars had an accident? I've just caught a glimpse of this purple bodywork.' There was a long silence and then someone came on the radio, 'What do you mean, have we had an accident?' 'Well, I've just seen some bodywork.' I think I gave them the heads-up that the accident had just happened. Win was just the other side of the barriers.

"We then had about two-and-a-half hours of safety car. Of course, your fuel lasts forever when you're under the safety car. While racing, the car used to run at 55-60° inside so you were sweating, but all of a sudden you're not sweating any more. You've got cold air vents pointing at you and I remember shivering in the car, absolutely freezing inside as I was trundling around behind the safety car, unsure whether one of my team-mates was dead or not. Inevitably, I was starting to wonder why the car crashed – turned out to be a puncture. Win had only just got in the car. So that was pretty terrifying."

"The 1987 Hungarian Grand Prix before the turbo failed. Great racetrack." (LAT)

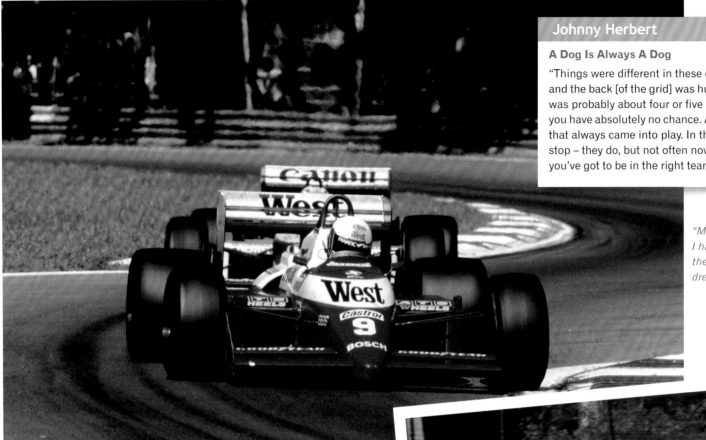

Johnny Herbert

A Dog Is Always A Dog

"Things were different in these days. The difference between the front and the back [of the grid] was huge. When he was in that Zakspeed, he was probably about four or five seconds off the pace, maybe more. So you have absolutely no chance. And then you also had reliability issues that always came into play. In this day and age, it's so rare for a car to stop – they do, but not often nowadays. But one thing never changes - you've got to be in the right team at the right time."

"Monza for Zakspeed. I have just lapped the Williams - in my dreams." (LAT)

"An important piece of silverware in my cabinet." (Abigail Humphries)

"First victory for Jaguar in sportscar racing was at Spa, in spite of crashing the car the day before."

Martin Brundle

Thought Provoking

"The only time I ever significantly damaged one of Tom's cars was at Spa in '87. Johnny Dumfries binned it on the first day which they fixed. I then got caught out on a wet kerb on the second day. They fixed that and we then easily won the race to the point where they put Boesel in our car so he could take the World Championship. So that was a positive experience. It probably helped me make the decision for '88, seeing Boesel become Champion. I would think that must have been a significant part of my decision-making process."

"Guiding the Zakspeed at the Portuguese Grand Prix before the gearbox cried, 'Enough'." (LAT)

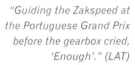

David Tremayne

Had Enough Of That

"It may have seemed like a good idea at the time but the Zakspeed really was a pretty poor car. However, the guys at Zakspeed all spoke very highly of what Martin did. By then he'd developed into a pretty savvy driver and he knew what he wanted from a car, and he was quite good as a car developer. The most impressive thing, though, was that at the end of the Zakspeed year he had the balls to say, 'I'm not doing another year like that.'"

Tony Dowe

Victory Drought Ends At Spa

"The first race I did [with TWR] was at Spa. Ian Reid, who was going to be the Chief Engineer, and myself were dragged over to Spa to run a third car with Martin and Johnny Dumfries. Nobody had a lot of confidence in what we were going to do and I have to say that, having been used to the normal American way of doing things for a few years, I was absolutely blown away as to how young Martin and Johnny were. They looked like school kids! We got into the lead and Tom took Raul Boesel out of the car he had been slated to be in and put him in our car and we won the race. So, first race, first win. That was pretty cool."

World Sportscar Champion
1988-1990

Not many young drivers have the courage to walk away from Formula 1 but the charismatic Tom Walkinshaw convinced Martin that his career and prospects would be better served by winning in sportscars rather than toiling around the rear of the field in no-hoper F1 cars. He joined TWR full-time for 1988.

There were TWR teams competing in both the World Sports Car Championship (WSC) and the International Motor Sports Association (IMSA) series, the latter in the USA. Martin would lead both teams and commute accordingly. He did 11 WSC rounds and 12 IMSA races. Additionally, he acted as a test driver for the Williams F1 team and, when Nigel Mansell had chickenpox, Martin stood in and finished seventh in the Belgian GP.

The IMSA series started superbly with a fine win in the classic Daytona 24-Hours. The Brundle XJR-9 (and 9D) he shared during the season with, mainly, John Nielsen clocked up four second-place finishes, a third and a fourth, plus four retirements. The season ended on a high note when Martin, together with Jan Lammers, won at Del Mar.

The WSC season yielded five wins, two seconds, a third and three retirements. The net result was that Martin became the 1988 World Sportscar Champion. Tom had been right! Another highlight that year was the birth of Charlie, Liz and Martin's daughter.

However, F1 is the pinnacle of the sport and Martin was lured back in '89, joining the underfunded Brabham team. Unfortunately, Bernie Ecclestone had sold the team by then and the great Brabham days were in the past. A fifth and two sixths were the best results from a frustrating season.

Not too surprisingly, Walkinshaw persuaded Martin to rejoin the TWR Jaguar team for 1990, the year that Martin and Liz produced a son by the name of Alex, who was destined to follow the family motorsport tradition. Ironically, 1990 was not to be a successful year for TWR. The team had ditched the old faithful Jaguar V12 engine in favour of a turbo-charged V6. The ultra-successful Porsche 956s and 962s had relied on turbo-charging for several years and this was TWR's attempt to do the same. The WSC season brought Martin just one win, some places and five retirements. He did only four US events, taking second place at the gruelling Daytona race.

However, there was one highlight to the year and something else special to add to the CV. Not a round of the WSC but nevertheless the most famous sportscar race in the world, Le Mans was the one to win. Martin acted as the hare to stretch and break the opposition and when his car retired, he joined Nielsen and Price Cobb in their TWR XJR-12LM to score another fine Le Mans victory for Jaguar.

"It's so exciting, even romantic, to drive a sportscar at night: man and machine versus the track and the elements."

Martin Brundle

Bold Move

"It was Tom Walkinshaw who talked me into leaving F1, which was a really tough decision - having made it into F1. Tom said, 'I think you'll be better winning in a Jaguar than driving a rubbish Formula 1 car.' And Zakspeed were going through some troubles and eventually stopped, so that ended up being a tremendous decision. In 1988, I drove for TWR Jaguar in the World Sportscar Championship, including the Le Mans 24-Hour race. I also drove for TWR Jaguar in the IMSA series in the USA, a team Tony Dowe and his guys put together in an amazingly short time."

Tony Dowe

Against The Odds

"First race we did [in USA] was the Daytona 24-Hours. From the day I started with TWR, which was October 1st 1987, to this race was 16 weeks and we started with nothing – no workshop, no cars, no transporters, no mechanics, nothing. It was probably the hardest I've ever worked. One of the things Martin does is get behind you and give you confidence in what you're doing.

"We had a test at a place in the middle of nowhere called Big Spring, down in Texas. The thinking was that if we could survive a racetrack that had zero facilities, at least it would highlight what we were missing. Then we did another test at Talledega which was fantastic. We were starting to get on top of running the cars. We turned up at Daytona and Martin and the guys in the car went on and won it. And we were 1st and 3rd in our first race so we thought, 'Well, this is easy! Ha ha.'

"The Lammers car dropped a valve and was chundering round – we should have been first, second and third. Tom grabbed Lammers and put him in at the end and Martin was bit iffy about it but it was all to the good and the victory was the first ever 24-hour race win for a TWR Jaguar sports racer."

"It was a dream to start the season with a victory against such tough competition."

Martin Brundle

Love Daytona

"We started off the season in the States and it began well with victory in the Daytona 24-Hours. What an amazing race! I love that race. It's the toughest race I've ever done, much more so than Le Mans. God, it's a physically demanding race.

"You've got 70-odd cars on the track, it's a much shorter track, you've got the infield, 13 hours of darkness at that time of the year, it's humid during the day, it's a typical Florida day in January. It seems the race has only just started and it goes dark. It's physically and mentally a very demanding event. Because it's a much shorter circuit, you can pass 10 cars a lap."

"The 31 degree banking of the Daytona oval generated enormous forces through the car and driver."

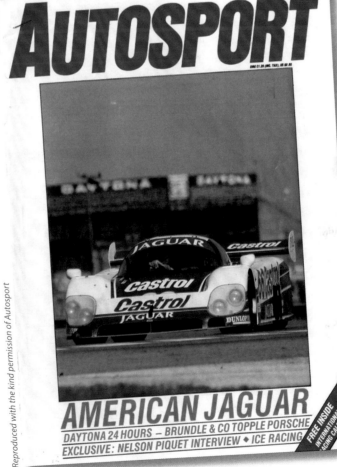

AUTOSPORT

4 FEBRUARY 1988 95p

AMERICAN JAGUAR

DAYTONA 24 HOURS – BRUNDLE & CO TOPPLE PORSCHE
EXCLUSIVE: NELSON PIQUET INTERVIEW ★ ICE RACING

FREE INSIDE INTERNATIONAL RACING CALENDAR

Reproduced with the kind permission of Autosport

Martin Brundle on ...

John Nielsen

"We won a lot of races together, Super John and me. He was just so strong. You could just keep putting Super John in, say, the middle of the night or like at Daytona. The pair of us won that as we lost Raul Boesel because he didn't feel well by about midnight. So Super John and I carried the Jag, for the next goodness knows how many hours at Daytona, and they often ran at 55°C inside - they were hot things, and physical: no power steering, they'd got a five-speed manual 'box, heavy clutch - physically incredibly hard cars to drive.

"I used to call him The Viking. He was great, and he had the speed. There was Davy Jones, Jan Lammers, AWOL [Andy Wallace], Eddie Cheever, Derek Warwick, Teo Fabi and all those guys. We had some great drivers in the Jaguars over the years."

Roger Silman

The Cat Pack

"The competition in the team was getting quite strong. He shared with Eddie Cheever in the WSR races that year, with Lammers and Johnny Dumfries in the other car. Jan was very strong when conditions were anything other than a bone dry track. He really excelled and Eddie was another accomplished driver in my eyes. So Martin had pretty stiff competition, I thought, but you could always put your money on him. He would always get the job done – he wouldn't come second to anyone. Very impressive, and a pleasure to work with."

"The Jaguar with sprint downforce set-up had truly impressive grip and cornering forces." (Sutton Motorsport Images)

Ole! Brundle the matador

Martin Brundle

Mutual Admiration Society

"Roger Silman and all his guys were absolute professionals and gelled brilliantly, as the results testify. I loved working with them and greatly appreciated the whole TWR team who never once let me down. Great bunch."

"I was lucky enough to be in the winning car at 14 international races for Jaguar. Victory in the Monza 1000 Kms was very satisfying." (Jaguar Heritage Archive)

AUTOSPORT

12 MAY 1988 95p

PORTS AUTOSPO 1000
E Silverst
SHIP th MAY 88

JAGUAR'S TREBLE
BRUNDLE/CHEEVER WIN CLASSIC DUEL AT SILVERSTONE
FORD'S TOUR DE CORSE VICTORY ♦ F3000 SURPRISES

Nigel Roebuck

Different Animals

"It could fairly be said that Martin was a great sports car driver whereas I don't think that many people would describe him in that way about F1. He had great days, there's no doubt about it. What he always says is that there were days when he could beat people like Hakkinen and Schumacher, but the point is it was, 'On my day.' Whereas he was an extremely good GP driver, without any doubt, in his era he was *the* best sports car driver.

"At a Silverstone sports car race when he was in the Jaguar, he was in that car much more than his co-driver and essentially drove a long, long sports car race, like a Grand Prix, and won the race. Talking [to me recently] about his son Alex being a born sports car racer, he said, 'Actually, I think I was really. Whenever I jumped in a sports car, I felt invincible. And, without wanting to sound arrogant, very often I was. When I got into an F1 car though, I didn't have that feeling. OK, in sports cars you do deliver a big lap in qualifying as you do in F1, but it doesn't really matter that much, certainly not like it does at a Grand Prix. A Grand Prix is an hour-and-a-half but at Le Mans you're going to be in the car for probably two hours and 40 minutes [per stint] and what you deliver over that time in terms of pace, consistency, fuel consumption, management of back-markers, using tyres over a triple stint, daylight-to-dusk, dusk-to-darkness, darkness-to-daylight, wet-to-dry, dry-to-wet... You're managing so much more. And the more I've thought about it, the more I've concluded that it's a completely different skill.'"

"Eddie and I were never the best of friends but we were a fast combination. He was much taller than me but somehow we made the cockpit fit both of us."
(Jaguar Heritage Trust)

"I found it mildly terrifying being jointly responsible for a newborn baby."

Martin Brundle

Monkey Tricks

"In '88, I was also the Williams test driver. They were developing a car with active suspension and it kept collapsing. The car did this a couple or three times on Mansell and Nigel said, 'I'm not driving that again. Put a monkey in it.' And I was the monkey they found to put in it!"

FAMILY DOUBLE

Brundles of joy — racing brothers Martin (left) and Robin Brundle pose with wives Liz and Joanne and new daughters Charlotte and Chloe. The babies were born last week within 36 hours of each other.

Saloon car driver Robin and Joanne were first to become parents, followed shortly by Jaguar ace Martin who had rushed back to Lynn from his Silverstone victory in time for the birth of Charlotte. The babies are a first for both couples and both weighed in at 6lb 14ozs.

"Yet another slick pit stop from the TWR team at Le Mans."

Martin Brundle

Why So Quick In Sports Cars?

"I have discussed this with Quentin Spurring, who is a Group C expert and author. I was team mates with Cheever and Lammers and all those guys, and apparently they could never work out how or why I was so quick in a sports car. And I don't know why. I think you can either do these things or you can't. I never performed in a single-seater really as well as I did in a sports car or, to an extent, in a touring car. I don't know if it's driving style, I don't know if it's confidence or mindset or what it is."

"It was an incredible coincidence. I rang Robin to tell him the news that Liz was pregnant and before I got round to it, he told me Jo was pregnant."

Martin Brundle

The Drive Of Dissatisfaction

"Like most sports people I've met - the vast majority - you have this fear of failure, and this dissatisfaction at all times with what you do. You're always driving yourself on. You're never happy. Occasionally you meet a sportsman, and I'm thinking Nigel Mansell or Nick Faldo or someone like that, who have this almost uncomfortable self-confidence and they drive themselves like that, with this total and utter belief that they're amazing. But most sports people I've met feel inadequate and feel disappointed in anything they've done at any time. They're always slightly unsure of themselves. And I think that's what drives you. Sports people are nowhere near as confident on the inside as they look on the outside. You keep driving yourself on."

Martin Brundle

Introspection

"Whenever I went to Le Mans, I was always the lead driver and I liked doing that. It's like when I took over my dad's garages when I was 18 - I like leading from the front.

"When I was racing the BMW, I was only 21. I didn't have the experience to be taking on some of those guys who were names. Why was I quick? Never really thought about it. I think it's just an instinctive thing. I also think I was really a bit of a later bloomer. I came on in my early-to-mid 20s where I really started to apply myself and I realised it was more than a hobby, it was now a profession. Also, if I saw somebody else doing something, I could take that and improve on it."

Martin Brundle

Bravery

"I think you've got to manage the risks in your mind, but I don't think that racing drivers are particularly brave. Would we be first in with our fists if there was a fight in the street? Unlikely. I've got fire alarms, burglar alarms, I won't walk down the side of a busy road, you wouldn't really get me jumping out of an aeroplane with a parachute on my back, or some kind of crazy off-piste skiing or that sort of thing because I don't want to hurt myself. Hang-gliding: I think that's bravery – or stupidity as some people might call it. I don't think we're necessarily brave. What we are is committed to going racing, having managed, mentally managed, the risks of, 'I might get injured, I might end up in a wheelchair, I might die. Am I prepared to do that? Yes I am. Therefore I'll go and race.' I think that's just a procedure to do what you have a passion and a skill for. I don't think it fundamentally makes you a brave person.

"If you talk to Formula One drivers, a lot of them don't like going on the road, or don't like going fast on the road. They feel uncertain and insecure in that circumstance. Some of them don't travel that fast on the road. Won't go in small aeroplanes. For me, that's what brave people do. Brave people are prepared to do anything at any time. All you're prepared to do as a racing driver is balance the risk versus the reward, and I don't mean financial reward. I mean the rewards of satisfaction and the achievement."

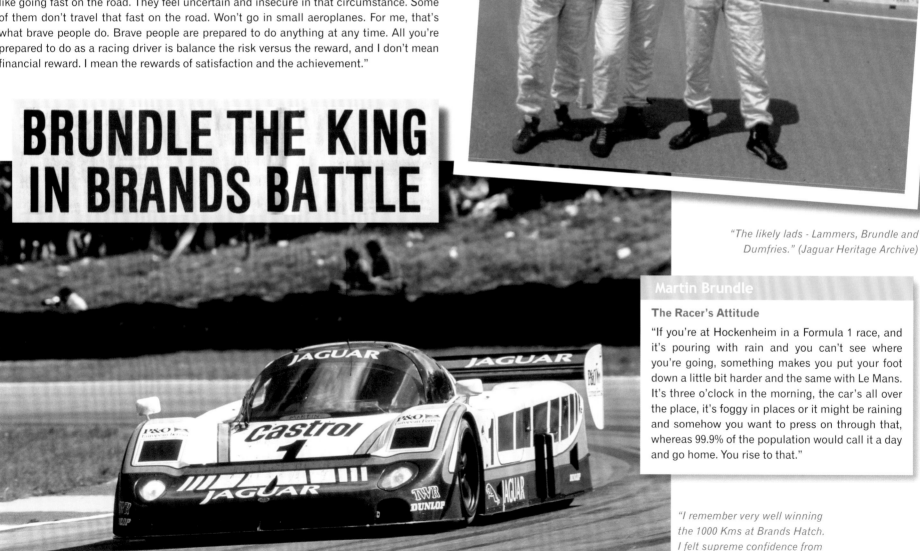

BRUNDLE THE KING IN BRANDS BATTLE

"The likely lads - Lammers, Brundle and Dumfries." (Jaguar Heritage Archive)

Martin Brundle

The Racer's Attitude

"If you're at Hockenheim in a Formula 1 race, and it's pouring with rain and you can't see where you're going, something makes you put your foot down a little bit harder and the same with Le Mans. It's three o'clock in the morning, the car's all over the place, it's foggy in places or it might be raining and somehow you want to press on through that, whereas 99.9% of the population would call it a day and go home. You rise to that."

"I remember very well winning the 1000 Kms at Brands Hatch. I felt supreme confidence from the moment I left the pits." (Sutton Motorsport Images)

Tony Dowe

Fiendish Foe

"That was a bit of an eye-opener. The Nissan [against which we were racing] was brilliantly suited to the US series; they'd changed to Goodyear tyres and they had a new electronically-controlled turbo wastegate system which helped them immensely. So, they had a car with a ton of grunt, a lot of downforce and really good tyres, and I have to say that we were struggling with the European mentality: 'Well, gosh, we've just won the World Championship the year before, therefore we must be good.'

"Although our car fitted the rules, it wasn't designed for that type of racing. It was good at Daytona because it was close to European-type racing. We knuckled down and we tried lots of things to improve our situation. In fact, we bookended the year at Del Mar and won the race, and Martin, in particular, was brilliant."

"Few remember that I did a Grand Prix for Williams, finishing seventh. The car had a level of grip way beyond anything I had experienced to date." (Sutton Motorsport Images)

Martin Brundle

Not Pussy-Footing

"Driving a Jaguar down the Mulsanne Straight at 235mph in the middle of the night is a brilliant experience. Do you know you might die? Well, yes you do. And the only drivers I've known that really appear to have no fear - like a Bellof – are dead. You've got to have a little bit of fear actually. You need some self-preservation."

"Sadly, it would be the only time I wore Williams overalls, despite later expectations." (Sutton Motorsport Images)

Nigel Roebuck

The Best

"There were some very good drivers around [in sports car racing]. I was recently chatting to Eddie Cheever - he was at Jaguar of course - about his sports car days and asked him who was the best. And he said, 'Martin, without a doubt.'"

"It caused a stir when I was fastest overall in wet practice." (Sutton Motorsport Images)

Murray Walker

Tom Cat

"Well, I think luck just happens. To some extent you make your own luck, but if Martin was unlucky in Formula 1, he was, by the same token, lucky in sports cars. He had this very close affinity with Tom Walkinshaw and as a result of that he drove the brilliant Jaguar."

"It was a very late call-up so I had to use Mansell's seat but his steering wheel was so small I could barely turn it." (Sutton Motorsport Images)

"My dad, always supportive, always behind the scenes."

Martin Brundle

Not Just Williams

"I was the Williams test driver and so, when Nigel got chickenpox, I got drafted into the team and I drove for Williams at Spa. So I was with Jaguar for two championships - I went to America 14 times - Williams tester, Williams racer - it was just mad. The only time I've ever been busier than that was 2012. I think I was actually busier with Sky, Le Mans, Silverstone, Goodwood and the million other things I was doing that year. I never thought I'd be anything like as busy as I was in '88 ever again, especially after I'd supposedly semi-retired."

"Another classic sportscar race - the Nurburgring 1000 Kms. Only second place this time but good Championship points." (Abigail Humphries)

Tony Dowe

Leader Of The Pack

"He was always the leader. Lammers could often do as quick a time in qualifying. Guys like John Nielsen and Davy Jones were good but Martin was inevitably looked on as the team leader. He also had had a long relationship with Tom – he could always tell Tom things that the other guys wouldn't. And that was good – as part of a team, it was good with Martin. He and I got on awesome. We had a great year."

Liz Brundle

Tom Walkinshaw

"I liked Tom a lot. I don't know why, but I think Martin had a special relationship with Tom and that then went on for years. We used to spend some social time with Tom as well. He had a house in France and we'd go down there sometimes at Easter to spend a few days with him. He was a lovely family man.

"As with a lot of powerful men, I think, there were two sides to his character. There's the side that you get in business that's quite hard, quite ruthless and demanding, and then behind the scenes there's a real softness and a family person that a lot of people don't see. I saw that side of him and it was interesting because we'd occasionally fly back in his plane. We'd have been there for the Easter weekend then we'd fly back on the plane and there was a transformation, during the journey, when he'd transfer back into businessman from family man. He certainly helped Martin. I've heard all sorts of things over the years that people have said about him, but he never did anything wrong to us. I liked him as a person and he was always very kind and thoughtful to me."

"The iconic colour scheme of the Jaguar." (Sutton Motorsport Images)

Win Percy

Getting The Best Out Of People

"People used to ask me, 'How did you get that drive?' I hope it's because you were up-front with people and they decided they would trust you. Tom's first words to me were, 'The boys like you and they'll work with you.' It meant a lot. It was the same with Martin. He treated everyone so well that he got the best out of everyone and it's very important. You can't sit on the start line and wonder if the wheels are tight, etc. – you have to believe in the guys. The more you work with them, and show them that they're equally as important as you are, the more you'll get the best out of everybody and consequently you'll get a good car."

"Second place at Spa, in treacherous conditions, claimed the Manufacturers' Championship for Jaguar but the Drivers' Championship was still wide open." (Sutton Motorsport Images)

Mark Blundell

My Mate

"I have memories of him before meeting him. Before Martin started in F1 in '84, I had begun my first year of motor racing as I was in Formula Ford. Because we both came from East Anglia and had similar names, I looked up to him and hoped to emulate his career, especially reading the regional press and seeing his name in lights. Then we caught up career-wise and we met in World Sports cars when he was at Jaguar and I was at Nissan and we hit it off quite quickly. We're chalk and cheese in many ways, as he would testify, but opposites attract. We've been team-mates, shared some great memories, had some great fun and tried to kill each other on the track as well!"

Roger Silman

Control

"I've seen Martin very upset but, thinking about it, I don't recollect ever seeing him lose his temper."

"This is the Japanese warrior's helmet I won in Fuji when clinching the Championship." (Abigail Humphries)

AUTOSPORT

BRUNDLE

22 SEPTEMBER 1988 £1.00

EIRE £1.47 (INC. TAX), US $2.95

JAGUAR'S TITLE

SAUBER'S SPA BUT TWR RETAINS WORLD TEAMS CROWN
BMW'S MANX SURPRISE ◆ SCHANCHE STORMS LYDDEN

Martin Brundle

World Champion

"We won a lot of Group C races. I used to love that Group C Jaguar. We didn't win Le Mans in 1988, much to my chagrin. We should have, but we didn't. However, I then won the World Sportscar Championship."

"A Randy Owens lithograph of an amazing victory at Del Mar - one of my best."

Maurice Hamilton

Respect For The Guild

"In 1988 the Guild of Motoring Writers chose him as their Driver of the Year which was great because that was recognition for what he had achieved. It's not exactly the Oscars and, over the years, many of the winners decided not to attend because they were Formula 1 drivers or something and why should they? But Martin came, and I remember him saying to me, 'You know, I'm really chuffed with this and I'm going to make the most of it.' He got up and gave a little speech saying thank you, which was again unheard of. Normally, if they were there, the winner would troop up, shake hands, have their picture taken and go and sit down with the trophy. Martin actually took the trouble to say thank you and to say what it meant to him. Again that stands out in my mind - smart guy."

WORLD SPORTSCAR CHAMPIONSHIP

DATE	RACE	HOW THEY FINISHED	
March 6	Jerez 800k	1st SCHLESSER	BRUNDLE Ret
March 13	Jarama 360k	1st BRUNDLE	2nd SCHLESSER
April 10	Monza 1000k	1st BRUNDLE	2nd SCHLESSER
May 8	Silverstone 1000k	1st BRUNDLE	2nd SCHLESSER
July 10	Brno 360k	1st SCHLESSER	2nd BRUNDLE
July 24	Brands Hatch 1000k	1st BRUNDLE	3rd SCHLESSER
Sept 4	Nurburgring 1000k	1st SCHLESSER	2nd BRUNDLE
Sept 8	Spa 1000k	2nd BRUNDLE	3rd SCHLESSER
Oct 9	Fuji 1000k	1st BRUNDLE	5th SCHLESSER

Final race to come: November 20. Melbourne 360k. In the Le Mans 24-hour race on June 11-12, Schlesser did not race and Brundle retired.

"In many ways, my finest hour, taking the Championship against Mercedes and Porsche and many others."

Robin Brundle

Mechanical Sensitivity

"When I was 17, we had done the Willhire 24-hour race. Consistency and kindness to the car was something that father had taught us both so when any of us got in a car you could just nurture it for 24 hours. That is yet another very important ingredient in Martin's sports car and Le Mans successes – not only understanding and feeling a car at an early age by building them and stripping them and doing his own maintenance but also then by actually driving them for 24 hours and understanding where the car feels stressed and where to change gear, given different temperatures, etc. All of those formative years were very important to him becoming a World Champion."

"As ever, the driver is only the final link in a very long chain." (Jaguar Heritage Archive)

Murray Walker

Best Of The Best

"Martin is a sports car World Champion – the best. So, he may have been unfortunate in Formula 1, but it was counterbalanced, to some extent, by his success in sports cars."

Roger Silman

1988 Conclusion

"I came to like John [Nielsen] very much indeed. He didn't have that sort of immediate air of being the thoroughly professional F1 driver that Martin had. He was almost too nice a bloke. I thought Martin was up against strong competition in our team but he always came out on top. I'd say that he never had an off-day which is also something that you do obviously get. My summary at the end of that season was – this is what I wrote at the time: 'That Martin is a very worthy World Champion is a gross understatement and he ended up in a class of his own.' It was very unfortunate for him that so few people in F1 understood at that point just how good he was."

"The accolades and awards came thick and fast. My much-treasured Segrave Trophy is shown below and my plaque to the left." The Segrave Trophy is awarded to the British national who accomplishes the most outstanding demonstration of the possibilities of transport by land, sea, air, or water. The trophy is named in honour of Sir Henry Segrave, and has been awarded in most years since 1930.

AUTOSPORT

Autosport Awards 1988

MARTIN BRUNDLE

• BRITISH COMPETITION DRIVER 1988 •
• AWARDED BY THE READERS OF AUTOSPORT •

"This was a very early Autosport Award at which time it was little more than a dinner with good friends."

BRABHAM DEAL IS FINALISED

BRUNDLE BACK IN FORMULA 1

"There was always a respectful friendship between Ayton and me but we were never close." (Sutton Motorsport Images)

"Racing with a fighter jet at RAF Abingdon - I will never forget looking straight into his after-burners as soon as he was airborn while I was doing over 200mph."

BRUNDLE ... world champion with a fresh goal.

Brundle back for a second bite at Senna

"Alongside my new team mate, Stefano Modena."

Martin Brundle

Back To F1 In '89

"Once again I had used Tom as a springboard and then left him because I was offered the Brabham drive for 1989. I just felt I needed to be in F1. Tom was very generous on that; he let me go again."

Martin Brundle

How Do You Do!

"Bernie had sold the team by the time I joined but he was still based at Roebuck House in Chessington, the Brabham base. I sat in Roebuck House and Bernie shouted, 'Brundle, come in here.' I sat down beside this kid; I had no idea who he was; he turned out to be my future team mate, Stefano Modena.

"So I met this guy called Joachim Luhti and they offered me a drive at Brabham. So I was back in F1. And it was a great little car: Judd engine with the Pirelli tyres, really neat little chassis."

Herbie Blash

First Choice

"Martin was thrown in at the deep end. Bernie had sold Brabham. Alfa Romeo took over and I personally went to look after the television side for Bernie. Then Joachim Luhti turned up and he wanted to buy the Brabham name and factory, and re-start. I must admit I was rather keen to get back to racing. It was a good experience but I preferred to look after a team. So one of the drivers that I wanted to see was Martin and I was very pro-Martin. I knew Martin's Manager, Nick Brittan, very well at that time, and Bernie assisted as well."

"With good friend and team boss, Herbie Blash, one of the few men who has been to significantly more F1 races than me." (Sutton Motorsport Images)

Herbie Blash

List Driven

"Unfortunately, both times he was with Brabham, the good days had gone. The thing that sticks in my mind is that, when Martin went testing, he was so methodical in listing down everything after the test. He did a full report on everything - what he felt had gone wrong, what was needed... And he continued to do that – I take it he did that throughout his whole career – because he also did that the second time he came back to Brabham. I've worked with quite a few drivers and I have never known a driver be quite so methodical and to, as I say, literally list every point down."

David Tremayne

Charge Turns Flat

"I worked with Martin at Brabham. I was doing their press releases at the races in those days. I remember Monaco in '89: Martin was on fire and he just destroyed Modena and everyone thought Modena was going to be the next coming man, the next God. Martin held his head up perfectly well against him. He has a good record of doing that with team mates. At Monaco he was dead set for third place, a really nice drive and then his battery went flat and he had to come in and have a new one fitted and then he finished sixth. Modena finished third and got all the glory. But that was Martin's glory that he should have had. That whole Brabham thing gelled pretty well actually. It was a nice little team of quick cars. Sergio Rinland's car was a really nice one. Again, Martin reminded everyone that he was a pretty talented guy."

Martin Brundle

Cruel Fate

"Stuck it on the second row at Monaco. Should have been on the podium. We were flying all weekend - I've always loved street circuits - I loved Monaco. Always went well on street circuits. I'll never forget Busby, my mechanic, saying on race morning, 'I've changed everything. We're going to have such a result today - I've changed this, I've changed that. I've changed the battery...' Anyway, the new battery turned out to be a dud and I lost over two minutes changing it late in the race while lying third. And that was the race where Herbie [Blash] was crying at the end because I had to cruise back to the pits, get out of the car, change the battery, get back in the car and I finished sixth.

"The Brabham-Judd on Pirellis was a great little car." (Sutton Motorsport Images)

Martin Brundle

On Fire In Monaco

"Had an incredible race actually - one of those typical Brundle situations where - as I was against Senna in '83, as I would be against Schumacher in '92 - I kind of had nothing to lose and I just went for it. If I could have driven like that every time I got in the car, I'd have been a World Champion. I don't know why I didn't!"

"Monaco '89 - probably my greatest F1 drive, although it only netted sixth place." (Sutton Motorsport Images)

"The Variante Alta chicane at Imola - nice to see I am very precise with the kerbs." (Sutton Motorsport Images)

Maurice Hamilton

Monaco Magic

"What a drive. What a really, really great drive. I was doing commentary then and there was a camera on his car, I remember that very clearly. It was fairly early days of cameras on the car. So we were really getting a good view of him driving that Brabham and you could see from it that he was absolutely in charge of the car, he was making it work, full of confidence, driving beautifully."

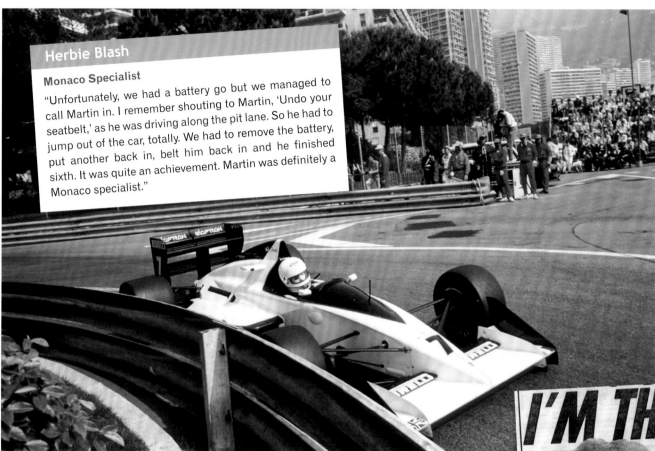

Herbie Blash

Monaco Specialist

"Unfortunately, we had a battery go but we managed to call Martin in. I remember shouting to Martin, 'Undo your seatbelt,' as he was driving along the pit lane. So he had to jump out of the car, totally. We had to remove the battery, put another back in, belt him back in and he finished sixth. It was quite an achievement. Martin was definitely a Monaco specialist."

"Portier Corner at Monaco, pushing my luck up against the barriers."
(Sutton Motorsport Images)

Martin Brundle

Slight Problem

"Then Joachim Luhti, the guy I did the deal with, ended up in prison. I remember Bernie had said to me, 'Look, Mr Luhti's in the financial world in Switzerland, and he's determined to keep a low profile, but he loves motor sport - wants to be involved with this.

"'Yes Mr. Ecclestone, that's fine by me.' That's how Luhti had presented himself."

Martin Brundle

Bully Boy Brundle

"After my pit stop in Monaco, I came steaming back through the pack and booted everybody out of the way as I came along. The British media - the gang of Allsop and Piecha and all those guys - bought me some 'Bully Boy' T-shirts, which I found quite amusing because a bully I'm not. I'm two personalities, though. I'm definitely massively more aggressive with a crash helmet on than without."

"My comeback drive at Monaco impressed the media. Tactical use of a library picture of me clay pigeon shooting was amusing."

I'M THE BULLY BOY OF THE TRACK

The Sun

BY STAN PIECHA

MARTIN BRUNDLE admitted last night he has become the bully of the track.

He has decided the best way to accelerate himself to the front of Grand Prix racing is to frighten off his rivals with displays of brute force.

Brabham driver Brundle, cruelly robbed of a top-three finish in the Monaco Grand Prix on Sunday when his battery went flat, said: "I've decided to become a lot more intimidating and it's working wonders."

Brundle, who eventually battled back to finish sixth, said: "I decided to go for it and pass everything. I threw the car all over the place and took a lot of risks.

"I bullied everyone in sight. I would make my decision to overtake and the driver of the car in front had two choices — to get out of the way or hit me. They all leaped out of the way."

Brundle, 29, will today be offered another year-long contract with the Chessington, Surrey-based team.

Show

And he believes having to go through the anguish of pre-qualifying just to get into the qualifying heats, has made him even more gutsy.

He said: "In pre-qualifying you have an hour to do the business. You come out of it sharper and more hardened.

"You are under tremendous pressure because if you fail to make the cut you are on your way home before the show even starts."

With Brundle's teammate Stefano Modena coming third, Brabham may finish with enough points to skip the pre-qualifying sessions when there is a mid-season review of the lower teams.

Points

Brundle, back in Formula One after a year's lay-off, flew to France today for a 48-hour testing session to improve the car even further.

He added: "I'm delighted with the progress we have made. It's beyond my expectations.

"Now that Stefano and I have managed to get into the points this weekend after failing to finish in the opening two races, we've put to bed a lot of ghosts.

"I've matured a lot and providing that I'm in a good car I feel I'm ready to win a race.

"Having to have the battery replaced in Monaco left me mentally destroyed because I was guaranteed third place and possibly second.

"It was such a daft thing to happen. It must have been a faulty alternator.

"But apart from that hiccup things were really starting to go well for the team.

"Stefano is the quickest co-driver I have ever had and we are working superbly together. We have total trust in each other."

Brundle revealed he had one moment's lapse of concentration during the tricky 77-lap Monaco circuit where he had to make 2,300 gear changes to cope with the sharp corners.

Brundle said: "It was two laps after I had overtaken Nigel Mansell.

Genius

"I was on a clear run and because I had lost my playmate my concentration lapsed for a fraction of a second and I clipped a barrier. I quickly knuckled down after that.

With Brundle's performance all five British drivers are now in the points for the world crown but he believes no-one will stop Monaco winner Ayrton Senna retaining his world crown.

"That guy's a genius. He's so quick and aggressive, no-one can catch him."

They can get out of my way or have a crash

Says MARTIN BRUNDLE

GUNNING FOR GLORY ... Grand Prix speedster Martin Brundle is aiming to be a hot shot on the race circuit as well as off it

"The story carried on with some appropriate T-shirts among my media friends, along with Liz and Herbie."

Herbie Blash

Arrest of Luhti

"It was at the Belgian GP when the owner of the team was arrested and I was left with this team where the only money we really had coming in was from a Japanese credit card company called Nippon Shinpan and somehow – and to this day I don't know how – I convinced them to stay with us to enable us to run to the end of the season, which fortunately we did. Then the team was on the market and then we had various people come along that were supposedly going to buy the team.

"My title was Managing Director – unfortunately! I was running the show on behalf of the various bandits that we had for owners!"

"My beloved Jet Ranger - quite an expensive leaf blower."

Martin Brundle

Joachim Luhti

"He turned up in the pit lane in Brazil for the first race with a knotted handkerchief on his head and a hooker on each arm. I had two team bosses who ended up in prison before the end of the calendar year that I drove for them! Luhti had two boats in the harbour in Monaco. It was all just a little bit weird.

"He was, theoretically, off the radar. I remember we went to Japan for a meeting with Nippon Shinpan, which was the Barclaycard of Japan at that time, probably still is. And he came down to breakfast wearing a T-shirt and headphones - he'd got little earpieces in, listening to some music. And his T-shirt said, 'I don't give a shit, I don't take shit, in fact I'm not even in the shit business'. It was quite a long message all down his T-shirt. I thought it was quite unusual attire to meet some very serious Japanese financial people. Anyway, luckily they sponsored the car through the year."

"But it wasn't always good news - the Brabham failed at Hockenheim." (Sutton Motorsport Images)

Murray Walker

Nursing The Situation

"There was the year of the Belgian Grand Prix, and James [Hunt] was my co-commentator and James didn't turn up for the whole race, and we were frantically looking for anybody who could help us out. James subsequently said that he'd been in bed with a stomach complaint. The stomach complaint turned out to be two Belgian nurses!

"We were getting anybody who would come into the commentary box and help me just to spread the load a bit. Martin retired and came into the box and was good. And that was in a situation where he'd just got out of a racing car in appalling weather and he was able to put more than two or three words together and be very intelligent and constructive about the whole thing."

"Nailing a Ligier on the pit straight at Estoril." (Sutton Motorsport Images)

"Deep in thought - pretty sure I am imagining a qualifying lap." (Sutton Motorsport Images)

Martin Brundle

Apprentice Expert

"James Hunt went on the missing list one day at Spa and anybody and everybody who had broken down, and who could speak English, was being asked to go and talk to Murray Walker. And I got up there and really enjoyed it."

(Sutton Motorsport Images)

Martin Brundle

All Change

"In Brazil we pre-qualified the Brabham but we had no pit garage. So, by nine we had pre-qualified, and then you're out at 10 until 11.30 for the first practice. And we had to move into a garage that had been kept free for whoever pre-qualified. We moved in and then discovered Stefano Modena had a jinx about which side of the garage his car was on. So they had to move it all around again, because he wanted to go on the other side - he didn't want to be on the left hand side of the garage. Lovely kid, Stefano."

"Spa '89 - Senna in my way again!"
(Sutton Motorsport Images)

F1 Teams In 1989

McLaren, Williams, Ferrari, Benetton, Tyrrell, Lotus, Arrows, Brabham, Dallara, Onyx, Minardi, March, Rial, Ligier, AGS, Lola, EuroBrun, Coloni, Osella and Zakspeed.

Martin Brundle

The Curse Of Pre-qualifying

"At that time there were a lot of F1 cars around. In '89 with the Brabham, we were pre-qualifying - there were 39 cars in F1. In Canada and Australia, you'd go all that way to a Grand Prix, and you might not race. Absolutely extraordinary times. Nine cars went out by 9am on a Friday and then another four went out by Saturday afternoon. So, 26 cars started the race, except for Monaco in the '80s when it was 20 cars.

"There were lots of cars but there were lots of rubbish cars as well and it was really difficult. Also, there were some good new teams in pre-qualifying like Onyx, like Jordan. You could get through pre-qualifying as I did at all the races bar two, and then be in the top 10 on the grid. So pre-qualifying was probably the stressiest thing that's ever happened to me in motorsport. You'd got one hour on a Friday morning and you had to get it done, irrespective of traffic, issues or mistakes. Your sponsors had come out to watch, you're in Oz, you're in Canada, all the money's been spent and you could be out by 9am. It's pretty soul destroying."

"I can see by the way I am holding my head, I am at one with this car." (Sutton Motorsport Images)

Martin Brundle

Lost At Sea

"The conditions were treacherous at Adelaide in '89. I had started 12th but was running seventh in the race, quite early doors. I was on Pirelli tyres which were not ideal in the rain. I was flat out in sixth on the Brabham Straight – about 150mph. And my Pirellis got up on top of the water. Before I knew it, I was spinning like a top in a ball of spray between two concrete walls. By a miracle, I avoided hitting them, selected first gear and drove off.

"As I accelerated away, I suddenly had the terrifying thought that I could be going the wrong way. With spray and grey walls all around me, I had no means of identifying anything. I had this horrible moment, 'Am I going in the right direction?' I couldn't slow down or stop in case someone piled into the back of me. Heart in mouth, there was nothing for it but to keep on the throttle, knowing that a car could come hammering out of the gloom and into me head-on. And then I saw a board that said, '200', with the writing on my side and knew I was going the right way. The relief was indescribable.

"That still haunts me to this day."

"The conditions were treacherous in Adelaide. Prost refused to start and Senna would crash into the back of me." (Sutton Motorsport Images)

"This picture confirms what an elegant car the Brabham was." (Sutton Motorsport Images)

Martin Brundle

Up Close And Personal

"Next lap, Senna hit me from behind on the same straight when I'm going along in fifth gear because I can't go flat out, as I could spin again. That's the famous occasion when the team were begging Senna to slow down because he's charging, he's a lap ahead or something. He was lapping me. I suddenly felt a huge impact from behind and Senna sailed past on three wheels."

Herbie Blash

Comparison With Modena?

"Oh, for me, there was no comparison. Modena was previously in F3000 and was looking as though he was going to be the new star in F1, but it never materialised. He was quite a strange guy, I have to say. Martin was definitely two or three steps ahead."

Roger Silman

Effective Partnership

"We'd progressed away from the Jaguar V12s to the turbo but raced the V12 at Daytona and Le Mans and Martin was second at Daytona, first at Le Mans. Martin and John Nielsen had developed a very strong relationship by this time. If you wanted to speak to them, you almost had to knock on the door and ask. I think they worked very closely to plan just how they wanted to drive the car, how to get it home at the end of 24 hours. I would say that they had total confidence in each other in the 24-hour races in 1990."

"Really should have won Daytona for a second time in 1990. I did the Daytona race again in 2012 and finished fourth, incredibly just a few seconds behind the winner. I really enjoyed that event."
(Sutton Motorsport Images)

Martin Brundle

Cat Calls

"Luhti disappears off the scene and Brabham's clearly going into a bit of a tailspin, or so it appeared. So Tom coaxed me back into the Jaguar again. By this time Tom's got a turbo Jaguar, which was the worst Jaguar I ever drove - horrible thing. The engine was based on the Metro 6R4 and it was just a bad car. We had some great races against Mercedes-Benz and I got on the podium with it but I knew as soon as I drove it in Jerez that it was a dog. And the turbo lag was horrible. It had downforce but it just didn't have any driveability. But we dragged it round. In fact, we had some reasonable results with the turbo car and some ding dong battles with Schumacher in the Sauber Mercedes."

Martin Brundle

Hare & Hound At Le Mans

"We had loads of Porsches to beat and all sorts but we had a strategy and it worked incredibly well. We sent our car out as a hare and then Tom kept me a space in the other car. I think he'd forgotten to tell Eliseo Salazar, supposedly that car's third driver, that that was what was going to happen. If my car had kept going, we'd have been fine but you can only have three drivers per car. Tom said, 'Just drive it flat out. Stretch the Porsches.' The car we won in was missing a gear and had no front brakes - they'd glazed over. It was run by the TWR IMSA team, Tony Dowe's guys, and they did a fantastic job."

"The Nissan of Geoff Brabham was mighty fast and our nemesis. The crowd are going wild as I lead him down the pit lane!" (Sutton Motorsport Images)

"This turbo-charged Jag was not a great racing car. It had plenty of downforce but driveability was poor."

One Into Two Will Go

"When we went to Le Mans, the relationship with Martin was pretty good. I pulled a number of stunts to get a result because I didn't want to go there and not win it again. We ended up keeping Salazar, who was supposed to be the third driver, out of the car so there was an opportunity, later in the race, for one of the other guys to get in, which happened to be Martin. So it was really appropriate that we got a 24-hour win with him in the car."

"Trading places with super-John Nielsen in the glorious V12-engined car." (Sutton Motorsport Images)

Roger Silman

Mix And Match

"Tom was a law unto himself as to how he'd mix up the drivers. All sorts of things were going on in the background. It was very difficult to get him to actually run the strongest drivers necessarily together. I suppose one word sums it all up – money."

Martin Brundle

Tom Walkinshaw

"Tom was a better team manager than driver. He was a very aggressive driver, a good driver. We all loved driving for Tom because he was a racer with an entrepreneurial flair. When Tom was on the pit wall, you knew he'd call it right - he understood races, he called them very well, he could wheel and deal, and he was good. When he was in the XJ-S and that sort of thing, he always made sure he personally got the best engine, the best tyres and all that lot, and why wouldn't you if it's your train set? I don't hesitate to say he was a *good* driver but I think he was a *great* team boss."

"Amusingly, the engine control unit was parked just beside our heads, away from any water in the cockpit." (Sutton Motorsport Images)

Win Percy

Walkinshaw

"He thought a lot of Martin. Tom was an unusual character. He was hard to deal with at times and unkind at times. He was OK, but he had to like you or want you, or he could be quite unkind. He let me down so often, but he also did a lot for me."

Purring cat lures Brundle back

"There are 13 hours of darkness at Daytona, just to spice up the challenge." (Sutton Motorsport Images)

MOTOR RACING — JAGUAR PLANS TO CONQUER WORLD AGAIN

IROC

"The IROC [International Race Of Champions] series was a fascinating one. I was over in America, driving for Jaguar in the IMSA series, and Tony Dowe said, 'I think you should do IROC, I'll get you in that.' So he rang up Jay Signore, and next thing is I'm at a test track with these IROC cars, which are NASCARs basically, all with the same body shells. I was there by dint of being the World Sports Car Champion. To be eligible for the IROC series, you'd got to have won a championship of some sort. And I'm in this trailer, and we've got a little changing area with a little locker each and it was Earnhardt, Fittipaldi, Unser Jr, Rusty Wallace, Mark Martin, Terry Labonte... It just went on and on and on, all these legends of single-seaters and NASCAR were there. And the token European boy was me. And I hooked up with Darrell Waltrip - he was a really good guy. I hit it off with his sense of humour."

"Around the streets of Miami, the turbo Jaguar was fearsome." (Jaguar Heritage Archive)

"The IROC cars looked pretty agricultural and they felt the same way." (LAT)

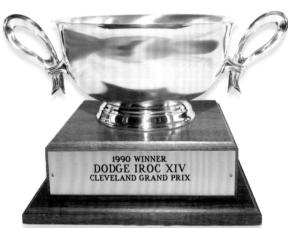

Martin Brundle

IROC Round One

"By a coincidence (!) Waltrip and I got knocked about a bit in the first lap and we ended up at the back, and I was behind him. And I just instinctively started pushing him down the straights to try and catch the front pack. And he was giving me all the thumbs up and I'm tentatively doing it and it feels good to me - I'm in the draft and we've got to catch the pack.

"So we worked together and, over the next 10 or 15 laps, we caught the leading pack, we went underneath the pack and as soon as we got to the front, he slotted up to the top, at the front of the pack and then 'he hung me out to dry'. So my best friend for the last 15 laps just burned me. And it was like somebody taking two plug leads off my V8, and I just went straight to the back of the pack. And you have to get on the back of the pack really quickly otherwise 10 laps later, you'll be lapped. You need the slipstream effect and the more cars you've got, the better it is. You'd be going along if you were in, say, eighth place and you'd look through all these rear screens and front screens and you were trying to see the track, and then guys would be making hand signals inside. Earnhardt and Co., in the pack were pretty spectacular. Anyway, somehow I muscled my way to fifth in this race at Talledega, which was pretty wild. And it was my first ever time on an oval. And it wasn't about going fast, it wasn't about going flat out, it was just working the traffic."

"IROC was one of the most enjoyable championships of my career - great characters and challenging superspeedways such as Talladega and Michigan. In many ways, I was at my peak - I could not stop winning races."

Martin Brundle

IROC Round Two

"The next race was a road course circuit at Cleveland Airport. I think it was some kind of reverse grid, so I started eighth. Nailed the lot of them into the first corner, took the lead, but we knew they were all going to run out of brakes on this road course. So there was a big water tank inside the cockpit, and I could feel the micro-switch underneath my foot on the brake pedal. This micro-switch squirted water from the tank on to the brakes to cool them. So I had my water tank filled right up, before the race. I'm going down the straight, and I could just feel the micro-switch click, as I pressed the brake pedal sufficiently to operate the switch but not the brakes, and in this way I kept cooling my brakes down the straights. So I led, and I just kept pulling away. Al Unser Jr made a good job of coming after me, but basically I just wiped the floor with them, and they weren't happy! They weren't happy at all. So now I'm leading the Championship, which I don't think was in the plans - $175,000 for the winner."

DODGE INTERNATIONAL RACE OF CHAMPIONS

Final Point Standings and Prize Money:

```
 1. Dale Earhardt, 60 points, $175,000
 2. Al Unser Jr., 44 points, $65,000
 3. Martin Brundle, 41 points, $50,000
 4. Mark Martin, 37 points, $45,000
 5. Terry Labonte, 36 points, $40,000
 6. Emerson Fittipaldi, 29 points, $38,000
 7. Dorsey Schroeder, 26 points, $35,000
 8. Rusty Wallace, 26 points, $34,000
 9. Darrell Waltrip, 23, $33,000
10. Bobby Rahal, 18 points,  $32,000
11. Geoff Brabham, 18 points, $31,000
12. Danny Sullivan, 13 points, $30,000
```

Tie-breaker: higher finishing position in final race.

The IROC XIV prize fund totals $608,000.

"You may read third place but I read this as being robbed of $125,000!"

"Whoever would have imagined that banger racing around the Pot Row grass track would have led to racing around the American superspeedways?" (LAT)

Martin Brundle

IROC Final Round - Gamesmanship

"Next, we go to Michigan. Michigan was pretty tough. I didn't really know it. Firstly, the race gets delayed a day because of the rain. Liz was expecting Alex any day. They'd made it quite a big story, as happens in America, 'Martin Brundle: is he going to make it home to see his baby born?' And I was on pole. Beside me was Al Jr, behind me was Dale Earnhardt, and beside him was Emerson Fittipaldi. We're sitting on the grid, and I'm there with my netting up the side, the windows down, ready to go, just contemplating what the hell it's all about and quite what I'm doing on pole position at Michigan. And Earnhardt, with his dark glasses on, with a thousand-yard stare, walked past the netting at my side window, and went, 'Don't forget your kids,' and just carried on walking! Talk about mind games! Liz was very upset when she heard this story, and understandably so. But that was Earnhardt. He was just trying to psych me out."

Martin Brundle

IROC Final Round – The Race

"I think, if I'm honest, I was out of my depth at this super-speedway with that pack of guys who were used to that sort of thing. I had ended up, through cunning and guile and a bit of good fortune, leading the Championship, sitting on pole. And I didn't quite know what to expect from this race, except I knew one of them was going to get me. Absolutely. The word on the street was, 'He ain't going home with the money. We're not having a European win.'

"I didn't really know how to control the pack, the rolling start. So we're going around and Little Al's showing me two fingers, like, 'Second gear, second gear!' just as I heard him snick it into first. So they're working the games on the warm-up lap and coming through the middle of Turn 4, I just let go. I'm gone. And they waved the start off – they call it an English Start apparently! You're not allowed to do that. So now they thought I was going too slow down the back straight – remember, I've never done this before – I'm going too slow, and then of course you're not allowed to just bolt, you've got to bring the pack to the line, I find out. So we're going round again. Now I've got Earnhardt coming up alongside me, 'Go faster!' I've got everybody trying to have a go at me. And somehow Earnhardt went underneath me down into Turn 1 on the first lap, and I got shuffled out of the pack and I wasn't quite following – you've got to follow so accurately to keep your car fully in the slipstream. But I was holding my own; I was still in a Championship-winning position. And then the inevitable happened: Rusty Wallace, who'd obviously drawn the short straw, gave me just a little kiss on the rear bumper – because you've got to remember the cars are staggered – they lean in at the front - they can't drive in a straight line. They're all geared up to go around left-hand corners. And you get unstable. And now I'm going round in circles. I heard all four tyres pop. Now I'm heading towards the end of the pit when I remember them saying, 'Whatever you do, don't hit the end of the pit wall!' Luckily it stopped on the grass, and they put four tyres on and sent me back out."

"The body langauge here tells me that Tom's not happy about something and I'm not particularly interested. He could be terrifying when he wasn't happy." (Martine Walkinshaw)

Martin Brundle

IROC – The Result

"I finished third in the Championship. Came home with 50,000 bucks. But there was just this lovely little yellow slice all down my back bumper from Rusty's yellow car. They were absolutely going to have me off. I enjoyed the experience. They wanted me to go back out and do it again. I'd love to have done it but I went back into F1, and the chances of trying to do the IROC and F1 was impossible, which was a great shame."

The Jaguar stalks its quarry at Le Mans

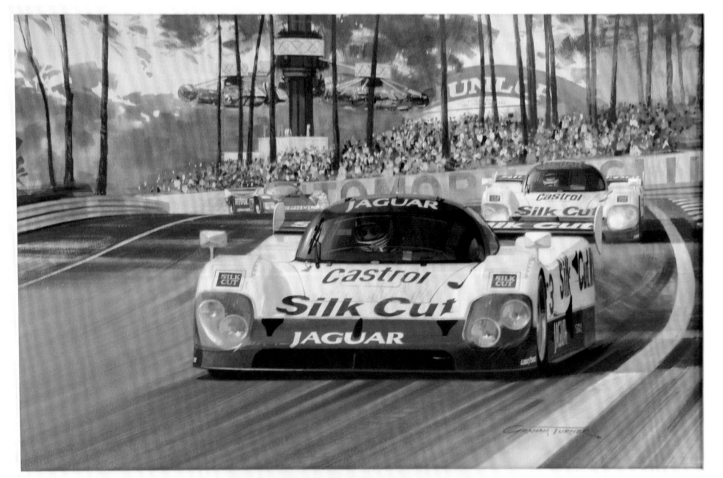

Mark Blundell

What's In A Name?

"In my early days I was testing for Williams before I made it into F1. I crashed a Williams car and in the headlines they used his name rather than mine. I was quite thankful for that! The best one would be when we were travelling from Japan to Australia. Martin was the big star and First Class travel was the norm for him. I was the new boy on the block, on peanuts and travelling in Economy. In Japanese an 'r' and 'l' are the same character. I presented myself early, as you do in Economy, and was given seat 4A or something. I thought I'd made it, that they'd recognised me and I was upgraded. But they'd got the names muddled up and I'd taken Martin's seat. Many people sitting on the plane that day would have witnessed Martin coming to the door, red-faced because he'd been arguing about being in Economy when he should have been in First Class. The Japanese air stewardesses came to ask me to move but I fronted it out and I refused to move. I took his seat for nine hours and he had to sit in the back of the aircraft. He's never forgiven me to this day!"

"A Graham Turner original of the Le Mans victory which I have at home in the bar, with the iconic fairground and Dunlop Bridge behind."

"It was a great privilege to drive this glorious car at Le Mans."
(Sutton Motorsport Images)

Martin Brundle on ...

Nigel Mansell

"Fearsomely competitive, determined, physically strong, an enigma out of the car. He sometimes has an unusual way of expressing things, but that's all part of Nigel's make-up and I have nothing but respect for him. I'm honoured to have shared a race track with him."

"I would drive both these cars in the race with over 13 hours at the wheel, combined." (Sutton Motorsport Images)

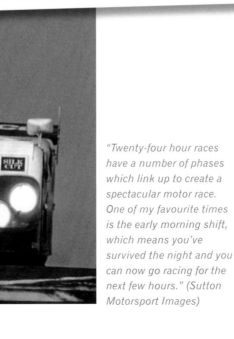

"Twenty-four hour races have a number of phases which link up to create a spectacular motor race. One of my favourite times is the early morning shift, which means you've survived the night and you can now go racing for the next few hours." (Sutton Motorsport Images)

Liz Brundle

Stamina

"Martin is not particularly big in build. His bones are not particularly large, he's not like Nigel Mansell who was quite big-built, able to build muscle and strength - that definitely helps you in a single-seater. Whereas with people like Martin there's only a certain amount of muscle they can build because they're small. But they do tend then to have good stamina. And Martin just had an inbuilt stamina.

"If we go abroad, and we have to drive back from somewhere, he'll drive for hours and hours and hours and not get tired. Whereas I would drive for a few hours and think, 'Oh, I've got to have a break now.' But he doesn't."

Martine Walkinshaw

Dropping In

"We used to go on holiday together. The Brundle family came to our house in France several times. Down in the South of France we used to have quad bikes and Tom and Martin used to go up into the hills at the back of Cannes. They used to be two naughty boys going out with those very fancy quad bikes. Once Tom was in front but he stopped because he had lost Martin. He waited and waited. Then he decided he had to turn back to see what had happened. But the track was very narrow and he was a bit worried that Martin would come round the corner flat out. But he still did it, to find Martin stuck on the outside of a corner, with one wheel hanging over the cliff. To put the quad bike in reverse, you had to lean forward to reach the lever. Of course, every time he did that the quad bike was leaning forward towards the bottom of the valley! I think it was an interesting moment for both of them."

"The Jaguar fans, mostly Brits, cheered us along every lap of the way." (Sutton Motorsport Images)

David Tremayne

Mutual & General

"Tom had huge respect for Martin and Martin had huge respect for Tom – that was key. It was probably the most cohesive and comfortable driving situation Martin ever had at a high level. So TWR showcased, perhaps better than anything else, what Martin could do in a fully competitive car and an environment in which he felt totally comfortable."

"I will never forget this moment as long as I live - just a sea of happy fans and a lot of satisfaction." (Sutton Motorsport Images)

After big achievement come the tiny feet

Reproduced with the kind permission of Autosport

AUTOSPORT

BRUNDLE

21 JUNE 1990 £1.35

US $3.95

JAGUAR 1-2 AT LE MANS

EPIC STRUGGLE DECIDED IN CLOSING MINUTES
NEEDELL/SEARS/REID UPHOLD PORSCHE HONOUR IN THIRD

Roger Silman

Technical Feedback

"He's always been brilliant at that. If you'd got a new car and wanted to sort it out, you could hardly ask for someone better. He's always been very strong at that."

"A trophy which takes pride of place at home - a good motivator during lesser times."

Ross Brawn

Helpful Experience

"Martin was very helpful to me, because I wasn't so familiar with sports car racing and Martin made that bridge if you like, between Formula 1 and sports car racing. He had involvements in both disciplines so he was able to help me a lot."

PIT & PADDOCK
EDITED BY TONY DODGINS

Brundle returns to Brabham

Reproduced with the kind permission of Autosport

Liz Brundle

Supreme In Sports Cars

"I used to love it, as I do with my son now, when he got in a sports car because I just knew there was a stunning performance about to happen. And I was so proud and it was such a pleasure to watch. You just knew that Martin was going to be able to put it on pole, win the race, do longer stints than other people, that type of thing. He was – perhaps some people wouldn't agree with me, I'm biassed obviously – but I think he was supreme in a sports car."

BRITISH IS BEST

Martin Brundle stepped in to help Jaguar take a Le Mans double. Five Britons crewed the top four cars in the world's greatest sportscar race. **26**

Reproduced with the kind permission of Autosport

Formula One - Part 2
1991-1996

For 1991, it was back to F1 for Martin. He rejoined Brabham who, in spite of financial shenanigans behind the scenes, completed the season. Unfortunately the Yamaha engine was too heavy and the results for Martin and his team mate, the confusingly similarly named Mark Blundell, were disappointing. A fifth and two Championship points were all Martin had to show for his season.

Frustratingly, Martin's F1 commitments meant he could only do three races in Ross Brawn's brilliant new XJR-14, which dramatically raised the standards in sportscar racing. Brundle and Derek Warwick, an extremely strong pairing, retired at Suzuka. At Monza, Martin took stints in both XJR-14s with the amusing result that he finished first and second!

In 1992, Martin joined the Benetton team and his team mate was a young man called Michael Schumacher. Although the team was still on their way up, this was by far the strongest team Martin had driven for in F1 and his best opportunity. His season started badly with four retirements. In Canada, he looked certain to win his first GP when the car failed. Meanwhile the 'wunderkind' was establishing a psychological, and points, advantage over his more senior team mate. As had happened when battling with Senna, Martin's spirits were down. As in '83, he bounced back in the second half of the season. Although always out-qualified by Michael, Martin used his experience to concentrate on having a more effective race car. He was often quicker in the races than Schumacher and beat him three times, including his second place at the Italian GP. Martin had four fourth places and was on the podium five times.

At the time, no-one realised how good Schumacher was and, partly because Martin did not blow him into the weeds and partly because the Italian team needed an Italian driver, Martin was not retained. It was a misjudgement that everyone now regrets.

The following year he joined Ligier-Renault, was reunited with his buddy Blundell and had just one podium. He did, however, score 13 points and finish seventh in the Championship, one place lower than '92.

In '94, he moved to McLaren, one of the great F1 teams. It was to be, probably, their worst year ever. The irony is excruciating. Powered by a disastrous Peugeot engine, it held together just seven times in 16 races. Of those seven, Martin had two podiums, including a second at Monaco.

Also later regretting the decision, McLaren replaced Martin for 1995 and he found himself sharing a drive at Ligier-Mugen-Honda with journeyman, Aguri Suzuki. For those races when he was not driving, Martin joined Murray Walker and Jonathan Palmer in the BBC commentary box.

For what would turn out to be his final season, Martin joined the Jordan team. His team mate was the very talented Rubens Barrichello who was at the beginning of his fine career. As ever, Martin gave it his all, matched Rubens and scored points five times but never appeared on the podium. The season had not started fortuitously when, through no fault of his, the Jordan took off on the very first lap at Melbourne, the first GP, and flew through the air before barrel-rolling to finish upside down. Most thought he must be dead. Martin ran back to get in the spare for the restart!

Martin Brundle
Back To Brabham

"In 1991, I was tempted back to Brabham with Yamaha. They had a new V12 Yamaha, which was a great engine but was very big and heavy. My passion for F1 was undiminished at this time and so unfortunately I had to dump Tom again. My team mate that year was Mark Blundell and we were to become great friends."

"Catching up with my old mate, Senna."

Herbie Blash

Shock Treatment

"When I took Martin and Mark over to Japan to meet the new Japanese owner [of Brabham], we were all expecting this multi-millionaire guy we'd heard so much about. He turned up at the airport to pick us up and he had this tatty old Rover V8, and it was just a heap. In Tokyo we expected to be in a good hotel but it was a really cheap one. Then we went off to Yamaha, which was my contact, and he turned up in a sort-of mini-van with a couple of seats in the back. It wasn't the Brabham that Martin, Mark or myself was expecting!"

"The XJR-14 was simply incredible around Suzuka. A fuel pump cheated us early on." (Sutton Motorsport Images)

Herbie Blash

Early Season Woes

"The Yamaha engine was just too big, too heavy and too thirsty on fuel. We also had a major gearbox design failure at the start when the first gear wouldn't fit into the gearbox. We went testing in South Africa and we actually had to have a second gear as our first gear. We had to push start the car because you couldn't drive off in the second gear. That was when Martin really started to do his homework. I have mentioned about him making lists – this one was about a six-page list of what was required. We weren't in very good shape.

"That was the first time Mark and Martin had been in the same team and was a really fun combination. Martin was maybe the more astute technically. It was fun apart from the fact the owners never had any money!"

Martin Brundle

Tom's Finest Cat

"I think Tom was compliant with my move back to Brabham. But in '91 TWR were running the XJR-14 with which I was involved. I remember the first time I met Ross Brawn - I can picture myself now talking to him sitting in a wooden mock-up of the XJR-14 at Kidlington. It would turn out to be the best racing car I ever drove, but I was always going to be part-time due to my F1 commitments. I think Tom always accepted I had this passion for single-seaters and he never wanted to get in my way. But, graciously, he was always there with a soft pillow when it went wrong for me."

"Ross Brawn's XJR-14 rewrote what was possible in sports car racing. It was a beautiful car, bursting with speed and purpose." (Sutton Motorsport Images)

(Ferrari)
Nelson Piquet - Bennet~~~~ (H) Yellow   28
Roberto Moreno - Be~~~~~~ Blue   30
RACE 2.
Graham Nickle~~~~~~~~~ Red
(Ferrari)
Annie Briggs - Cee~~~~~~~~~~~ Green
(Williams)
Mark Blundell - Br~~~~~~ Yellow
Martin Brundle - B~~~~~~ Blue

"The Brundell Brothers - we even had to beat each other at Scalextric - just look at that concentration."

Derek Warwick

World Class

"Martin was one of the best drivers ever to come out of the UK. He was very competitive against some really strong opposition like Nelson Piquet and, of course, Michael Schumacher. And anyone who could compete with those sort of drivers is what I would term a world-class driver. Also in F3 on his way up, he beat Senna as many times as Senna beat him. The quality has always been there – he's been a fantastic driver. I drove with him in sportscars with Jaguar and, of all my team mates, I have to say that he was always one of the strongest team mates I ever had. Whenever Martin was in the car, I knew very well that I was in for a tough session because he was so bloody quick."

James Allen

Up For That

"I first started working with Martin, would you believe, in 1991 because I joined Brabham, doing all their media relations stuff and was the Press Officer, essentially, of the team - my first job after university. We had a very interesting relationship. He was very focused and very determined, but he was more obviously intelligent than a lot of the drivers, and particularly articulate, being able to put into words quite complex things.

"I had to try and find things that people could say or write about the team, which, considering they were towards the back of the grid, was always a bit of a struggle. With Martin, it was always great because I'd say, 'Look, I think people might be quite interested in this,' and he'd go, 'Yeah, that's a cracking idea, why don't you do that? I'll help you with that.' And so I'd come up with something and produce it. He'd give me some quotes, I'd write it, people would pick it up and use it."

"Mum looking particularly glamorous today."

Martin Brundle

Derek Warwick & The XJR-14

"Derek would pick it up by the scruff of the neck and go for it, just like he did in the F1 Toleman. We had all the bases covered, me and Del-boy."

"My team mate Derek attacking the XJR-14 - check out that rear wing."

"Let battle commence - between the two MBs."

Ross Brawn

Comparison With Warwick

"There were a lot of similarities between Derek and Martin. I think Derek could sometimes be a little bit more emotional than Martin. But quite comparable, I'd have to say. I wouldn't honestly be able to tell you if one was quicker than the other. I think it depended on the day and the circumstances. So I don't think there was very much in it in terms of track performance, probably either one of them will point to events that would prove otherwise, but I don't remember a massive distinction in my mind. I think Martin was always very good with the fine engineering detail of what the car was doing, and understanding what the car was doing. Derek could give you the same information, perhaps with a little less understanding of what was going on from a mechanical point of view. Both very, very good drivers and both great members of the team."

"I drove both cars in the race at Monza to finish first and second - a rather unusual result." (Sutton Motorsport Images)

Martin Brundle

Trying In Several Senses

"It was a difficult F1 year. I retired five times and did not qualify twice. I finished fifth in the penultimate race, in Japan, which was good, but those two points were the only ones I scored that year. And nobody seemed to want to pay me so we had to get really punchy to get the money that year."

"I only hope Derek was getting paid to wear that crash helmet." (Sutton Motorsport Images)

James Allen

Careers Advisor

"We always got on well and about two-thirds of the way through 1991, he said to me, 'You're wasted doing this. You should become a journalist.' And I replied, 'Well, that is where I wanted to go. I do want to get into TV and writing and stuff.' And he said, 'Well I wouldn't waste any more time, if I was you. I'd just get on and do it.' The following year I joined *Autosport* and then started working in TV at the same time and went on from there. So I have always been grateful to him for spotting something in me at the time."

Martin Brundle

Talent Scout

"A journalist did a no-show due to travel issues and so James asked me the questions instead and I realised he was a natural at it, more so than at PR."

Mark Blundell

Room Wanted

"We were at Brabham and we were both driving for an F1 team but we were staying in a derelict barn at Magny Cours because that was what the team had put us in. There was a hole in the roof, it was freezing cold and we were about to do a Grand Prix that weekend and we ended up sharing a room. I wouldn't even call it 2-star. So we're driving around at 10 o'clock the night t before the race trying to find other accommodation. Quite comical really."

"I drove single-handed to finish third. It would be the first time I would meet Michael Schumacher who, a few months later, would be my team mate." (Sutton Motorsport Images)

"Mark and I at Silverstone. It soon became very well-known that where you found one of us, you'd find the other one close by."

Martin Brundle

Top Two Steps Lead To Step Up

"I drove the XJR-14 single handedly at Silverstone after we had lost 10 minutes in the pits with a broken throttle cable. I came back through the field and had the race of my life to score a podium. It impressed Tom and Ross. Also in Monza, I had finished first and second in the same race, and for the first time in my life, I think by August, I'd signed for the Benetton F1 team because they were both going there to help run the outfit."

"The V12 Yamaha sounded glorious but made for a very long Formula 1 car." (Sutton Motorsport Images)

A family that lives life in the fast lane

Evening Telegraph

Jaguar Racing Revue, 1991 - Silverstone, May 19

"Brundle described the new Jaguar in glowing terms. 'This car, you can be sure, will go down in history as one of the greatest racing cars of all time.' It was Brundle who claimed pole position with a lap just 0.046 second faster than Warwick's best effort in the sister car. At the start, however, Brundle momentarily had a problem getting his car into third gear and the poleman was swamped by [team mate] Fabi, Keke Rosburg and Philippe Alliot in the Peugeots, and Wendlinger in the latest Mercedes. Brundle was busily making up the lost ground when, on only the second lap of this 83-lap event, his throttle cable broke. Martin was able to coast into the pits on tickover, but lost six laps while his crew fitted a new cable. Establishing the sportscar lap record for the new track, Brundle crossed the line 20 seconds ahead of the Schlesser/Mass Group C Mercedes, having taken two of his lost laps back from the race leader. He was cheered to the echo by the 20,000 spectators. 'I'm not kidding,' said a shattered Brundle, 'that was the hardest race I have ever driven. We hadn't foreseen that one of us would have to go the distance, but there was no choice in the circumstances. I don't think I've wept since I was 12 years old, but that was what I was doing as I drove into parc fermé. It was a mixture of exhaustion and relief that the pain was finally over...'"

"Living in Norfolk, a helicopter seemed a good way to head out into the big wide world."

"On the face of it the '91 Brabham looked a very good car, but it was heavy and thirsty." (Sutton Motorsport Images)

"Bell supplied, serviced and painted my crash helmets through the latter part of my career." (Abigail Humphries)

Professional Friends

"You knew you had a true professional as a team-mate, you knew that he was going to be fast, you knew you had a chance of winning. When he handed the car back, it was in the same condition as you left it. A lot of drivers, when you share cars, are not very sympathetic to the car. Martin had this amazing ability to go very, very fast at the same time as being gentle on the equipment, because you had to be in those days. I wouldn't say in those days that we were the best of buddies because we were two very focused, determined young drivers who always wanted to have the upper hand. It was more of a professional friendship in those days. We had a lot of respect for one another as professional racing drivers; it's difficult to be friends."

"I love to see the wide tyres and suspension from that period of Formula 1." (Sutton Motorsport Images)

James Allen

The Insight Of Jenks

"Denis Jenkinson, who was a really important mentor for me, showed me the timing sheet breakdown of the Belgian Grand Prix, 1991. He was looking at the way that the two drivers were coming out of the pits on the new set of the Pirelli race tyres, and what was very interesting was that Martin was very aggressive as a driver. That's perhaps surprising to people, because he's not a particularly aggressive individual – he certainly doesn't come across that way on television. But, if you actually look very closely at the way he drove then, he was a very aggressive driver and that's one of the reasons why he didn't leave anything on the table during races. He was always absolutely on it, making sure his in-laps and his out-laps were as quick as they possibly could be and very aggressive on the throttle. I remember Jenks, who was a genius beyond measure at understanding racing drivers and what made them fast, pointing this out to me."

Herbie Blash

No Money

"Unfortunately the money ran out. But Martin, as a person, gave 100% all the way. One of the last races that we had was in Japan and, of course, for Yamaha it was essential that the team went to the Japanese Grand Prix, their home race. So Yamaha bought the old Brabham factory and that was what enabled the team to go to Japan."

"Those eye socket balaclavas were always really annoying to wear for a race distance." (Sutton Motorsport Images)

"I wish I could have raced the Jaguar XJR-14 more often in 1991.(Sutton Motorsport Images)

James Allen

Debt Collector 1

"We'd had some problems with the owners of the Brabham team called Middlebridge, a Japanese company. We'd all had difficulty getting bills paid and Martin, I think, was owed a few payments on his driving retainer. He was running fifth, with all the Yamaha top brass, and the owner of Middlebridge who was a Japanese guy called Koji Nacauchi, in the pits. We all had our radios on and Martin, with about three laps to go, said, 'Tell Koji unless I get my payment, I'm going to pit.' There were these white faces, everyone looking at each other in the pit box! 'Does he mean it? Yes, he means it!' So it was all hastily agreed. 'Don't worry, everything's fine.' He'd driven his nuts off that day, he was absolutely brilliant, and he was running fifth in a Brabham at Suzuka which is a real drivers' circuit, and also a real circuit that rewards downforce, something we didn't have that year."

Mark Blundell

The Full Business

"Martin is an incredibly sharp operator. He doesn't give up much. He probably gave me more than most as we had a strong bond as friends. Saying that though, as strong as our friendship was off the track, it was dog-eat-dog on the circuit, and maybe even more so as we were that close and there was probably always something we were trying to prove against each other. I learned a lot from him. He was very smart on the way to handle the team members around him, very astute about the politics of the business. He'd been around longer and had a big name already and he made sure that he used all of his contacts and his experience to maximum effect. When it came to the bottom line in terms of pace, he was an extremely quick driver. He's a magnificent racer - a better racing driver on a Sunday afternoon than in qualifying and a smart driver as well. He always thought ahead. He was always in check with the balance of his car, his time management and fuel consumption. I think he's a man's driver."

"The Brabham looks like a missile from this angle. Adelaide would be my final race for the team and I failed to qualify through a brake issue." (Sutton Motorsport Images)

Martin Brundle

Debt Collector 2

"I said I was going to pit and I meant it. They had made so many promises and I was generally very frustrated at how the whole year had gone. I had just pulled a great move to pass Modena in the Tyrrell Honda and I knew they would be happy. So, I used that moment. Still didn't get paid though at that point, despite assurances."

Ross Brawn

Working With Martin

"Just top quality. Martin was very good on all fronts: very constructive, very good relationship in terms of getting the car to work and function. He was very good with engineers, very constructive and very objective, which was a great help. And, of course, quick. Any racing driver can have all the qualities in the world, but if he's not quick, then they're not much use to you. And so he was very quick, very competitive, a good racing driver, great experience. He just had all the attributes that we needed. I think the unfortunate thing about the XJR-14 year was that he was still splitting his activities between F1 and sports car racing, and it meant he couldn't put 100% effort into the sports car programme. Teo Fabi won the Championship that year, but it might have been different if Martin had been able to put his effort into it full-time."

Martin Brundle

Tom's Boy

"I didn't have to desert Tom at that point because he and Ross basically swept me up and took me to Benetton with them. There was a slight issue in that I was Tom's man and Michael Schumacher was Flavio's man, and there was a power struggle going on to say the least. Flavio very much won that one so it didn't help my cause really. But I was Tom's boy. Since 1979, I'd been Tom's boy."

"My new team mate: Michael Schumacher. Despite his doubtful sense of humour, he would turn out to be one of the all-time greats!"

"I finished second to Senna in Monza. On the podium, he told me we would be team mates the following year at Williams." (Painting by Michael Turner)

Ross Brawn

Group Move

"Tom and I both had aspirations to get back into Formula 1, perhaps get back in a stronger position than when I left Arrows, which was a nice team but it got frustrating with the resources that were available. Jackie Oliver and Alan Rees did a great job of keeping the team alive, but it was always going to be limited in what they could achieve. The opportunity came up with Benetton. And Martin joined us as a little group that went there. For us, it was very important to have a driver on whom we could rely, as to quality and standards. With Martin we knew we had a really good reference point for where we were and where we were going to be."

"I was Tom's boy at Benetton, which was both a positive and a negative."

Ross Brawn

The Cost Of Comparison

"The unfortunate thing for Martin in that period is that no-one really understood how good Michael was. Martin certainly gave Michael a hard time, but I think Martin would have benefited more from the comparison if people had appreciated how exceptional Michael was or was going to become. Martin certainly held his end up. But of course Michael was a really tough reference point. I think it's all credit to Martin that he was able to hold his own on several occasions with Michael, who obviously went on to prove that he was one of the greatest racing drivers in the world."

Dave Redding

Phraser

"He was a good guy to work with. We'd had non-English drivers before so having an English driver made quite a big difference. With the common language, sarcasm and humour could be used when we worked together so it made life quite easy. He certainly had a few phrases for describing a car - 'pointy' being one that comes to mind which means a car that's very sharp to turn in. He had a few phrases that stuck after he left. He sometimes said that it felt like the car was towing something - that didn't stick but 'pointy' was in use long after he left."

"There was a vibrancy about the whole Benetton company and team, not just the overalls." (Abigail Humphries)

"The colour scheme obviously made it through to the family jeep."

Martin Brundle

Unlucky Start

"The magic year of '92 and I started off very badly. I had clutch problems in my first race, an engine problem in my second, contact in the third race and then I spun off in the fourth. Meanwhile Schumacher's looking pretty bullet-proof.

"I just couldn't get on the leader board. Had the most terrible time. I was very unlucky with the contact, very unlucky with the unreliability. We were at the end of the era where you had to look after the tyres, the clutch, the brakes, the car in general, the motor. You'd drive your car with the old Alain Prost-style of trying to win in the slowest possible manner. Michael turned up as the cars were starting to get more and more robust and with a level of fitness that meant he could drive every corner of every lap of every race, flat out. And we all had to raise our game big time."

Dave Redding

Team Mate - Schumacher

"The year was difficult to start with – Michael was the new kid on the block. Martin was naturally the senior figure and obviously Michael turned out to be the talent that he is. So, I think that was a difficult one to manage when you're being beaten by the upstart. It wasn't always the case, though. I think they got on in a professional way, as work colleagues."

"We started with the year with the B191. I spun at Kyalami and then burned out the clutch." (Sutton Motorsport Images)

*"If I'm describing a big over-steer, sliding moment, no wonder I have fear in my eyes."
(Sutton Motorsport Images)*

Martin Brundle

Overcoming The Challenge

"In terms of his speed, his fitness, his commitment, Michael definitely, in my view, rewrote the rules at that time. I was getting pretty down about this. It was tough. I'd come back to the team's motorhome and I'd have to move loads of journalists out of the way who were waiting to talk to Michael Schumacher so I could to talk to my engineers. Everything was pointing at Schumi – he was the new king. And, as I did in '83, I thought, 'I've got nothing to lose. Just go for it. Just let your natural skills and juices flow.' I was quicker than Michael in a practice session in Imola and he had the courtesy to come and congratulate me. And it was one of those moments, it was one of those switch-over moments, where I suddenly knew I could do it, and so did he. I just took off. I felt great. And I finished in the points in 11 of the next 12 races, five podiums and, the one where I didn't finish, the car broke when I should have won the race, in Canada."

*"At Interlagos I was flying along but would end up making contact with Jean Alesi and then the pit wall."
(Sutton Motorsport Images)*

Ross Brawn

Good Technical Feedback

"I think Martin did have a very good understanding of what was going on with the car. I think drivers of that era, and I'm comparing it now with the modern era, had a deeper understanding of the mechanics of the car. Nowadays we have such comprehensive data analysis/data acquisition and modelling simulation, that we can tell from the data exactly what the car is doing – what level of under-steer it has, what degree of over-steer, how it reacts to the throttle. Those things weren't available in this period that we're talking about. So the engineers were much, much more reliant on the driver to give them an accurate picture of what was going on on the track, and having recall of what was going on in individual corners and helping give direction as to what was actually going to make the car go faster. And it was always a great strength of Martin's that he was good in that area."

David Tremayne

Caught In The Crossfire

"For Benetton he signed at Monza in '91 but there was a war going on between Flavio [Briatore] and Tom [Walkinshaw] and they were both running Benetton. From the minute Martin signed, which was obviously Tom's idea, Flavio was suggesting that he could be replaced at any moment, which is not conducive to a driver feeling welcome and comfortable. But that was Flavio's style: if it wasn't something that he had invented, he didn't want it. So I think he was uncomfortable at Benetton. The TWR years were Martin at his finest and I think that shows where his real potential was, what he could do when he was really comfortable and happy and had a decent car under him. His sports car career was second to none, I think."

"Moving on to the B192, this was the best F1 car I raced. It was way behind the Williams on technology but it was a dream to drive." (Sutton Motorsport Images)

Ross Brawn

The Ideal Pairing

"I think Martin probably came to terms with the fact that Michael was going to be quicker in qualifying in raw speed, and Martin used his experience and intelligence to make sure that he was always in good shape for the race. I don't think it was fully appreciated by everybody at the time, but it was a great combination, because we had the sort of raw talent of Michael, still unpolished, and we had the experience and ability of Martin. For me, it was a great combination."

"Montreal was the race I should have won. On great form and fastest in the warm-up, the transmission failed in the race." (Sutton Motorsport Images)

Martine Walkinshaw

Role Play

"Tom was much more involved with the engineering and technical side. Flavio was more on the commercial side which usually includes the choice of driver."

Martin Brundle

Senna Traits

"I followed Michael closely in races, and I tended to be a better starter, most likely because I was a weak qualifier, and he got into a little bit of a panic - a little bit like Senna. And very early on, I saw some traits in Michael I saw through his career. He'd be pretty quick to run you out of space on the race track and be quite aggressive. He struggled to know quite where the line was between being an aggressive winner and being out of order and unreasonable. And I think he always did struggle a little bit on that."

"My first F1 podium since Detroit '84. I had a lucky schnapps before the race and it would become a regular feature. Nigel was very magnanimous on the day." (Sutton Motorsport Images)

"Two men I am greatly indebted to: Tom Walkinshaw and Ross Brawn." (Sutton Motorsport Images)

Martin Brundle

Good Cars

"We had the Benetton B191, then the B192 was used from May. Great cars, very easy to set up, very easy to drive."

Martin Brundle

Aura Of Expectation

"I really started to get my head round the car, the set up, where I needed to be. I'd been in Formula 1 eight years at that point but I'd never been in a front-running team and it's a completely different scenario where you turn up to a race meeting and the team expects to be on the podium and probably winning the race - as opposed to eight years of teams that, if you went home with a few World Championship points, you'd had a fantastic weekend. And all of a sudden now I'm in a team where, if you don't score points and you don't score podiums, 'What's gone wrong? This is terrible!'"

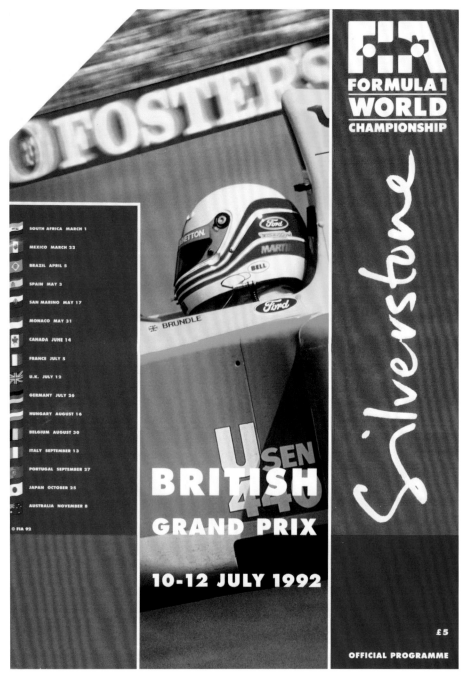

"Quite an honour to be chosen for the cover for the official programme."

Martin Brundle

Liquid Support

"I knew that was a key moment in my life. I was very close to tears at the airport and poured myself a huge whisky in the departure lounge"

"At the Silverstone F1 tests, Mum and Dad used to set up camp with the hospitality unit on the inside of Copse Corner and entertain garage clients for three days. I'd go along at lunchtime to update them. Those were the days..."

Martin Brundle

So Near

"In '92 of course, not only did I have Schumacher as a team mate, but we were up against the incredible Williams, with the paddle shift gearbox and lots of other goodies - the fully dominant '92 Williams of Mansell and Patrese. We did a good job hanging on and were pretty much best of the rest.

"There were two races I could have won. One was Canada. Michael held me up for a long time, which he later admitted was stupid, but then I eventually passed him in traffic. I was catching Berger, who was leading, at a ridiculous rate. I was seven seconds behind him with 20-odd laps to go and gaining on him, the thick end of a second a lap. He was having gear selection problems and he'd buzzed his engine too, but I was in great shape. And then the differential broke – they'd put the bolts in the wrong way round. It was a crying shame because, usually, the car was pretty reliable.

"Senna had broken down in the same spot earlier and he was leaning over the fence. I was destroyed because I really thought I was going to win that race. I'd been quick all weekend, my car was superb and I was hooked-up - it was just easy. It was one of those where you get into a trance-like groove and rhythm, and off you go. Gerhard in the Ferrari was going to be no problem at all to pass. And then the car broke. Ayrton looked at me and said, 'Tough, isn't it?'

"Senna intelligently radioed his McLaren pit to let them know the state of my tyres because Schumacher was still in the race. After he got a lift back with a marshal on a scooter, I jumped in his McLaren and had a good look around at the controls!"

Dave Redding

Bad Luck

"When he was at Benetton, we were renowned for being quite reliable so it was doubly ironic that the time he was in a reliable car, the time he had the chance of a win, the car let him down."

Dave Redding

Experience Tells

"Grid position is important but performing well in the race is even more important. I see that with drivers I have worked with. Last year [2012], it was Jenson and Lewis. It's taken Lewis several years to realise that you can't drive every lap like a qualifying lap. And Michael was much the same. You have to manage the car, the tyres and the conditions, and you can't force yourself on it all the time. It takes guys with a bit of maturity and a few seasons of experience to realise that."

40 DAILY EXPRESS Saturday July 11 1992

SILVERSTONE SPECIAL

Real Brundle of joy!

By CHRISTOPHER HILTON

MARTIN BRUNDLE squeezes into his Benetton tomorrow bidding to build on his greatest Formula One success.

Brundle was a superb third in France last week, his first visit to the podium in a career embracing 91 Grands Prix.

But Brundle's eight years in Formula One have not always been in the fast lane.

"You get used to the highs and lows," he says. "It's the type of sport in which you have to, otherwise you just couldn't cope."

There were lows for Brundle and his team at the start of the season. He added: "I threw the car off the road a couple of times.

"I had a couple of reliability problems—the one in Montreal robbed me of

Martin chases more success

my first Grand Prix win. I think I'd been driving the perfect motor race." Something else made the start of the season difficult. Brundle partners the gifted young German Michael Schumacher and says: "He is naturally quicker than I am.

"There is also no doubt that my strength is as a race driver not as a quali-

fier. You've got to be good enough as a qualifier but I think I have raced extremely well. I've not had a bad race."

Schumacher's was seen in France, where he shunted Ayrton Senna. Brundle's experience was equally evident when he spun in the wet, gathered the car safely and kept on.

When will his first win come? Silverstone? "You've got to string 59 laps together and I think it will be one of the most physical races of the year.

"It's going to be a very hard race but if we can get ahead of the Williams and the McLarens . . ."

Damon Hill, on the other hand, is hoping Silverstone will mark his breakthrough.

His contrasting career includes testing for Nigel Mansell's Williams—"I feel like a love-struck teenager"—to driving for Brabham, which Hill has so far been unable to qualify for a race.

That is no reflection on him. Even Mansell might not be able to qualify it.

Problems

Hill, son of twice world champion Graham, originally intended to do a season of Formula 3000 to get more "race craft" but financial problems prevented that.

There was a vacancy at Brabham and he took it. "What I need now is to do a Grand Prix, get the best out of the car and not fall off."

He is preparing to sustain his career by "slogging it out in anything I can get" but I wonder how long he will have to do that. Frank Williams has been impressed with his testing and if you impress Frank you are good.

Mark Blundell is another Briton on hold.

"My thoughts on the season? What can I say? I've only done one race—Le Mans."

Le Mans is for sports cars and is nothing to do with Formula One. Blun-

dell, partnering Derek Warwick, won it.

He says: "The rest of the season I've been testing for Marlboro McLaren, which is very enjoyable but it's not racing and I'm getting to the point where I want to be racing very badly."

Blundell, 26, accepts the frustration of being a test driver at McLaren. "I'm not in a position to do a flat-out lap. My role is to

go through a number of variables and collect data, try and improve the car.

"Your feedback has to be precise, it has to be strong and everybody has to believe in you.

"There are chances to do a fast lap. At the beginning of the year we were testing, Ayrton Senna set a competitive time and I matched it to the tenth of a second. That bodes well for me."

Hill . . . contrasts

On the charge: Martin Brundle is on a high

Daily Express

Martin Brundle

The Price Of Indecision

"At Spa, I could see the Williams just up the road. It was a wet day. Schumacher was third and I was right on Schumi's tail all race. And I just felt a little bit of grip coming out through a drying Les Combes chicane and I started to think about changing to slicks when Michael went off the track in front of me, bouncing down the grass. Benetton always had a very low front wing and it was so easy to knock it off if you went over some rough ground, or if you hit a kerb too hard. He rejoined behind me and I thought his front wing had gone.

"Michael fell back a little bit behind me in Blanchimont and that convinced me even more he'd lost his front wing. Then at the old Bus Stop chicane, Michael saw my rear tyres, saw just how blistered they were - you can see your own fronts but you can't easily see your own rears in the mirrors when they are rotating, and he went in for a set of slicks. If I'd have gone in, he'd have had to queue behind me..

"That moment of indecision - 'Right, you're third now, I think Schumacher's lost his nose...' I knew slicks were a bit of a gamble and I thought, 'I'll leave it one more lap.' I pitted at the end of the next lap, but that was one lap too late – Michael had got the slicks and won the race. I came out side by side with Patrese and he out-dragged me up the hill in the Williams. And so I finished fourth. That was Michael's first victory. And that moment of indecision was entirely my fault – I should have stuck with my instincts and grabbed the slicks because I would have won the race. Instead, I wasn't even on the podium!"

Helen Dickson

Cheerleader

"I've been to Silverstone on several occasions. Martin very kindly used to helicopter us in and we'd have a wonderful experience – always such a good atmosphere at Silverstone with the British drivers. I can remember 1992, the year that Mansell won and Martin came third. It was the year that the crowds invaded the track. We were in the hospitality suite, in the old BRDC building and thought we'd go down to the area underneath the podium. So we were running like the devil to get there and we sweet-talked a marshal and he opened the barriers for us. There was a huge surge of people who were trying to get under the podium as we were. So we were enveloped by this crowd who started chanting, 'Mansell, Mansell'. So I thought, 'That's all right, Mansell's done really well but what about my brother, so I started, Brundle, Brundle,' and a couple of chaps said, 'Why are you chanting Brundle?' And I said, 'Well, he's up there, look,' so they all began chanting 'Brundle' too. It was a lovely atmosphere. It made up for all the times he didn't even make it round the track."

"Signing for a front-running team was like changing championships. Suddenly podiums and victories were expected and not simply to be celebrated."

"Couldn't touch the Williams on the track but at least, with the help of Roebuck and Tremayne, I could beat Nigel in the media quiz." (David Tremayne)

Martin Brundle

Disputed Territory

"I had a big run-in with Alesi that year. We often found ourselves on the same part of the track. It started when he felt I blocked him in qualifying at Imola and we had a nose-to-nose in the pit lane. He threatened to kill me next time. It came to a head when he ran me into the pit wall in Brazil. Now, when we meet, we man hug!"

Martin Brundle

'Strong' Tactics

"The one thing Michael Schumacher could never get his head around was why he was vilified for doing things that he perceived Senna was revered for. The difference, for me, is that with Senna it was purely an emotional, almost out-of-body kind of reaction, whereas with Michael it was his default mode. I don't want to beat up on Michael because I have a huge amount of respect for him as a man and as a racing driver. But I think Michael crossed the line and I was on the receiving end of it a few times. Senna crossed the line occasionally. You could debate all day long whether there's any difference between what Senna did and what Michael did? And I personally think there is a slight difference, but some people don't."

"During the British Grand Prix, I had an epic fight with Senna in the McLaren which brought back memories of our F3 days."
(Sutton Motorsport Images)

David Tremayne

The Throw Of The Dice

"If you look at '92, he should have won in Canada. Why didn't fate let him have at least one win – he deserved to have one. Then at the end of the year at Spa, against Michael, he was as quick as Michael there and it was whichever one of them came in first for the pit stop. That's the kind of thing that fate turns on."

Dave Redding

Practical Experience

"If a driver says, 'I need to change the mechanical balance, or put a stiffer rear bar in,' for example, and they know what those bits look like, it certainly helps. Martin used to spend a lot of time in the garage so he would actually know what the physical bit looked like on that car. Take a rear roll bar: on one car it looks like a torsion spring, on another car it might look like a blade. So, whilst the phrasing is correct and the effect it has on the car's balance is the same, the bit may look different from car to car and from year to year. He would definitely make sure he knew what the physical bits looked like and I think that is helpful. It's good to visualise what's going on when you are talking about it, rather than just saying, 'I'd like to move the mechanical balance by 2%' and having no idea what that meant or what was required in terms of parts. So, I think Martin's practical knowledge was a help."

Johnny Herbert

Mr. Reliable

"His best opportunity was when he was with Benetton with Michael. Again he showed that, although the qualifying was his difficulty, the racing was where he was always reliable. This is where Martin's very good, always reliable. And that was why he was able to get those results. Unfortunately, he never got that race win. In F1 that is, sadly, how the cards are dealt."

"This image reminds me of just how much oil the cars used to throw out."
(Sutton Motorsport Images)

"At Silverstone, I had the wildest slow down lap I have ever experienced - it was a struggle to drive to the podium through the enthusiastic crowd who had invaded the track."

Martin Brundle on ...

Michael Schumacher

"Schumi: the most complete driver but I think it's touch and go with Alonso. Eventually Vettel will trump them both, I would imagine. I always said with Michael if he'd have given away two or three races that he won questionably, and a championship because of that, he'd have been revered as one of the all-time sporting greats. There was just half a dozen things he did, including 2006 in Monaco where he parked it. I think that's the one that probably upset me the most, if I'm honest, of his misdemeanours. But inevitably here we are, immediately talking about the dark side of Michael, when all we should be talking about are the incredible results. When we were team mates, out of the car he was absolutely correct. I never once saw him playing games. We did have our ups and downs when I got into the media."

"A thoroughly satisfying day at Monza, beating Schumacher and finishing second only to Senna." (Sutton Motorsport Images)

Martin Brundle

Eez A Not Italiano!

"I drove some dogs. What I didn't do was navigate myself into the best cars. And when I did in '92, for a number of reasons outside of my control I got binned. Two things destroyed my F1 career: one was breaking my ankle in 1984, and the other was losing the Benetton drive, despite having done a very, very good job. To this day Flavio apologises to me once a year, saying, 'I shouldn't have done that.' And, 'Sorry, I had no idea how good Michael Schumacher was.' This kid came along, and although I beat him quite a lot in races through that year, he looked good and to have great potential. Flavio saw this new boy pretty much giving the old boy a run for his money and Michael won in Spa when I should have won the race.

"Also, he was getting ribbed by the Italian media, because they said, 'You call yourself an Italian team at Benetton? You're based in the UK, you race under a British licence, you've got a Scottish team principal in Tom Walkinshaw, a South African designer in Rory Byrne, a British technical director in Ross Brawn, and you've got a British and a German driver – tell us which bit of that's Italian?' For '93, they entered under an Italian licence and had Ricardo Patrese in the car. So that cost me very dearly. Especially as I thought I was going to Williams for '93, and Damon got that job."

Murray Walker

Realist

"Martin was very co-operative, always. And always very straightforward. I was interviewing him somewhere on the Continent, because I remember we were sitting outside a restaurant in the country, and we'd both got a glass of beer in front of us, and I said, 'How about your team mate, Michael Schumacher, how are things going with him?' 'Why's he beating me,' he said. 'Is that what you mean?' Now not many drivers would be prepared to admit that someone was beating them."

Liz Brundle

The Good Life But...

"It's been great! Motorsport has given us so much, but it's a tough life and it pushes you right to the limit. It demands everything, and that particular year with Benetton, I think I struggled because I could see how much pressure Martin was under. It was beginning to get to him, and hence it was getting to me because obviously my role in the background is to make sure that 'my' driver's got his head right, and that I say the right things and help him with his confidence and all that. You feel the pressure as well, and you find it hard."

"I am not quite sure what we are looking at in this photo." (Sutton Motorsport Images)

Ross Brawn

Unfortunate Parting

"There were occasions when if the car hadn't let him down, or there hadn't been some other issue, then he would have got that victory. And I think he did a great job. Within the team there were some political tensions between Tom and Flavio. Martin was very much seen as Tom's boy, and unfortunately Martin suffered some of the fallout from that situation. I think the team would have been much better placed to have continued with the same structure it had than the changes they made. History shows the changes that were made weren't a step forward. I didn't have the influence or power within the team at that stage so I went with the flow. But I think that, from my own personal perspective, it was a great shame that Martin wasn't able to continue with the team, because I think it would have put the team in a stronger position."

Maurice Hamilton

Too Late, Was The Cry

"There were times when he had Shuey on the go. I remember an interview with Flavio Briatore who, much later on, admitted that, because he was so besotted with Michael, he overlooked Martin a bit and didn't appreciate that Martin was as quick as he was. It was only afterwards he began to realise how good Michael was, and therefore how good Martin was. Canada: such a shame that he didn't win that. That would have changed a lot of things, I think. The diff bolts - your whole career can pivot on little things like that."

"Now that's how a Formula 1 car should look." (Sutton Motorsport Images)

"I had been in bed with food poisoning and missed second qualifying at Suzuka. It was incredible I made it to the podium, with Berger and Patrese." (Sutton Motorsport Images)

Herbie Blash

Odds Against

"It really is a crying shame that he never won a Grand Prix. He was definitely World Champion material, not just a Grand Prix winner, but he just wasn't in the right place at the right time. I think he really showed his worth when he was at Benetton. You could see from that very first race, with the Jordan, how special Schumacher was. Obviously Schumacher was the Golden Boy at Benetton, even if Martin was quicker. It was Schumacher's team as far as Flavio was concerned – Flavio was Michael's manager."

Williams leaves Brundle in cold

"The B192 at speed - my head is down - I am willing the car along." (Sutton Motorsport Images)

Ross Brawn

New Kid On The Block

"I think Flavio favoured [having] an Italian driver. There was some commercial deal as well with Patrese, in terms of sponsorship, that was attractive to Flavio, and I don't think he really appreciated the level that Martin was at because there was this new kid on the block who was giving Martin a hard time. But no-one really appreciated the level Michael was at, because he then went on to give everybody a hard time. There was nobody who really, at least at the peak of his career, who stood up against Michael. Of all the team-mates he had, none of them were really able to compare. So I think Martin did a very credible job. And I think it was a mistake to make the change, but it's easy to say in retrospect."

"On the podium with Berger and Schumacher, my final race for Benetton was at Adelaide. It's easy to see why they fired me..." (Sutton Motorsport Images)

Martin Brundle

Press Revelation

"I found out in August at the Hungarian GP that I was being replaced. An Italian journalist asked me what I was doing the following year and I said I was hopefully staying at Benetton. He said, 'Don't you know they've signed Patrese?'"

British talent carries the French flag

Ligier pinning hopes on Brundle and Blundell

Liz Brundle

"I was lucky to get a seat at Ligier as Mark had already signed."

Dave Redding

Bespoke For One

"I think Martin had done more than enough to keep his seat [at Benetton], particularly towards the end of the season. He scored some very good points for the team. I think some of the issue was that Schumacher was beginning to steer the development of the '93 car which Martin probably didn't like, in terms of its characteristics. It was becoming pointier and pointier, so more and more front end of the car and harder to drive and I'm not sure whether the big bosses necessarily believed Martin's comments so they thought they'd bring Patrese in and he said the same thing. They developed a car that really only Schumacher could drive."

Martin Brundle

Tough

"I finished second to Senna at Monza, beating Schumacher. That same weekend, Mansell announced he was going to race in America the following season. Subsequent meetings and conversations very much led me to believe I was going to drive for Williams in 1993."

Cruel Fate, Again

"I believe he'd been told that he was likely to get the Williams drive, and was expecting a call to go down to sign the contract the next morning, and we even got to the point where we were going to open a bottle of Champagne here to celebrate, and then next morning the call didn't come. And then we heard that Damon had been given the drive, and we'd missed out. He was the Williams test driver at the time."

"Two rosbifs in a French state-funded team seemed unlikely. In this picture it appears somebody has left something sharp in my seat." (Sutton Motorsport Images)

David Tremayne

Williams

"One of the tragedies was that he didn't get the Williams drive. Nobody quite knows why. At one stage, it looked like they would be quite happy to sign him and they changed their minds."

Louise Goodman

Trophy Friend

"Driving from Imola, to the airport, Mark Blundell and Martin got stopped by the police. Mark was speeding and he suddenly came back to the car and said to Martin, 'Give me your trophy, give me your trophy'. So the minute he produced the trophy, claiming to be Martin Brundle, who'd just finished on the podium, the police waved him through. They used to get up to all sorts."

James Allen

If Only...

"In a way Martin is a little bit like Button in that perhaps he wasn't always right where he would like to have been in qualifying, but his races were always very, very strong. Obviously it's well-documented that he outperformed Schumacher a few times in the Benetton in '92 and I think, if he could have had the opportunity to stay there into '93, when obviously Patrese got moved in for political reasons, and maybe even for '94 as well, it would have been a different sort of Formula 1 career. He was certainly capable of winning plenty of races; he was a really, really good racer."

"I thoroughly enjoyed driving for Ligier, even if the French handshake ritual was mildly challenging on arrival at the factory." (Sutton Motorsport Images)

Martin Brundle on ...

Ayrton Senna

"Drove from the heart. He had the most God-given skill of anybody I've seen, ever, in my racing life. Had a sixth sense and knew where the grip was before the corner, instead of in the middle of it, or just after. I remember at Silverstone one year in F3 in the rain when it was red-flagged. The race was therefore run in two parts and, in the second part, I tried a line he'd taken to pass me in the first part of the race and I so nearly aquaplaned off the track. I said to him afterwards on the podium, 'Your line into Stowe didn't work in the second part?' and he said, 'I don't know, I didn't try it, it was too wet.' How did he know that? How did he know it was too wet? Why didn't I know it was too wet? Extraordinary driver."

David Coulthard

Men And Boy

"I guess the first time I really spoke with him was at a test at Imola, when I was the Williams test driver. He was having dinner with Mark Blundell and I was eating on my own so I asked to join them. I was the young hopeful and they were the established drivers. They said I could join them if I paid, which I did!"

Mark Blundell

No Quarter

"There's the competitive side to him, the dog-eat-dog side. At Estoril in a GP, he put me off the road at about 170mph and only an hour or so later we were sharing a private plane going back to Norwich airport and neither of us would look at each other over the top of the newspaper because we were both fuming at each other. Then it was one of those surreal moments when we then got off the jet and looked at each other and said, 'Talk to you tomorrow, then.' 'OK, yeah, talk to you tomorrow.' And that was the end of it. We were as competitive with each other as we were with anyone else but, over and above that, there was a friendship that meant a great deal to us both as well. So we always ended on a good note."

Alex Brundle

That's My Dad

"When Dad brought home a trophy, it was a really exciting thing for a youngster. You'd see this trophy, this artefact on the podium, and then all of a sudden it came to visit you in your home which was a really exciting moment. We used to watch the start of a Grand Prix, then sit playing with Lego or something while all the business was done, and then come back and see how he'd got on at the end!"

"Blue skies at Imola - I looked pretty confident here." (Sutton Motorsport Images)

Sir Jackie Stewart

'Murrayisms'

"Martin was the fall-guy for some of these because Mark Blundell raced at the same time as Martin Brundle. For Murray, it was Martin Blundell and Mark Brundle, more times that I would like to remember, and Martin handled it so well!"

"An Imola podium was my reward. Michael's comment on the podium was, 'Welcome back'. Alain Prost won the race." (Sutton Motorsport Images)

Martin Brundle

Not Only Helmets Have Peaks

"I think you peak as a racing driver. For me, somewhere between 28 and 34 is a crossover point of your experience, your youth, your fitness, your determination, your will to win, your ability to absorb all the media pressure and that sort of thing. I think there's a sweet spot. It might have extended now because the guys are so much fitter and pampered by lots of PR people around them and media people to protect them. And of course, they don't get killed and they don't get badly injured."

James Allen

Rough & Tough

"He's one of those guys who's always on the look out for how he can learn, and if you look around, not just Formula 1 but the world in general I think, people who are successful are people that, however old they are, and however well established they are, they never stop learning. They never feel that there isn't anything they can learn from somebody. Having said all of that, he's somebody who absolutely doesn't suffer fools gladly. I've seen people get on the wrong side of Martin and he just doesn't have any time for people who waste his time. He can be very, very tough. But that's what you have to be when you're in Formula 1 as a driver.

"If you look at Schumacher, you look at Senna, all these people, they felt that they were in a war against others. And so Martin - this nice chap from Norfolk, who's managed to make his way up through the ranks - has pitched in against some of the hardest bastards who have ever drawn breath. And the team principals are even worse, and he had to survive in that jungle. So he built himself a really tough protective shell and also was quite prepared to do the hard thing if it needed to be done, and you have to admire that because that's the side of the sport that people just don't really understand at all.

"Those guys were animals in those days and it was a really brutal world that he was racing in: Senna, Mansell, Prost. I did Mansell's autobiography with him and the stories - just unbelievable stuff that happened. Incredible. And Martin was in that world as a driver and trying to survive. So I admired him for being able to play that game and be able to have those tools in his toolbox, but at the same time be able to be a compassionate and understanding sort of person who would listen to others, who would learn from other people."

Derek Allsop

Media Man

"I got him to do his first [newspaper] columns and they were fantastic. So you can see the guy developing, not just as a racing driver, but as a rounded press man if you like. I remember saying to him in the early 1990s, 'You have been a good racing driver, but you'll be an even bigger name in the commentary box than the cockpit.' He didn't like it at the time, but I think I may have been right there. He is a natural, and you can see that developing through the years. He's also a very practical guy and a salesman: all that comes out in his personality."

"Descending to the lower paddock at the Hungaroring but I'm hot and sweaty for some reason." (Sutton Motorsport Images)

Mark Blundell

Shared Fun

"If you went into the F1 pit lane most people would know that if you found one of us, the other wouldn't be too far away. We were connected at the hip so to speak. We'd share a lot of time together and we liked it that way. We get on extremely well. We have shared several drinks, several dinners and probably several hangovers along the way."

Martin Brundle

Steady Year

"I ended up with Blundell for the second time as my team mate. Mark's one of my best friends and remains so to this day, and we just had a great rapport. We were super competitive against each other but had total mutual respect on a professional and personal level. I would trust him on anything. I don't think there was a single day at the races that I didn't have breakfast and dinner with Billy Blundell. We had a lot of fun. So we were two rosbifs at Ligier which was amusing, with a French state-funded team. Cyril de Rouvre was a great boss but he ended up in prison at the end of the year. I got a podium in Imola and we really did well. I scored points in seven of the 16 races. We had the Renault engine and it was great and then Williams were very keen for Benetton not to get the Renault engine and so they started sending us bits and some help - we had a fantastic car mid-year."

"I lost a wheel during the Grand Prix which cost me a strong finishing position." (Sutton Motorsport Images)

Derek Warwick

Hard But Fair

"I think he was a hard driver. He gave no quarter. He took every advantage he could get but he wouldn't put you in danger. And that's why in those days we had more respect than the drivers of today maybe. I think he was fair, yes. Fair in the sense that he wouldn't try and put you into the trees, but aggressive enough to know that when you wanted to pass him, he would make it bloody difficult."

"The Ligier had a one-off paint scheme (also seen on the opposite page) by Hugo Pratt for the Japanese GP." (Sutton Motorsport Images)

Mark Blundell

Je Ne Comprends Pas

"Martin was more on top of things as he had a bit of a handle on the French language whereas I had zero and he used it to good effect. We had some great times. The cars were more competitive at some tracks than others. Dealing with a foreign organisation is always going to be a bit tricky. We had quite a lot of testing over there and we would go from Stansted Airport to Magny Cours – there was always a bit of a race to see who would get there in the quickest possible time!"

Martin Brundle

The Waiting Game

"So with de Rouvre's problems I left. I wanted to drive the McLaren and I played a dangerous game. I put all my chips on the hope I was going to get it and I waited the whole winter. I worked on Ron Dennis and I knew he was talking to loads of drivers and that he really wanted Prost in the car. When we went to Estoril to test, Prost drove in the morning; I drove in the afternoon. You could tell Prost wasn't keen; the Peugeot engine wasn't really very strong at that point. He was nonplussed which I was quite pleased to see.

"I actually signed for McLaren on the Tuesday before the first Grand Prix. Talk about preparation - you'd laugh now if a driver did that in F1. I signed on the Tuesday, got on a plane and went to the first Grand Prix. But that first test day - I should have known really. I got in the car after Prost had finished with it, just after lunch, and on the out-lap it threw a con-rod so hard it went through the bottom of the sump, out through the undertray of the car and damaged the racetrack. At the first race in Brazil, I spent two days with the throttle sticking open before I nearly died in the race."

"Unfortunately fire proof overalls were rather necessary in the 1994 McLaren."

"After three days of filming at Catalunya for a simulator game, I borrowed Randy Mamola's leathers and tried the 500 two-stroke Yamaha GP bike. It was quite a challenge, as my only previous experience was on my 50cc moped when I was 16!"

Martin Whitmarsh

Traumatic Stress

"He drove for us in '94 alongside Mika and effectively he stepped into Ayrton's seat – he had left at the end of '93. It was a very traumatic time for the sport with a series of accidents and it was a fairly traumatic time for McLaren with Peugeot."

Mike Greasley

Brinkmanship

"Lovely bloke to work for. He has a hell of business brain so he always knew exactly what he wanted to do and where he wanted to go, and when. I remember that McLaren year, he hung on for that drive and did all the negotiations himself. Everybody thought, 'You're leaving it too late Martin and you could end up with nothing' – but he got it."

Martin Brundle

Near Death Experience

"The accident in which I really came closest to dying was Brazil '94 when my flywheel came off. I was slowing down, the team were on the radio to me. The French driver Eric Bernard in his Ligier, who I had just lapped, was caught by surprise by me slowing. Meanwhile behind him, Verstappen and Irvine were fighting each other. Irvine moved to the left to avoid hitting Bernard. Verstappen, in Irvine's slipstream and unaware of my problems in front, went to the left of Irvine, didn't lift, put a wheel on the grass at 180mph and was pitched sideways. He hit my left rear wheel, took off and barrel-rolled across the top of my car, one of his rear wheels hitting my head.

"All I knew about the accident was that I mysteriously found myself in the gravel trap at the next corner. I got out, tried to walk back to the pits, passed out, crawled back to a marshal, couldn't get his attention, crawled half way to the pits, felt better, got up, walked to the pits, debriefed and went home. A week later the family said to me, 'We're taking you to hospital, you're not right.' I was heavily concussed. I've seen a picture of the accident where you can't see my head - it looks as though my head's been knocked off!"

"Showing off to somebody that I could fly helicopters. I love the freedom of the skies."

"Sadly this was an all-too-common occurrence in 1994." (Sutton Motorsport Images)

Murray Walker

Explosive Situation

"Martin was very brave actually that year because he knew that there was a seat going at McLaren, and he was determined to have it. So he hung on and hung on and hung on and turned down offers from other teams and, if McLaren had appointed someone else, he would have been without a drive. But it's an indication of what a determined bloke he is. Unfortunately, he went to McLaren when they had the Peugeot engine which was a sort of mobile hand grenade – it was just a question of when it went off!"

"The '94 McLaren was fundamentally a good car. In Aida, in Japan, I was homing in on third place when the engine failed."
(Sutton Motorsport Images)

Martin Whitmarsh

McLaren Shoot Out

"We had an issue with Martin that was mildly amusing. I don't suppose Martin felt it was amusing. Peugeot Motor Sport, our partner, was headed by an ex-racing driver, Jean-Pierre Jabouille, and he was a clear fan of Philippe Alliot's right from the get-go. I'm sure Martin felt that Peugeot were anti-him because they were continually saying, 'Let's drop him. We can put Philippe Alliot in - he's much quicker.'

"In seeking to appease our new partner, Peugeot, we undertook to do a drive-off at the Paul Ricard circuit. Martin turned up to drive the car, as did Philippe Alliot - it was literally a drive-off on one day. The circuit was unnaturally quick, even for that era, so cones were positioned as a chicane in the middle of the straight to slow the car but also to make the circuit more representative of other circuits in terms of its speed profile. So Martin went out, did his normal professional job, set a competitive lap time and came back. That was fine. Jabouille turned up with his protégé and Alliot got in the car. He was one second or more off the pace for a series of laps. Then made some adjustments, went out for a run, still slow, then suddenly – bang – did a lap time that was faster than Martin's and came back in the garage. We had a jubilant Alliot and Jabouille. 'There you go. Shows you that this guy has much more potential than this bloody Brundle.' Whilst we were scratching our heads, one of our engineers pointed out that somehow Alliot had gone through the chicane without pulling any lateral G on the fast lap that he'd just done. This either meant his mates on the circuit had pulled the cones out of the way, or he'd driven effectively outside them down the side of the track, so he could straight-line the chicane. He had dabbed the brakes; there was a brake trace to make it look like he'd done something!"

"The tragic weekend of Imola '94. I will never forget dodging around debris from Senna's crash and the incredible events which followed." (Sutton Motorsport Images)

Martin Brundle

When The Flag Drops...

"I did have to cope with the Alliot nonsense until he stepped in to replace the banned Hakkinen as my team mate at the Hungarian GP and I thrashed him. Nothing heard again. Although I was on a race-by-race contract at McLaren, which was a ridiculous position to put me in."

"I stepped into the seat that Ayrton vacated at McLaren. He came by to wish me luck."

Martin Brundle

Reflections On The Senna Accident

"You inevitably do a bit of soul searching. 'Do I want to do this. Is it right?' And the answer is always yes, you do want to do it and you get back in. Also, if you're competitive and you're a little bit tough and brutal, you get hardened along the way, and there's almost - it doesn't sound right - but, 'Well it's him and not me. It's one I haven't got to beat, and statistically there's less chance of me getting killed now.' You actually come at it fairly hard-nosed in the end and, 'I'm either going to stop doing this, and then what I am going to do because this is my whole life, or I carry on and hope it doesn't happen to me.'"

Martin Brundle

Ayrton's Fatal Accident

"Senna's death was tough for us all because we were going through a very strange time then. Barrichello had a big accident on the Friday, Ratzenberger was killed on the Saturday and Senna on the Sunday. Then, two weeks later, Wendlinger was in a coma. We had a similar thing happen in sports cars in '85 when we lost Bellof, we lost Winkelhock and Palmer had a big shunt, all within 14 days and you can't help wonder, 'What's going on? What's going to happen next?'

"I went to Bellof's funeral which I found very distressing - to see his family and his girlfriend, and the absolute destruction of those people at the funeral. So I didn't go to Senna's funeral, which I very much regret now, but I couldn't. I'd made up my mind at Bellof's funeral that I wouldn't go to another racing driver's funeral while I was racing because, when I saw that destruction... You then translate that to people close to you and that matter to you, and you think, 'God, am I putting them through that?' And I'd had a couple of fairly miraculous escapes at that point anyway, even by '94."

NOTES of meeting of Formula 1 drivers held at Monaco - May 13, 1994 at 09.30.

Meeting attended by all current Grand Prix drivers with the exception of Karl Wendlinger. Also in attendance Niki Lauda.

The meeting opened with Berger and Lauda relating their past experiences regarding drivers meetings.

1. Brundle was appointed chairman of the meeting.

2. Brundle and Schumacher agreed to take notes. It was also agreed that a secretary be available to take notes at the next planned meeting.

3. It was agreed that all proposals should have 60% approval from those in attendance in order to be carried.

4. It was agreed that the following drivers should represent the GPDA (Grand Prix Drivers Association) : Schumacher, Berger and Christian Fittipaldi. These drivers will represent the GPDA to the FIA, FOCA and race circuits.

5. It was agreed that a former Grand Prix driver should be appointed as official spokesperson. The drivers nominated Lauda who agreed to undertake this role until at least the end of 1994.

    Lauda was adamant that the GPDA should seek full recognition and voting powers with the FIA.

    It was agreed that an office and database should be established. Lauda agreed to investigate the costs and to report at the next meeting.

    Concerns were expressed over Lauda's links with Ferrari and assurances were given. These were accepted.

    It was agreed that at a later date that some or all super licence fees should be redirected to cover the costs of the drivers activities concerning safety issues. It was proposed but not necessarily well supported that the GPDA should enlist the support of the ASN's of each country staging a Grand Prix.

David Tremayne

Post-Senna

"Martin talked a lot about Imola and he said that the oddest, spookiest thing was the thought that during the rest of that race he passed a patch of Ayrton's blood. Ayrton had been a massive part of his life and had actually made Martin. If Martin had just dominated F3 in '83, would people have really thought as much about him as if he hadn't fought Senna? Ayrton validated Martin as a driver. That was what really attracted Ken about him – everybody knew this Brazillian was quick, but if this British guy on a low budget who could actually keep up with him, he must be something pretty special. In 1994 Martin was part of the GPDA [Grand Prix Drivers' Association]. You can imagine what it was like back then. Martin did a lot of track inspections that year on behalf of the GPDA and he said in the end he had to stop because he was an active driver and was going to so many places and thinking, 'Jesus Christ, I could be killed at this corner, or that one,' and he said it started to gnaw away at him to the point where sometimes it's better not to know that kind of thing."

"I always seemed to end up in charge of things and the Grand Prix Drivers' Association was another example of that."

"On the grid in Monaco, the young drivers were like rabbits in the headlights. I steered through it all to finish second."

Martin Brundle

Taking A Lead

"We re-formed the GPDA at Monaco with Schumacher and Berger. I became the Chairman. It would mark the beginning of a very combative period with Bernie and Max Mosley."

Brilliant Brundle

Norfolk ace puts torment behind him to finish second

Martin Whitmarsh

Monaco Specialist - Again

"Skimming through '94, the highlight for me was Martin's drive in Monaco. He came through the field so he overtook on a circuit, and in an era, when overtaking was particularly difficult. To my mind, it was probably one of the greatest drives of his career."

"My dream of driving for McLaren at the British Grand Prix lasted a few hundred metres. The official Peugeot press release said I should have carried on from this. I was angry when McLaren refused to correct that." (Sutton Motorsport Images)

Martin Brundle on ...

Mika Hakkinen

"Hakkinen seemed to live in a little bubble of his own really. Very simple life, his only distraction was his pet tortoise. And I think he just turned up to the track and, while we were all busy doing other things or getting distracted, he just went race driving. And he was brilliant. He had a driving technique with his left foot braking that was good. He had bravery, especially after his accident. You often see, when people get into a world championship position, they transcend to a new level. Damon did it, I think, when he won the title. They get their head into a different place. Mika found that. He was apolitical. He was also significantly faster than me, albeit with first access to McLaren's best equipment."

Martin Brundle

Ditching The Dirt

"'There's so much wing on it feels like I'm towing a caravan.' I knew exactly what I meant. And of course I say all those things now on TV, and people like it, because that's the bite-sized bits that make them understand what's happening inside the car. But the engineers didn't use to love it when I explained the car like that! No, they used to take the mickey out of me. I remember coming in once and Pat Fry said to me, 'What's it doing, is it stage-coaching today?' So they used to try and pre-empt my expressions! Talking of silly things you say to engineers, I remember Giorgio Ascanelli, who was my engineer at McLaren - a very typical, emotional, Italian who was dedicated to his job. We were at Magny Cours in the McLaren in '94, and I'd always been quick at Magny Cours. I knew the place like the back of my hand from racing with Ligier who were based there. And we just couldn't get the McLaren to work and we were getting frustrated. He'd elected to go back to base set-up without telling me, and I went out and I knew it wasn't right. And I came back in, I stood about 14th or 15th and I just hadn't got the speed that I knew I could have round that track, and it was Peugeot's home race.

"I came in and he said, 'So? How is it?' And I'd sussed what he'd done, and I said, 'It's shit.' And that was all I said, which was a really stupid thing to say. So he pressed the button on his headphones and said, 'OK guys, we need less shit all round, please.' Normally it would be something like, 'Three mil on the front ride height, two steps up on the rear roll bar.' He then took off his headphones, laid them on the top of the toolbox alongside, walked out of the garage and I never saw him again until the end of the session.

"He was right. It was stupid what I'd said, but I was just frustrated. It was a frustrating year."

"In the face of adversity, you have to keep smiling." (Sutton Motorsport Images)

"Surprisingly it all hung together at Monza for a fifth place finish. The car was better towards the end of the season." (Sutton Motorsport Images)

Liz Brundle

Blown Out Of Proportion

"The engine blew up, I think, nine times or something out of the whole season. He'd be doing well and then the engine would go. At the Hungarian GP, the alternator and battery packed up a few corners from home. I was with the children in Spain; we were watching television. Alex was tiny and he was, 'My daddy's going to win a trophy!' And I said, 'You have to wait until the flag comes down because anything can happen.' And sure enough, he had problems when almost in sight of the flag. 'My daddy didn't win a trophy!'"

Nigel Roebuck

Taking The Mika

"I think Martin has a very balanced attitude to his own ability and his own standing in the sport. I think he's come to terms with the fact that, while having great days, he simply couldn't be considered a great GP driver - a very, very good one and certainly a great sports car racer. He said to me once about Hakkinen: they would get to the end of qualifying and Mika would produce a [stunning] time. Martin always reckoned that, certainly over one lap, Mika was quicker than Schumacher but there were times with Mika that Martin would think, 'Where did that come from? I just don't understand where that came from.' Martin was always very realistic with himself. Having said that, on some days he could match and sometimes beat Mika but fundamentally Mika was on it every weekend and perhaps Martin wasn't."

"It was a post-Jerez bullfight - I am second from right, Hakkinen is third from left. We stopped smiling when they sent the feisty bull after us and we ran like hell."

Martin Whitmarsh

Divorce Power

"The car wasn't a bad car. I don't think it was a great car, but it got eight podiums during the course of the year which was more than Peugeot ever got again. It was a difficult year because by about halfway through the year, frankly, we were divorcing Peugeot and getting out of the contract we had, and we were going into a relationship with Mercedes. I think Martin was aware of what was going on, the fact that we were divorcing them, so it was frosty with them. There were lots of reasons for him to be distracted but whatever he does, he does it in a very professional way."

"This shot looks a bit like I'm playing myself in a movie." (Sutton Motorsport Images)

Martin Brundle

Wheel Of Misfortune

"I got two podiums that year. Monaco was a miracle because it had no oil or water left in it and Australia at the end of the year when it was going a little bit better. But I was in a podium position five or six times more when the engine broke. Its party trick was throwing its flywheel off at high revs and the flywheel then would go and hit the floor and come back up through the oil tank."

Martin Brundle

Faint Praise

"After Monaco, Ron Dennis chose to congratulate me by saying, 'Don't forget that second is first loser.' I don't think many people could have nursed that car home, beaten only by Schumacher."

Martin Whitmarsh

Tribute

"We went into a multi-year contract with Peugeot and it was no coincidence that we paid Jordan to take the contract away from us at the end. So we ended up the following year having to pay for the pleasure of not using their engines. It was a tough year for F1 and the team. It's very easy for drivers to let their heads drop, to get distracted and to lose motivation. I think we've got to record a lot of gratitude to Martin for being professional enough to come through that year as it would have been a tougher year for us with other drivers."

Martin Brundle

Timing Is Everything

"Jaguar, Nissan, Toyota, Bentley: they hired me because I could develop their car, which I did. That was my strong point. I would work hard on developing the cars. But I was never in the right car at the right time. Even when I went to McLaren I was in the right car at the wrong time. And had it been the right time Prost would have driven anyway. There were many things I would do differently now if I had the chance again, but we can all say that."

"My final race for McLaren and I finished on the podium. Along with Berger and Mansell, our combined age is probably still a record."
(Sutton Motorsport Images)

"In Suzuka, in torrential rain, I was on the radio calling for the race to be stopped, just before I aquaplaned off, and hit a marshal, breaking his leg."
(Sutton Motorsport Images)

Martin Whitmarsh

Reason For Not Retaining Martin

"It was entirely my fault. It felt that there was an opportunity – it was an error – to recruit Nigel [Mansell]. Nigel had left F1 and gone Indy racing. I believed that Nigel in the early '90s, despite the personality idiosyncrasies, was a brilliant racing driver and I felt at that time that Mika was still a young driver and unproven. A team like McLaren needed a star for our sponsors, for our profile, for whatever, and Nigel was that star. It turned out to be my mistake, and in fact we would have been far better in the following year to have kept Martin. Nigel's career was even shorter lived with us and he did no more than two races and we mutually terminated that one. I've got to put my hand up – it was primarily my fault."

Martin Brundle

Back To Ligier

"Tom Walkinshaw was my pillow to land on - again. He had this Ligier-Mugen-Honda deal and it was a great car - basically a Benetton with a Mugen Honda in it. But he had this political problem with the Mugen deal - he had to run a Japanese driver for some of the races. So I had to share the car with Aguri Suzuki. But I still had some great races in that car."

"Caught red-handed at the tea machine, and probably biscuits too, but the shot above confirms I used to take my fitness very seriously and always had a gym at home." (Martine Walkinshaw)

"However, I wish I had known then what I know now about specific exercise, nutrition and hydration for Formula 1 drivers." (Sutton Motorsport Images)

Keith Sutton

A Late Lunch

"We were mates and we had a good rapport. I found out that Martin, before the start of the F1 season, always used to take all the British newspaper journalists out for lunch. They could all interview him. It was a good idea. It was an opportunity to fill in everyone with what was going on and get a good rapport going with the journalists. I joked with him about this and said, 'What about the British photographers? What about taking us out for lunch?' He said, 'Yes, we should do that.' But it never happened. And then once I said, jokingly, 'Look, the British photographers are not happy with you and we're not even going to take pictures of you any more.' And Martin said, 'You're joking. You can't do that. What is it?' 'Well, this lunch you promised us, when is it going to happen?' We were in Argentina, but he wasn't racing the Ligier in that GP and he said, 'Sort the boys; we'll go out for a big steak.' We had a great time and it was good that he kept his promise."

Guest Appearances

"When he was driving in the Ligier team and sharing the seat with Aguri Suzuki, Mark Wilkin, who was the BBC producer, got Martin to come into the commentary box, at a time when Jonathan Palmer was sharing the commentary with me, and Martin was bloody good. And when the BBC lost the contract and ITV got it, ITV didn't ask Jonathan Palmer to continue, but they asked Martin Brundle to."

"I was always so happy challenging the street furniture of Monaco."
(Sutton Motorsport Images)

"My good friend Jaques Laffite appears animated but we have never had a cross word and we were just having fun." (Sutton Motorsport Images)

Martin Brundle

No Fixed Abode

"Through '95 I was doing Eurosport on Saturday with Ben Edwards and John Watson. And then BBC on Sunday with Murray and Jonathan. I was probably not welcome in either commentary box if truth be known. For half the races, I was kicking around. The other half, I was kicking arse to be honest. I was going pretty well. One of my very strong seasons '95 and I was only in the car half the time. It was a good little car that '95 Ligier."

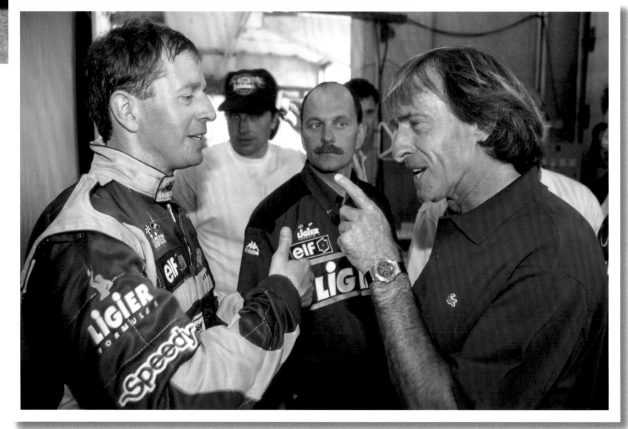

Murray Walker

Two Pundits

"It was quite a difficult political situation actually in '95, because there was me doing the commentary and there was my official pundit, and my number two pundit, if you like. So Martin sat in the background, more-or-less, with a pair of headphones on and a microphone, and spoke when he was spoken to!"

"That was a hard-earned trophy in the rain at Spa - my final podium in Formula 1."

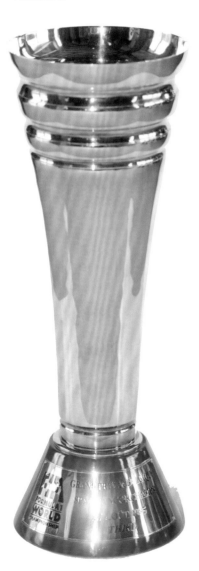

Martin Brundle

Wet Spa

"I finished on the podium in Spa. Had a great race with Damon. I stayed out on wets, and somehow got it to the end with, I think, every tread block of the wets, front and rear, blistered. Damon stopped for tyres and passed me on the last lap. I had some good results in that car, in '95."

"Unusually the engine failed in Hungary which was a shame as it was another one of my favourite tracks." (Sutton Motorsport Images)

James Allen

Gee, That's Simple

"So then I started working for ESPN, American TV, and doing that coverage for the US in early '93/'94 and '95/'96 and whenever you needed a driver to explain something, in simple words, you went to Martin Brundle.

"I was once doing a piece on the basics of Formula 1, and I wanted someone to explain of G-force. So, of course, I went along to Martin, and I said, 'Right, Martin, I need someone to explain G-force.' And he said, 'No problem. You rolling? Right.'

"'Martin, can you explain G-Force to us?' 'No problem,' he said. 'G-Force is the force that makes your granny swap seats in the back of the car when you go too fast round a roundabout.'

"It was gold, absolutely fantastic. So that's an example of the ability he has always had to just nail it, and with a nice touch of humour."

"By now it was 20 years since I had met Liz at technical college. I have no idea how she put up with all the ups and downs." (Sutton Motorsport Images)

Martin Brundle on ...

Gerhard Berger

"Gerdy - good friend of mine. Like him a lot. He's very smart. I don't actually think he was any better than me. He operated at stratospheric levels. He was very smart in how he manoeuvred with Bernie, Ron and Max, and Dietrich Matterschitz later on, and now he's with the FIA. He's got a clarity of thought and he's very black and white in terms of how he views things, and he's management material. Post-Bernie I could see somebody like Gerhard playing a role. Not surprised he ended up in charge at BMW motorsport for a while. He got himself in a position where he earned a huge amount of money and won races, and I think he did that through cunning and guile, and just being worldly, rather than necessarily being faster than the rest."

"This would be a set-up shot of me pretending I can play snooker, although I do have a full size table." (Sutton Motorsport Images)

Martin Brundle on …

David Coulthard

"Pretty much the most popular driver there's been in recent times, I would say. Still is. Very popular guy, DC, in the paddock, amongst the drivers - mostly because of the parties he used to throw as much as anything! As a driver, very smooth, very fast. His dedication to his fitness was scary. I had the ability to be a Formula 1 winner, and didn't put myself in that position. He had the ability to be World Champion, and didn't put himself in that position. He used to get distracted by people or events that he shouldn't have let happen, or some stuff going on in his private life. Some of his victories were supreme. There could have been a bit more 'tough bastard' in him, that's for sure, but I managed him for 11 years and learned a great deal from him, as I do today. We have remained friends through intense rivalry and a long business relationship which is rewarding."

"The 1995 Ligier-Mugen was a great car and I enjoyed driving it." (Sutton Motorsport Images)

"I am challenging the Monza kerbs and, it seems, winning the battle so far." (Sutton Motorsport Images)

Martin Brundle

Great Days

"It makes me smile today when people say, 'Oh, this is without question the best era of F1.' And I'm like, 'Just think back a little bit...' We all think whatever era we were involved in was the best era. I had Senna as a rival for 11 years, Schumacher and Hakkinen as team mates – the three greatest drivers of my generation. And I occasionally beat Senna, Schumacher and Hakkinen in the same car on the same day. So, clearly the skills were there, but I didn't do that anywhere near often enough. You have to take your chances."

Derek Warwick

Why Quick?

"What makes any driver quick? It's a multitude of things. Firstly, you must have the natural ability which he had heaps of. Fitness. He struggled a little with fitness at times because of his broken ankle but that was not to deter him at all. His determination, his ability to focus on the job ahead and, like all racing drivers, we all, unfortunately, have to have a little trait of selfishness in us otherwise we couldn't do the job that we do. Remember, he was just after the really bad times of a lot of drivers being killed so you had to be very single-minded, very determined and, like I said, selfish. Selfish is not an easy word to use because none of us like to see ourselves as being selfish, but I'm sure we are. I've always thought of myself, and I'm sure Martin thinks exactly the same because he comes from a very strong family, I am the most selfish/unselfish person you would ever meet: selfish because when I want to do something, I do it; unselfish because when it's the time for the family, when I'm not racing, they were the most important thing to me. Martin was very much in the same mould as myself in terms of being able to keep a family going as well as being a professional racing driver."

"New Year's Eve in the Alps with the Walkinshaw and Brundle families. Tom got the bill." (Martine Walkinshaw)

Charlie Brundle

Model Daughter

"We had a nanny who used to look after us and she used to make little cardboard racing cars for us to sit in to watch the races – little models of Daddy's racing car."

"The race in Adelaide 2005 still torments me. I tripped over my old mate Blundell in the McLaren and it cost me a second place finish." (Sutton Motorsport Images)

Robin Brundle

Chopper Pilot

"Helicopters were great – he owned a Bell Jet Ranger and we would fly from his garden to Silverstone where they would use the helicopter as an air ambulance when they decided it would be good to have a helicopter on site. Very competent pilot. He once showed me how you have to practise an engine stall and auto-rotate down to a safe landing. He decided it was a nice clear day and a nice piece of land and he would practice this manoeuvre. I have to say that it was the first time I had broken into a sweat in an aircraft with him. But it was absolutely perfect."

Rubens Barrichello

Welcome, Mate

"I rate MB very highly: a very technical driver with lots of input on the car set-up. When he came to the Jordan team, I felt like I had a good chance to prove myself as MB had been Schumacher's team mate so it was going to be a good comparison for me."

"This is one of those moody shots where a photographer is trying to make me look good." (Sutton Motorsport Images)

"The first team photos with Jordan before the Benson & Hedges sponsorship was announced. We had clearly been told to look serious."

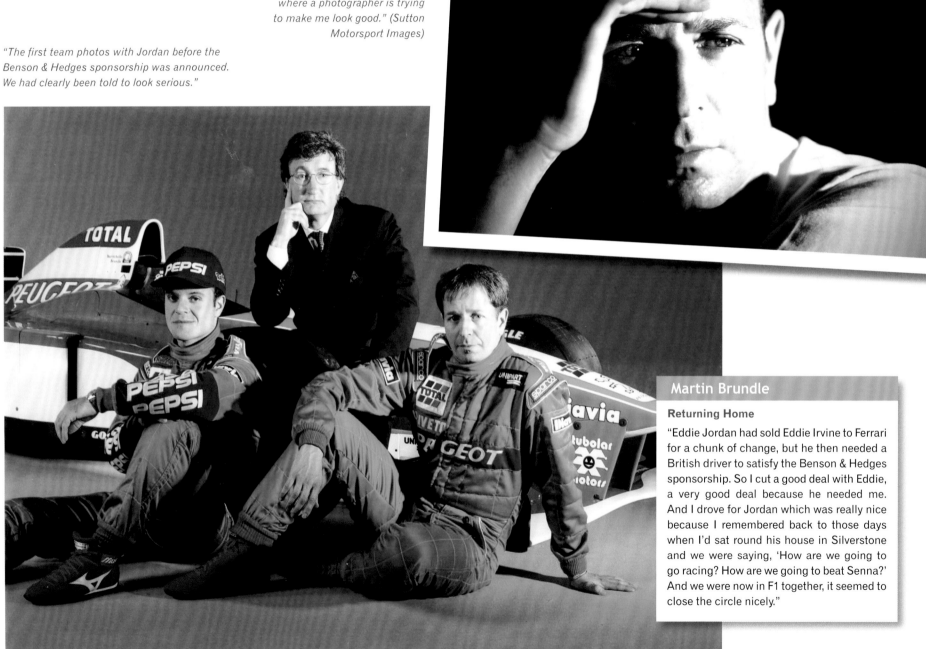

Martin Brundle

Returning Home

"Eddie Jordan had sold Eddie Irvine to Ferrari for a chunk of change, but he then needed a British driver to satisfy the Benson & Hedges sponsorship. So I cut a good deal with Eddie, a very good deal because he needed me. And I drove for Jordan which was really nice because I remembered back to those days when I'd sat round his house in Silverstone and we were saying, 'How are we going to go racing? How are we going to beat Senna?' And we were now in F1 together, it seemed to close the circle nicely."

"Unlike many F1 drivers, I love driving on the road. Whatever I've got, I am always planning my next car." (Sutton Motorsport Images)

Keith Sutton

Dream Cars

"In '96, I worked for a Japanese magazine and we did some 'at home, lifestyle' features and I went over to Norfolk to photograph Martin. We did pictures of him and Liz with the kids, in the gym working out, and all that stuff. He's always had the road cars I dreamed of. He said that something had just arrived that morning that I might be interested in: a Ferrari 355 Berlinetta, my dream car. He said, 'Come on, let me take you for a spin around the Norfolk country lanes.' When you get in the passenger seat with a racing driver, especially of his calibre, you realise the talent and the car control of these guys like you can only dream of. They're in another league. I'll never forget that drive. He jokingly said, 'You really like this car.' I said, 'I love it'. He said, 'Well, if I ever win a GP, it's yours'. I thought, 'Bloody hell, that's generous'. Of course, he never did. However, when he was up for selling it in '97, he remembered me and called me and said, 'I'm selling the Ferrari. I'll do you a fantastic deal. Are you interested?' And I thought, 'Bloody hell, that's a fantastic deal and if I don't do it now, I might regret it in years to come.'"

"One of my all time favourites was the Ferrari 355GTB. I once drove it 100 miles home from Oxfordshire and enjoyed it so much I sat in the drive for a full 10 minutes, contemplating driving back again." (Sutton Motorsport Images)

Martin Brundle

Flying Start

"The car was quite difficult in the early part of the season. I rolled it into a ball on the first lap ever of my Jordan Grand Prix experience and survived that. Everybody thought I was dead."

Louise Goodman

A Revelation

"Looking after Press & PR for Jordan, I came into much closer contact with Martin when he joined us and that's when I really got to know him properly. He was quite a revelation for me at the time. The vast majority of the drivers I'd worked with up until then had been younger guys. I'd had people like Eddie Irvine and Rubens Barrichello, and a lot of young blokes with whom it was like herding cats a lot of the time, and suddenly Martin: turned up at the right time, wearing the right clothes, saying the right things to the right people... It was, 'Ooh, this is like having a grown-up racing driver suddenly. I'm not used to this!'"

Eddie Jordan

Keep Going

"I thought Martin was dead. As soon as I knew he was OK, I just concentrated on readying the spare car."

Liz Brundle

The Worst Accident

"The worst one for me was Australia, '96, where the car flew through the air. I was at the back of the pit garage. I've seen a lot of accidents over the years, and you become a little bit blasé about them. Basically if somebody's spinning along the floor and bits are flying off, you don't worry too much, because you know that's what's supposed to happen. The ones you worry about are the ones where the cars are flying through the air. And I saw it was a Jordan, and I just knew it was Martin. I saw the helmet and I thought, 'Oh my God, this is the one I've dreaded.' And there were a group of us sitting at the back of the pits watching the screen, and everyone said, 'It's not him.' I said, 'It is, it is him.' And I stood up and went, 'NO!' And as the car took off and then slid along upside down, the tears began to pour down my face. Then I saw him climb out! And I thought, 'Oh my God, pull yourself together girl, he's going to be back here in a minute and you've got tears rolling down your face and he needs you to be strong and be there...' So I took some deep breaths and pulled myself together. He came back to the pits and gave me a wink and I said to him, 'You OK?' and he said, 'Yep. I'm going in the spare car.' So I thought, 'Hell, I've got to watch another start!' That was the worst one."

"This was my first ever racing lap for Jordan F1 and I broke the car like an egg. It's always your fault when a single seater crashes as there is only one person in it." (Getty Images)

Brundle, the man who ran from death

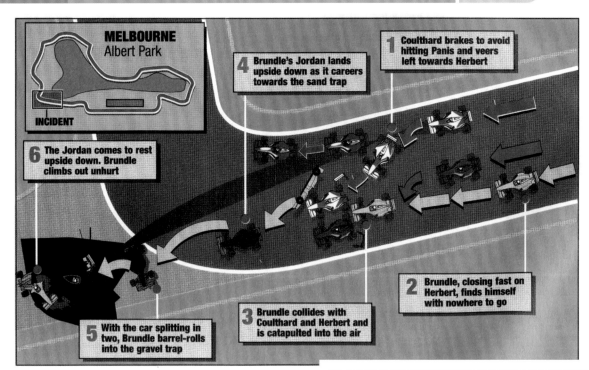

MELBOURNE
Albert Park

INCIDENT

1 Coulthard brakes to avoid hitting Panis and veers left towards Herbert

4 Brundle's Jordan lands upside down as it careers towards the sand trap

6 The Jordan comes to rest upside down. Brundle climbs out unhurt

2 Brundle, closing fast on Herbert, finds himself with nowhere to go

3 Brundle collides with Coulthard and Herbert and is catapulted into the air

5 With the car splitting in two, Brundle barrel-rolls into the gravel trap

Liz Brundle

Parental Guidance

"When he retired after the re-start, he came back to the pits and I said, 'You have to ring home'. Being Australia, being so far ahead in time, I knew the children would be getting up to watch the race; his dad was probably watching it live because he used to get up early. And I thought the family, particularly the children, are going to be freaked out by it. 'No, I don't need to do that; it's not a big deal.' And I said, 'Martin, I saw it! And that's what they'll see, and you have to ring home. And it has to be you ringing. It's no good me ringing. You have to speak to the children.' Eventually I persuaded him to, and Charlie, our elder daughter, understood about it. Alex was little and he didn't understand. So I said to Alex, 'Right, you're going to watch the race, and daddy's going to have a crash, but he's fine. So although it seems that he's having the crash then, he's already had the crash!' I was trying to explain it all to them, and of course to my parents, and everybody else I thought might be watching. It wasn't a pleasant experience! I remember saying to Eddie Jordan, 'Thank you for building such a strong car, Eddie.'"

"The misery continued in Argentina when I was attacked from behind by Tarso Marques after a safety car restart." (Sutton Motorsport Images)

Nigel Roebuck

Immortal Mortals

"One of the things I always admired about him as a racing driver – he was extremely brave. The example which is always cited was in Melbourne when he was shunted on the first lap and [it was] one of those shunts that you see and wince. I remember that day that the press room went completely silent for about a minute. Then he gets out of it and immediately is intent on doing the re-start in the spare car. I remember a similar thing happening with Warwick at Monza with an enormous accident coming out of Parabolica on the first lap, coming down the road upside down. He then ran back to the pits. Both of them were just intent on finding Sid Watkins and getting the OK to do the re-start. Things like that are really quite hard for ordinary people to comprehend."

Sutton Motorsport Images

"In Monaco the team did a great pit stop for me but I got caught out on a damp track in Casino Square." (Sutton Motorsport Images)

"In 1996 having achieved 150 Grand Prix starts; today it is pretty average."

Jonathan Palmer

Survivor

"Martin ended up racing much longer than me, and I was then commentating about him on BBC F1 coverage. I certainly remember being massively relieved when he climbed out of his Jordan after his horrific first-lap Melbourne cartwheeling shunt in 1996."

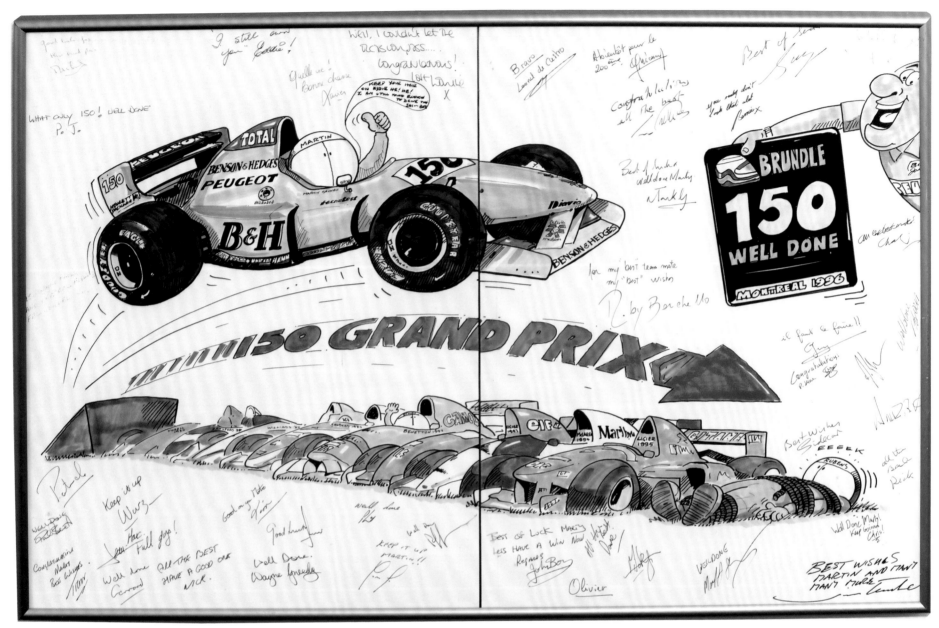

Helen Dickson

Brave Faces

"He had a huge amount of support but Mother was always worried – she was worried senseless really. As we all have. I remember the race in Australia where he just went over and over and over. We were relying on the BBC to tell us what was happening and they weren't really telling us much. It was at about 3am. Then they showed him climbing out of the car and we spotted him running down the pit lane. My mother who was asking, 'What's he doing? He can't get back in the car; he can't start that race again.' So we've always had this terrible knot in our stomachs every time he's been racing. The race that Senna died in was a terrible weekend – and Martin's was racing alongside him. It's been really nerve-wracking for the family but you never dream of saying, 'What on earth are you doing?' My mother would never have dreamt of stopping him from doing it when he was younger. She used to watch him crash his cars in the banger racing; then go home and cook Sunday lunch for him!"

Louise Goodman

Smart Guy

"He would make a point of knowing, if he had a sponsor function, who they were and what they did, and he'd talk to them. He'd iron his own shirt, or wear a shirt that somebody had ironed for him – he looked presentable and respectable. That's not to say that the other guys were unprofessional, just different characters. Martin is quite fastidious; that's part of why he's had the success he has. He crosses all of the t's and dots all of the i's."

"It is an impressive team line-up but this is just the team members who attended the race meetings."
(Sutton Motorsport Images)

Johnny Herbert

Risk Assessment

"Protection has moved on so much. Our shoulders were sticking above the sides of the monocoque - it was normal then. That was the height of racing technology at that time. You knew there was a risk and you were willing to take that risk. It was the latter part of the dangerous era but it was still a good era all the same. You still had a lot more safety than you did when it was aluminium [construction] or even the steel tubing in the late '60s. It was better with carbon fibre but, in the early days of carbon fibre, it wasn't nowhere nears as strong as it is today. It was all we knew then."

Louise Goodman

Staying Power

"We had a vast turnover of drivers at Jordan over the years. Some only lasted one race. So the fact that Martin lasted a whole year is testament to his fortitude!"

Louise Goodman

Smart Guy

"He would make a point of knowing, if he had a sponsor function, who they were and what they did, and he'd talk to them. He'd iron his own shirt, or wear a shirt that somebody had ironed for him – he looked presentable and respectable. That's not to say that the other guys were unprofessional, just different characters. Martin is quite fastidious; that's part of why he's had the success he has. He crosses all of the t's and dots all of the i's."

"A Jordan pit stop in the Silverstone pit lane, literally a few hundred metres from the Jordan factory."
(Sutton Motorsport Images)

Martin Brundle

Seasonal Survey

"The Jordan 196 was initially difficult although we improved it through the year and I finished in the points five times. I made too many mistakes. I crashed in Imola, in Hungary and two or three other places where I dropped the car and shouldn't have done. It went better in the second half of the year and of the races both Rubens and I finished, he beat me three times and I beat him three times. Taking the whole season, he out-qualified me 11-5, but in the second half I out-qualified him 5-3. And, in my final ever Grand Prix, I finished fifth just as I did in my first ever Grand Prix! As pleased as I was, I didn't realise it was my last race at the time or I would have savoured the moment more."

"By 1996, F1 was very much a data-driven sport, as it remains today."
(Sutton Motorsport Images)

"One of my favourite days ever - a car swap with rally legend Colin McRae."
(Sutton Motorsport Images)

Louise Goodman

Toy Swap

"When I was at Jordan we did a cross-challenge with Prodrive. So we put Colin McRae in the Formula 1 car and Martin in the rally car. It took us about 20 minutes to persuade Colin to get in to the rally car with Martin whilst Martin was driving it. That was no reflection on Martin; it was just that no rally driver wants to sit alongside somebody as a passenger."

"We swapped car models too - a treasured possession at home." (Sutton Motorsport Images)

David Tremayne

If A = B, And B = C, Then A = C

"You've got to say that Rubens Barrichello is not a slouch. In '96, one would be quick one time and the other would be quick the next. If you fast forward to 2009, you wouldn't say that Jenson Button was slow and Jenson showed up pretty well against Lewis at McLaren. Jenson and Rubens together at Brawn were pretty well matched. So, that's a nice little line of perspective of where you could argue Martin was in '96. Martin and Rubens were pretty evenly matched and they were forever slugging it out and there was a lot of intra-team rivalry between the two of them. Unfortunately by then, the magic with Martin and Eddie had evaporated and Jordan was a much more commercial enterprise then than it had been in '83."

"Colin was mightily impressive in the F1 car, except for a practice start where he nearly creamed it into the pit wall." (Sutton Motorsport Images)

"The experience motivated me to fulfill my dream of doing the Rally of Great Britain."

Martin Brundle

Rally Driver

"I fancied myself as a rally driver, I loved rallying and I did some events with our Celica back in the late '70s. In '96, we managed to organise through Ford and a sponsor for me to do the Rally of Great Britain, which was the hardest thing I've ever done in my life behind the wheel of a racing car. I think rally drivers are the most skilful drivers in the world. They have to cope with unknown surfaces and they drive at such incredible speeds."

Brundle: 'As good as Jim Clark'

Martin Brundle got down to some serious training for next weekend's Network Q RAC Rally at Silverstone on Monday and his tutor, Roger Clark, reckoned the Formula 1 ace was potentially as good as the legendary Jim Clark.

'I did this same job with both Graham Hill and Jim Clark when they tried to do the RAC Rally many years ago,' said the man who last won the event 20 years ago this year. 'They were both very good drivers but they tackled the learning curve differently. Jimmy was a natural and got the right gear every time. It took him no more than 10 minutes to be as quick as me. Martin isn't far behind that, if indeed he's behind at all,' enthused Clark.

Brundle began the session being too erratic for Clark's liking but he soon got him driving more tidily and in a style that gives him a chance of finishing the event.

Brundle admitted that he was getting plenty of help from the rally stars. 'I learned a lot from my session with Colin McRae a few months ago and my good friend Juha Kankkunen has offered to help. Carlos Sainz has also said I can ring him at any time as of course he knows the Escort Cosworth very well. There's a lot more rapport in rallying than in F1.'

In Spain last week McRae warned: 'Martin will have to concentrate in a style that will get him to the finish. If he does that then he'll be going quite quickly when he reaches Wales. If not he won't get that far! I'll be quite happy to give him another lesson if he wants.'

Brundle's main fear is going off on the opening stage, Kershope...

Martin Brundle puts one of Mike Little's Escorts through its paces at Silverstone on Monday, with 1970s rally legend Roger Clark on hand to give advice on how to win, or finish, the RAC Rally

Reproduced with the kind permission of Autosport

Regional Press

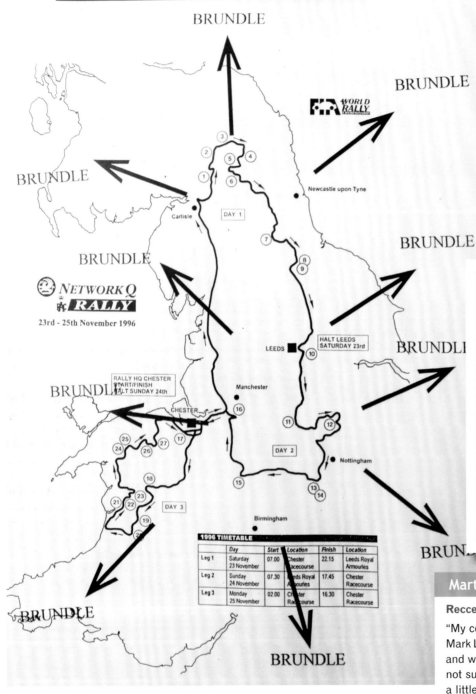

BRUNDLE

BRUNDLE

BRUNDLE

BRUNDLE

BRUNDLE

BRUNDLE

BRUNDLE

BRUNDLE

BRUNDLE

BRUNDLE

BRUNDLE

NETWORK Q RALLY

23rd - 25th November 1996

Newcastle upon Tyne

Carlisle   DAY 1

LEEDS   HALT LEEDS SATURDAY 23rd

Manchester

RALLY HQ CHESTER
START/FINISH
HALT SUNDAY 24th

CHESTER

DAY 2   Nottingham

Birmingham

DAY 3

1996 TIMETABLE

	Day	Start	Location	Finish	Location
Leg 1	Saturday 23 November	07.00	Chester Racecourse	22.15	Leeds Royal Armouries
Leg 2	Sunday 24 November	07.30	Leeds Royal Armouries	17.45	Chester Racecourse
Leg 3	Monday 25 November	02.00	Chester Racecourse	16.30	Chester Racecourse

"A great way to see the countryside, if only you had time to look. This press release seems to suggest I was everywhere."

Martin Brundle

The Mysteries Of Pace Notes

"We'd done about 400 metres on the recce and Roger said to me, 'And?' I said, 'And what?' 'Well, what do you want me to write?' And I said, 'What do you mean, what do you want me to write?' So, I stopped the car. He said, 'Well, you have to tell me the note. I write it down and then read it back to you.' I didn't even know how to make a note. So there I am, going to do one of the hardest rallies in the world and I didn't even know what to do. I thought the co-driver made the notes, and told me what was coming up. That's laughable when I think back, but it's a true story! Learning to describe a forest road in a way that means something to you when you're going along it at 100 mph is hard. Then you realise that you might recce at night and do it in the day, or vice versa. Or recce in the snow and do it without snow and it is nearly impossible. For example, in daylight you might call an 800 metre long stretch a flat out straight with no big crests or anything. Then on that same straight at night, your headlights pick out the little dips and peaks and troughs in the road, and it looks like several 200 metre stretches, Then, you can't remember how far you've gone, but you know there's a hairpin left at the end of it. Talking later on to Juha Kankkunen, Didier Auriol and Carlos Sainz, for them it just painted a picture in their minds. And, of course, they'd get to know some stages as well as I would know Silverstone."

"It's a long day in the seat when rallying with little time for sleep or to reflect." (Sutton Motorsport Images)

Martin Brundle

Recce, Recce

"My co-driver was Roger Freeman, who very sadly got killed with Mark Lovell. I will never forget, we went to make the first pace notes and we started the recce in a car which I actually crashed. You're not supposed to go above 30 mph but I had to try out the course a little bit. I hit a sheet of ice and crashed. So, we had to borrow a car off Gwyndaf Evans's Ford garage forecourt on the absolute undertaking with his sales manager that we did not carry on with the recce. And of course we did. So I had to do the honourable thing and buy the car."

Nigel Roebuck

Ambassadors In Waiting

"What we [the press] always said was that the great tragedy was that Mansell had the Williams years and neither Derek [Warwick] nor Martin did. Either one of them, had they been in that car and winning races like he was... What a wonderful thing that would have been for British sport to have a driver up there of that type and character, winning, winning, winning – it would have been a wonderful thing."

"Had done some local stage rallies in Norfolk but this was a whole new challenge."

Louise Goodman

Breaking The News

"Martin always says that I was the one who informed him that he was no longer going to be a Formula 1 driver. Eddie, being Eddie, had still not quite got around to telling Martin that he wasn't going to be driving for Jordan the following season. He never likes to be the bearer of bad tidings. I knew that we were about to announce the two drivers for 2007 and Martin still hadn't had the call to officially tell him that. So I just thought it was polite really to inform him that a press release announcing our drivers was about to go out."

Martin Brundle

Slide Role

"So it snowed like crazy, we went off and got towed back on by Louise Aitken-Walker. It was just pure lack of experience that I went off. I then managed the next day to slide off on a sheet of ice and into a culvert – car on its side. Turbo caught fire, Roger's popped a rib out, he's uncomfortable and I've got to climb on top of him to get out of this Escort that's on fire!"

Brundle to tackle RAC

"Then it snowed and I was completely out of my depth." (Sutton Motorsport Images)

Martin Brundle

Out Of Work

"I was at the Racing Car Show and Louise Goodman was our media girl at Jordan and Lou said to me, 'How long are you going to be here?' I thought I was driving the Jordan again in '97, though there was a lot of talk that I was going to TV which annoyed me because some people had stopped talking to me about going racing. Lou was grimacing a bit and she said, 'When are you leaving?' I said, 'I don't know, about 5 o'clock. Why, do you need me to do something?' She said, 'No, er, no, Eddie wants to announce Ralf Schumacher and Giancarlo Fisichella as his drivers.' So that's how I found out I wasn't a Grand Prix driver any more."

David Croft

Character Building

"I don't know of anyone who has had such bad luck with the teams that he was joining. Benetton were on the up but sadly Schumacher was calling all the shots. Could have joined Williams but Damon Hill got the drive. And Hill went on to become a World Champion. And you only have to look at what he did in sports cars to know that in terms of F1 there is more to Martin than the guy who flew through the air with the greatest of ease in Melbourne. And you look at the scars now from his driving career – that crash in practice at Dallas – the year Tyrrell got booted out and therefore that crash never happened despite the fact he still suffers from it now. And to do Le Mans in 2012, finish 15th, after getting fit once again and going through the pain barrier once again, it shows what he's got about him."

RALLYING ■ Norfolk ace crashes out

Brundle's brave bid goes up in flames

Martin Brundle's dream of completing the Network Q RAC Rally went up in flames yesterday when his car crashed and caught fire, after careering off the road into an icy ditch.

The Formula One star had endured a traumatic first competitive rally after crashing into a gully on the opening day which left him well down the classifications.

He had battled his way up to 73rd position after the second leg, but was forced to retire after the smash on yesterday's section in the forests of mid-Wales.

Brundle and co-driver Roger Freeman escaped uninjured from the burning Ford Escort Cosworth.

A Ford spokesman said: "The car hit something hard and stopped within inches, turning on its side.

"The turbo was still running and flames started coming from the engine, prompting Martin and Roger to clamber out of the car as quickly as possible."

The spokesman added that Freeman had suffered "a few bumps and bruises" from the impact, but that neither of the pair would require hospital treatment.

Brundle said: "We were running beautifully through the stage and had not had a single moment of trouble. We were catching the car in front when we arrived at a left-hand corner which was cautioned in our notes.

"It was a bit deceptive because there were two roads coming together and in the middle of the two there was a dyke.

"At the end of the dyke was a vertical face and we hit it doing about 50mph. It was a pretty serious stop.

"We got out of the car pretty quickly when it caught fire and the poor Escort is now looking very sad. It was my first time in the Welsh forest at speed and I was enjoying it. I feel very disappointed that it all came to grief when it all seemed under control.

"I probably made the classic rallying mistake of losing concentration while behind another rally car."

However, Brundle said the prangs had not put him off rallying.

"There's so much to learn because of the hugely variable nature of the surfaces.

"I have certainly learned rallying the hard way, but would love to come back and do it again."

A faulty fuse blew David Mann's chances of an RAC rally finish – after he had survived two days of driving on snow and sheet ice.

Mann's challenge ground to a halt just two miles from a service area, which could have fixed an electrical problem which left him with failing lights, wipers and eventually engine.

The Bungay mushroom farmer, who started 44th, was lying 18th overall and fifth in his group when his Proton car broke down.

German Armin Schwarz won the rally after leading from the first stage in his Toyota Celica.

At the finish, Schwarz was seven minutes 52 seconds ahead of Subaru Impreza driver Masao Kamioka with Sweden's Stig Blomqvist third and Mark Higgins, the leading Briton, in fourth place.

Eastern Daily Press

"I struggled to get my head round the fact that spectators were effectively the barriers in places, and having someone else in the car I was responsible for." (Sutton Motorsport Images)

Liz Brundle

Unfinished Business

"I think it was unfortunate that he finished racing when he did. He wanted to carry on for another couple of years. Unfortunately, the decision was left quite late so by the time he knew that he wasn't going to be driving with Jordan, there weren't other opportunities available. And that was it for Formula 1."

"Despite the dramas, I loved doing the rally." (Sutton Motorsport Images)

Brundle gets grip of life on skids

Nigel Roebuck

No Justice

"The great Chris Amon never won a Grand Prix. Anything can happen. There were definitely races that Martin should have won and deserved to win. His team mates included Schumacher and Hakkinen. There were days that in equal cars he beat them - he was quicker. Somehow the cards never really fell: he didn't spend the majority of his F1 career in ultra-competitive cars."

Rubens Barrichello

Politics, Again

"We had a good relationship, for at least two-thirds of the Championship. After that Eddie Jordan became a bit political on his choice of drivers for the following year and that put us apart a little. In the end, EJ chose two different drivers... Hee hee hee! And so we were friends again."

Adrian Newey

No Wins

"That is the nature of F1. It is all 'ifs' and 'buts'. There are drivers who are probably less deserving that have won races but that's the way it fell for him."

"That's quite a rear wing set-up I am dragging through the air. Despite that, I managed to spin off and rip the suspension apart in the gravel. It was a poor error on my part." (Sutton Motorsport Images)

For 1997

"Martin was quite keen to join Stewart Grand Prix right at the very beginning when we were choosing the original drivers and he certainly was very much in the loop but, in the end, we chose Rubens because we thought he had more potential as Martin was coming toward the end of his F1 career. However, he would have been very good. But to get our sponsors together and to see the potential, Rubens, at that time, was seen to be a rising star."

"I had a fantastic race at Monza with my team mate Rubens which I won and came home fourth." (Sutton Motorsport Images)

Eddie Jordan

Money Talks

"I took Fisichella and Ralf Schumacher for 1997 because they both had sponsorship from Deutsche Bank and DHL, and Michael was paying for Ralf. So, two young chargers with sponsor money was more appealing, and the reason I dropped Martin and Rubens. It was financially driven."

"In the pit stops, Rubens got ahead of me but he mistakenly switched off the ignition just as I was repassing him." (Sutton Motorsport Images)

Derek Warwick

Deserved Better

"He very much comes from the same background as me. I started on the ovals with F2 Superstox; he started on the ovals with Hot Rods. So we both come from a fairly aggressive, harsh background and a good family background, but different from these drivers coming through today. I think that because we were good businessmen, because we understood how it all worked, one thing Martin didn't do is have somebody that managed him and was able to put him in the right car at the right time. He had the right cars when he was at Benetton but people don't understand the politics that went around that time. When you have people like Briatore running the team and you're not the favourite driver, and I don't think that Martin was ever the favourite driver, it's really difficult to keep your morale up, race after race. For sure, in the right car, say a Williams like Nigel Mansell or Damon Hill, he would have been a multiple GP winner, without any shadow of a doubt. I would put him up there amongst the great British drivers, even though he didn't win a Grand Prix."

"Racing drivers are regular people who happen to be very good at driving fast, and are prepared to accept the risks. Otherwise, like everyone else, family and friends are extremely important. We've tried hard to give Charlie and Alex a balanced and family environment." (Sutton Motorsport Images)

"After my fourth at Monza, it was a bit of letdown to only finish ninth at Estoril in the Portuguese Grand Prix." (Sutton Motorsport Images)

Martin Brundle

Reflecting

"First of all, I didn't create the right chances. Secondly, I didn't make the best of the chances I had. Now I look back I don't think I was focused enough on some things in F1. F1's hard, F1's harder than everything else by some margin, I would say. I think I also had a confidence in - particularly around Tom - in a sports car. I had a belief... I felt invincible in a sports car, and I usually was. I never felt that invincibility in a single-seater. Maybe because the competition was tougher."

Murray Walker

Beating The Best

"As a racing driver in Formula 1, Martin drove for eight teams and he was on the second and third steps of the podium. He never actually won a Grand Prix, but he came mighty close to it. By virtue of finishing second, as he did, it means he beat people like Senna and Schumacher."

"I would finish fifth in my final Grand Prix just as I did in my first race. Unfortunately, I had no idea it was my last Grand Prix." (Sutton Motorsport Images)

Sir Jackie Stewart

Luck?

"You make your own luck. It's a question of making the right decisions to be in the right place at the right time. It's the same in business. And to achieve that, you usually require experience. Natural ability is given to you by God, if you like, whether you're an athlete or a business person or in any sphere of life. And then from that experience, you gain knowledge. And after a while, you sometimes get wisdom. But you've got to go through a series of experiences to get to where you really want to be. I think Martin, right now, must feel that he is in a place that he would have wanted to be.

"He probably wouldn't have made those early choices had he had other experience. I think all of these things come as part of the jigsaw puzzle that makes you the person you are and I think Martin has matured really well and he runs his life well. All of that has come together in connection with his motor racing experience and knowledge as a driver. He was a Le Mans winner and he won the Sportscar World Championship. These were, if you like, the rewards to set against some of the disappointments that he had within F1. Sometimes there is an element of luck – when Ayrton Senna happened to be in F1 at the same time as Martin Brundle."

Sir Stirling Moss

The Greatest Sums Up

"He was better than his results."

The ITV Years
1997-2008

Reluctant to retire from F1, Martin looked around for another drive. There were none available, even for a man of his experience and ability. The cards had just not fallen well for him in F1. Supreme in sports cars, he had built a team around him with all the advantages that brings. He had never been in a position to do that in F1. He had beaten Senna, he had outshone Schumacher on occasions and, on the rare occasions they both finished, he had beaten Hakkinen at McLaren. Also, he had proved he was unusually versatile, being seriously quick in touring cars, F1 and his beloved sportscars. However, it was time to move on.

There had been rumours circulating for some months that Martin would take up commentating. To his considerable annoyance, initially, these prophesies became self-fulfilling when he accepted ITV's invitation to join the great Murray Walker in the commentary box as the resident expert.

Traditionally, F1 racing had been on BBC television but, to everyone's surprise, Mr. Ecclestone, the F1 ringmaster, decided to take the coverage from the complacent BBC and offer it to their great rivals at ITV from 1997. The decision certainly set the cat amongst the pigeons at the time and many enthusiasts were appalled by the idea of adverts punctuating the drama of a Grand Prix and the concentration required to seriously follow a race.

This annoying trait was more than made up for by the winning team of Murray and Martin. Hitting it off immediately, they became an immensely popular duo. Murray was an institution; Martin was a natural. Combined with the innovations of the dynamic new production team, ITV set new standards.

When, in 2001, Murray decided to retire, James Allen was promoted from covering the pits to the role of main commentator. James, who had the unenviable task of following Murray, did a fine job. Meanwhile, Martin had become famous for his grid walks, his quick wit and his ability to explain complex subjects in an easily-understandable way. The team, and Martin individually, were showered with Royal Television Society awards and BAFTAs.

Martin Brundle

Bereft

"I was lost personally at the time. I wasn't clear about my next step and so I tried a number of things. Also, being so busy was a way to smother the pain of losing my F1 seat."

TEAM: Martin Brundle, Louise Goodman and Murray Walker at the launch of ITV Sport's coverage of the 1997 Formula One season.

Brundle signs up for TV race job

Eastern Daily Press

The TV Decision

"In that January/February, when he realised he didn't have a Formula 1 drive, I remember we had some long discussions because he was offered a number of opportunities. One was to be an F1 tester, another was to be involved with the management of an F1 team, yet another was to go on TV, and a final one was to drive at Le Mans again. And everyone said, 'You should go on television; do the TV job.' But he did all four. It must have been quite tough for him to handle so many things. This is where he's very bright actually - he's a very clever person and he reckons that he can do anything. He's got a confidence, and I'm always thinking, 'Right, I'll think of you something you can't do!' And I can never really think of anything because he'll have a go at everything!"

❝ Hug the inside of the first corner like it's your favourite granny. ❞

"Early days in the commentary box with the maestro. Note my left hand on his shoulder." (Sutton Motorsport Images)

Martin Brundle

Foundations

"Through the second half of '96 there'd already been a lot of speculation that I was going to ITVF1. I think it suited one or two people to sow those seeds and also to give it credence. One of the groups bidding for the ITV contract was Meridian, Anglia and Chrysalis - MACH 1 they called it. Anglia TV was based in Norwich. Several friends there had looked after me over the years and given me coverage through my career. It was simply 'Right, we're going to put a bid in for the F1 contract. Will you give us some advice? Give us a bit of knowledge.' 'Yeah, sure.' So I met them in a pub in Norwich and I just downloaded what I thought they could do and where I thought they could improve the coverage of F1 from a driver's perspective. Anyway, they were a smart bunch and they won the thing. And still I had no idea that I was going to be involved – and no intentions whatsoever of doing so."

"Murray and I had a friendly relationship which stretched back to the F3 days but we really got to know each other well at ITV." (Sutton Motorsport Images)

"A rare shot of Murray Walker sitting down in the commentary box. He loved to wallpaper the place with information."

Louise Goodman

Career Placement

"I think Eddie [Jordan] was very keen on promoting Martin to the guys at ITV and saying that he'd make a brilliant commentator for them and he was dead right in all of that but, being EJ, I think part of it was that he didn't believe he was going to re-sign Martin the following year, so it would make his life easier. He could then turn round to Martin and say [Irish accent], 'I got you the fookin' job with ITV,' rather than saying, 'I fookin' fired you.' Typical EJ stuff!

"That's not to say that Eddie didn't think he'd do a good job because I think we all thought he would. From our experience of how he worked with sponsors – he could explain things to guests in the garage in an interesting, entertaining and informative way, which was something I could never get the other drivers to do. I always thought it was the used-car salesman in him – the fact that he was a motor-trader. Not so much gift-of-the-gab, because he's not a person who gabs a lot, but he's a good salesman, whether that be selling cars or selling himself as the professional Formula 1 driver to the sponsors."

" The drivers know this circuit like the backs of their hands, and that's with their gloves on. "

Martin Brundle

Wrong Job

"So I went kicking and screaming into the commentary box. Didn't really want to do it if truth be known. And when the race started on the Sunday in Melbourne, just a year after I'd had my somersault, I felt empty and destroyed. I was in the wrong place. I wanted to be on the grid. I didn't want to be in the commentary box."

" Those mirrors are about as useful as a chocolate fireguard. "

Martin Brundle

Working With The Master

"Then, after Melbourne '97, I read all these very nice reports about my job in the commentary box. And I'd made a couple of smart moves. I'd decided that if Murray stood up to commentate, I'd stand up, because I felt I needed to communicate with him. Also, that he was the master and I was the boy, although we had a microphone each, and it just gelled from day one. How lucky was I to be able to be able to learn from the greatest TV sports commentator of all time?"

Executive Producer

"I first met Martin in '96 when Bernie had sold the F1 rights to ITV and we'd been selected as the production company. So from that summer, we were actively putting the team together on and off screen. It had become reasonably well-known to me, although Martin was in complete denial about it, that Eddie Jordan wasn't going to renew his contract and I think Martin was getting a bit tetchy with everybody who kept saying, 'Oh, you should go into TV,' because he figured he would still carry on driving.

"He was always the guy we were very keen on because he is such a smart bloke and we figured that he would be a really good co-com for Murray and we wanted to use him to do other things as well. But in all fairness, I don't think any of us could have foreseen just how good he would turn out to be. In all the years I've been in the business - about 30 years - I haven't come across many people who are a complete natural in this world, who have come from a different world, mostly sport - we worked on a lot of different sports - and who have made the jump into TV and who have done it with consummate ease, which he did. And he just got better and better and better. From day one in the commentary box with Murray, it just worked like clockwork and then we got him doing other things and doing features."

"Working once again with Roger Silman and the TWR team at Le Mans in '97."

"The Nissan looked great but the programme was compromised." (Sutton Motorsport Images)

My Successor

"Our careers have mirrored in many ways, latterly with Martin taking over my TV commentary role when F1 moved from BBC to ITV in 1997, something he is better at than I was, to be honest."

❝ They're so brave, the mechanics: they just form a human garage and wait for this boiling hot missile to come at them. ❞

"The traditional photographs at Le Mans while signing on downtown, with Jorg Muller." (Sutton Motorsport Images)

Murray Walker

Standing Together

"I always stood because I got very excited and I just felt more relaxed standing up – I could see out of the window better and move about the box if I had to. James always sat beside me. Now Martin thought, 'If old Murray could stand up for the whole race, then I could stand up for the whole race.' And I was notorious, I'm afraid, for getting so involved with what I was talking about that I wasn't too anxious that anybody else should talk about it, especially if it was James Hunt or Martin Brundle! It was very difficult to get the microphone away from me. And Martin used to stand beside me with his hand on my shoulder and if he had something urgent he wanted to say, he would shake my shoulder and if he had something really urgent to say, he would really, really shake my shoulder. I didn't realise it, but I apparently swayed from side to side and Martin said, 'In order to avoid bumping into him all the time, I had to sway with him and we must have looked like a couple of windscreen wipers!'"

❝ Sometimes F1 drivers look absolutely awesome and sometimes they look like they couldn't drive sheep. And today is a sheep day. ❞

Louise Goodman

With Respect

"I think the rapport that he and Murray built up was great. There were times when Murray would 'get things wrong' through his excitement and his passion. And whereas James Hunt would kind of belittle him, Martin would correct Murray, as and when required, but in a very gentle fashion. I think there was already a lot of respect between the two of them, so that showed through straight away. I think they made a great partnership straight away."

"A much bigger budget went into the Toyota programme to create this sensational car." (Toyota)

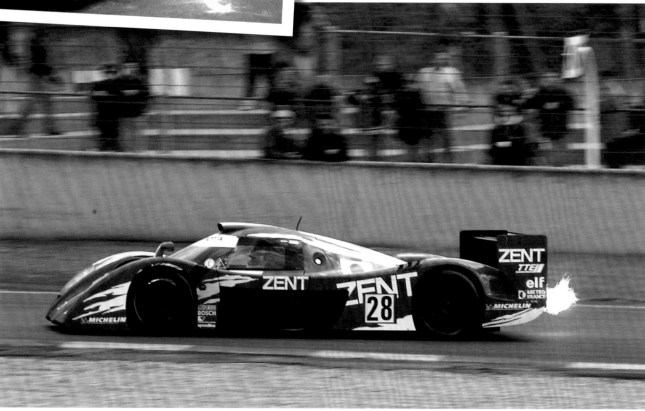

Win Percy

1998 Goodwood Revival

"I remember the first Goodwood. Martin was driving John Coombs's Ecurie Belge D-type, Stirling was in an Aston and they were going through the first corner and Stirling went through on the inside of Martin and did his usual polite putting his hand up. And I was just behind with Valentine Lindsay's 'D', struggling to drift it, and Stirling's politely putting his hand up! I thought, 'Blimey, this guy doesn't change at all!' It was just amazing and Martin respected that."

"At the same time my relationship with the Goodwood Revival began. This is John Coombs' D-type." (Philip Porter)

John Coombs

Culture Shock

"When he came in, after doing two or three laps in qualifying, he said, 'It's go no adhesion.' So, I just opened the bonnet and pointed at a tyre. 'Oh, I see what you mean.' Rather narrower than he was used to. He went very quickly and was very good. If you watch him on a video, it's quite frightening: he really had a big go. Another time, he was in my Lotus 15 which he drove equally well."

Murray Walker

Martin

"I really got to know Martin, working together all the time at all the Grands Prix. It's a very stressful situation in the commentary box. I won't say that James and I didn't get on, but there was a lot of friction, and I thought that James was lazy and James thought that I talked too much, so there was often a difficult atmosphere in the commentary box. It was never like that with Martin. I found Martin to be, first of all, an absolutely super bloke - a human being with a good sense of humour, a really, really hard worker, straight, honest, decent."

Martin Brundle

Murray

"He's a lovely man. And genuine. And he was very generous to me as well. I think with James and with Jonathan, he'd had a more competitive relationship. James was upset that he didn't get the microphone from him from all the stuff I've read. Obviously they were a great combination and they motivated me big time when I was a kid. Now suddenly, Murray realised he didn't have a competitor in the commentary box, he had somebody who wanted to work as one with him. And he opened up and he became more generous I think, with the microphone, and in other ways. And then I found this way of gently correcting him that I think the audience came along with me on. It was respectful. And occasionally I'd come up with a one-liner which became my speciality."

Martin Brundle

Jaguar D-type

"I scared myself in a D-type, in John Coombs's D-type. Phew – what a difficult car they are to drive. Little tiny brake pedal. Just felt like it was going to crash everywhere. Frightened the life out of me."

"The great thing about TV is that you get to interview motor racing royalty, such as Luca di Montezemolo." (Sutton Motorsport Images)

Adrian Newey

F1 Chauffeur

"After he retired, he drove the McLaren two-seater for celebrity-type demo runs at the Grands Prix. Certainly, watching him then, he seemed to get that two-seater into all sorts of fairly alarming looking angles though I don't think he ever spun it. I remember thinking, 'I hope he doesn't crash it,' because I am not sure it would have stood up particularly well. Structurally, it never looked to me a particularly nicely put together piece of kit!"

"It gave me immense pleasure to take Murray Walker round Silverstone in the two-seater McLaren. He's braver than me - I wouldn't have got in the back of it."

❝ The track gets more and more like a building site every lap. ❞

Martin Brundle

Racing After F1

"I was completely lost in '97, so I did everything, basically. I became a Director at Arrows and a test driver. I drove for Tom – always returning to Tom - in the Nissan. It was the last time I drove for Tom actually - 1997, at Le Mans. It was a bit of a mish-mash of a car from former TWR Le Mans cars, and it was to the new GT regulations. Always doomed to break down, I'm afraid."

"Testing the Toyota at Spa, which would eventually be snowed off and abandoned." (Toyota)

Roger Silman

Nissan

"My next brush with Martin was when he came to drive the TWR Nissan at Le Mans - a disastrous programme. An absolute nonsense from beginning to end. When we went to the test day, Martin was fastest, and then for the race itself he qualified fourth and we were right off the pace. It was only after the event that Tony Southgate could establish that we had nothing like the horse-power available during the race compared to the test day. They never told us. I wasn't a party to this but I think Martin was extremely annoyed. And I think that was the end – Martin went off to Toyota following that."

❝ **Raikkonen's down here somewhere – let's see if we can get two or maybe even three words plus VAT out of him today.** ❞

"I started on pole in '99 and led the race easily but a puncture would ruin our chances." (Toyota)

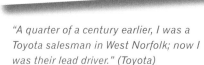

"A quarter of a century earlier, I was a Toyota salesman in West Norfolk; now I was their lead driver." (Toyota)

❝ **Ambition gets well ahead of adhesion in this weather.** ❞

Martin Brundle

Not Me

"The grid walk wasn't my idea. I'm not a creative person. I'm all about content and delivery."

Alex Brundle

Father's Time

"Le Mans was the first time I really understood my father's job. He put the Toyota on pole and I remember the build-up and the excitement. It was a really key moment for me in terms of understanding what motorsport was all about."

Murray Walker

Father Of The Grid Walk

"I've always been very slightly miffed, in the nicest possible way, about the way that Martin has got this great reputation for doing the grid walk. I actually started the grid walk! Not with the BBC, but with Australian television. Australia were looking for something different to do and I said, 'Now look, if you give me a cameraman with a Steadicam, somebody who can walk backwards, I will walk through the grid, totally unprompted and with nothing planned, and I will just talk to whoever I see.' And I did that in the knowledge that I knew an enormous number of people on the grid, and there was bound to be someone I knew and could talk to, no matter where I was. And it was enormously successful and I like to think that that was what started the grid walk.

"But fair do's, Martin is the chap who perfected it. Any of the others I've seen who've tried to do it are not a patch on him. Because Martin's got the personality to do it, he's got the experience, he's got the knowledge, and everybody likes him and enjoys talking to him - and he has a quick wit."

"Feeling pretty pleased about the perfect lap of Le Mans for pole." (Toyota)

"The eyes have it. The intensity of Le Mans is all too clear." (Toyota)

Neil Duncanson

Grid Walk Is Born

"We didn't start doing the grid walk until the Silverstone of the first year. We had Louise Goodman and James Allen doing interviews on the grid and I'd said to Martin, 'What I think we're missing is a real understanding of what's going through the minds of the drivers, the pit crews and everybody that's on the grid. Who are all these people and what are they doing?' And what I wanted him to do was to stand at the front of the grid, introduce himself and the British GP from that angle and then to walk back down the grid, talking to people as he went, ideally as many drivers as he could get to do it, and finish up at the back.

"He looked at me askance – he wasn't entirely sure what I was on about. He umm'd and ahh'd. Then he said, 'Well, it's all at the wrong angle. I'm always sitting in the car...' So, the first grid walk we did, he sits on the ground, and starts with, 'This is my normal view at a British Grand Prix,' then he gets up and starts walking from the back to the front. That easily became the most popular part of the races and our F1 coverage. Not only did he not know what was going to happen next, but neither did we!"

"The pole position trophy - the heaviest one I have - you wouldn't want to drop it on your foot."
(Abigail Humphries)

Toyota At Le Mans

"In '98 I drove for Toyota, which was great. They had a beautiful car and it basically was a wide single-seater with bodywork. It was just a stunning car but the first day I tested it I broke a vertebra in my back. I hit a wall at Paul Ricard with the throttle sticking, and I went off in a corner where Villeneuve had gone off in the Williams the week before, and they hadn't put the tyres back. Our car hadn't been through its crash-testing yet. Actually, the front of the car was too strong. So it didn't give. So my back gave. I remember getting out of the car and squealing my head off, I was in such pain. That set me back a while. And it still hurts to this day. As a driver, your back and your ears get routinely knocked about."

 That didn't work... You hit the wrong part of him, my friend. 🙙

"I met some fascinating people driving the McLaren two-seater, not least the King of Spain."

Liz Brundle

Grid Walks Out Of Character

"He's not at all like that in real life. And it's so unlike him to push himself forward and barge people out of the way and I know he hates doing it. It's just not him, but he has to do it. Because he's live on television; he can't stand there for five minutes. His time's gone! I think he was a bit cheeky, from what I hear from the family, when he was little. I love the grid walks."

🙙 **It's a badge of honour: if you don't come in from this track having wiped some of the paint off the side of your tyres, you're not trying hard enough.** 🙙

Martin Brundle

Royal Patronage

"I took out some awesome guests in the two-seater, not least the King of Spain who would come to support me later in the Bentley at Le Mans in 2001."

To Martin Brundle with my thanks for a wonderful drive on the two-seater F.1. with my Hector.
30.V.99/

Martin Brundle

Grid Walk – It's Not Me, Honest

"My alter ego is on the grid. I've never ever watched one in full. People seem to like them but I cannot bear the thought of watching myself on TV. I've seen bits and pieces on YouTube and I absolutely don't recognise the person that charges round the grid being rude, butting in, but there's no other way. All the other media just simply stand and wait for an interview and throw to the studio, whereas I'm on the hoof for 10 minutes. It's car-crash television!"

❝ You need to be one of the Daleks to understand what he said on the radio. ❞

Martin Brundle

Rallying With Toyota

"In '98/99 I was a works Toyota driver for the Le Mans effort, which was rewarding if ultimately frustrating. And I said to Ove Anderson, I'd love to do the Rally of Great Britain again in a Toyota. So we went testing, and I got really close – in testing – to Sainz and Auriol and everyone was like, 'Wow, this is impressive.' But of course it was literally going over the same special stage again and again, which was my kind of driving – finding time by relentlessly going over something and I got within half a second per mile of them."

"I'm a glutton for punishment - I tried Rally GB again in 1999." (LAT)

❝ He's covered himself with more gravel than glory this year. ❞

"This time it was in the works-prepared Toyota so everything was guaranteed to be fine..." (Toyota)

Martin Brundle

1999 Rally Of Great Britain

"Got to the rally itself in the Welsh valleys and it had been raining so it was saturated on the forest stage, and it was foggy. And they had been logging since we'd recce'd: they'd taken some logs away and it was all muddy around that area. I was 15 seconds-a-mile slower than the works boys. I had a couple of near misses and my co-driver Arne Hertz had already saved me from a couple of offs, where he'd remembered other people had crashed. He'd go, 'Slow down, caution, slow down, I remember this!' And we'd slow right down, and sure enough there'd be something over the edge, upside down or in a tree or something.

"Then I decided I was faster than I was going; I wasn't pushing hard enough. I'd got a bit of confidence and, inevitably, I stopped listening to my co-driver. The hardest thing I found to do was listen to a co-driver. It's not what you do. Sure, when I'm flying or when I'm in a racing car, I can work a machine and listen at the same time, but that's generic information. It's not the same as having specific information coming two or three corners in advance, so you can set the car up. I found that alien. Inevitably I hit a tree. It was really a shame because it did very little damage to the car, I'd managed to slow it right down mostly before we connected with this little tree, but the oil cooler was broken. So my rallying career came to an abrupt halt twice. And I wasn't as good as I thought I was. And I already respected the rally drivers a lot before I dipped in! I honestly think they are, overall, the most skilled drivers in the world. It never surprises me when Loeb wins the Race of Champions, or the rally drivers are very strong in other competitions."

The Art Of The Grid Walk

"We were in a pre-production meeting at Silverstone and we said to Martin, 'You should come down on the grid and just do something.' And he's like, 'Yeah, I might do that.' Because it was really easy to get from the grid because there was a back gate up to the comm. box. In some places it's quite a long way, but there it was really close. So I said to him, 'You should do that.' And of course he did but, being him, he didn't just come down and bosh about for a couple of minutes. He thought about it, planned it. And you just thought, 'Oh, wow! This is telly gold! This is brilliant what he's doing here.' He then went on to make that an art form."

"Waiting around for camera crew and sound crew can take forever but it is usually worth it."
(Andrew Parr)

"Keith Wilson, to my right, was our first ever grid walk cameraman. I have no idea why we are doing a jigsaw puzzle."
(Andrew Parr)

Grid Walks – A Victim Speaks

"I think it is a good feature for television. It can be slightly annoying when you get a microphone thrust in your face, as a generality, but having said that I think Martin's very good in that respect. He won't thrust a microphone if he senses you don't want to talk or will respect it if you say, 'I am busy at the moment.' Having been a driver, and having been under pressure, and knowing there's a focus prior to the race, he understands and is discreet which is, unfortunately, more than can be said for some of his journalistic colleagues."

❝ Before I got a serious job in TV, I used to drive these racing cars a bit. ❞

Grid Walks – Another Victim

"All of us actually recognise what a great element of presenting Formula 1 to the public that is. You do get occasions when Martin will jump in and you're in the middle of something and you just can't deal with it, but he understands. Martin's the first one to take a step back and say, 'Actually no, we're not going to go there at the moment,' and I think because we know that – if you give him the look, or just give him a, 'Not now, Martin,' then he understands and he's happy to step back and leave you alone. And I think, with that caveat that we all have with Martin, we're all very pleased to have someone promoting the sport in such a great way. And we want more of it."

Lynn News

Brundle in Bentley team for Le Mans

Murray Walker

Preparation Is The Secret

"When we became the pairing that did the job together, he was absolutely meticulous in preparation. I was well-known for marching in with reams of notes and sticking things all over the commentary box wall to remind me if I needed reminding. Martin had a big binder which Margaret, his secretary, I suspect, had assembled with his guidance, and referred to it frequently. But Martin had got things in his head, of course, that would never have entered mine, because of the experience that he had in his particular field, that I hadn't got, which is why, I like to think, we worked so well together."

❝ A face like a bulldog chewing a wasp. ❞

"I was very excited, and pleased, to have the chance to go back to Le Mans with Bentley."

"As I was becoming a Bentley Boy, I read up on their fascinating origins and history."

Bentley boy Brundle back at Le Mans

EXCLUSIVE BY BOB McKENZIE

MARTIN BRUNDLE is to lead Bentley's stylish return to Le Mans this year for his eighth drive in the 24 Hours Race. The ITV Formula One commentator and Express Sport columnist will drive one of the two EXP Speed figure eight cars, which Bentley has created especially for the legendary race.

"It is a wonderful opportunity to go back to a historic race with a legendary name like Bentley," said 41-year-old Brundle.

"I have not had a lot of time to myself until recently and had not given much thought to driving this year. When Bentley approached me it did not take much convincing to join their team.

"Bentley have not been to Le Mans for 71 years, but they had a hat-trick of wins before stopping. That's a great memory for a great

name but this is not a nostalgic return, it is a properly put together assault on the race.

"Winning in the first year after starting fairly late will be tough, especially with the Audis which won last year competing again. It is going to be fun trying."

Brundle will be joined in the three-man team by another Englishman, 26-year-old Guy Smith from Hull, and a former Le Mans winner, Stefan Ortelli.

The Bentley cars, powered by 3.6 litre twin turbo-charged V8 engines, will compete in the GTP class for fully enclosed prototypes and are being built not far from Brundle's home by Racing Technology Norfolk, with Richard Lloyd in charge of the two-car team.

Brundle will not be able to get behind the wheel until later in March because of Formula One races in Australia and Malaysia.

"It's going to be hectic because we have test programmes all over Europe to find differing circuits, but I am excited by the idea of racing again," said Brundle. "For the first time in 28 years I had no racing events in 2000

and, although I kept my hand in with some Formula One cars and the McLaren two-seater, I missed it very much. I may be seen as a commentator but I still feel like a racing driver.

"The car looks great and I love the heritage of the Bentley name. That was a big attraction about getting involved in a lot of work again."

Brundle, of course, is a Le Mans winner with Jaguar in 1990 and has also led challenges by Toyota and Nissan in recent years. His long Formula One career spanned 158 races, but last year he was fully occupied in Silverstone's business battles as the circuit tried to remain on the grand prix calendar.

That was successfully completed and he now finds himself the chairman of the British Racing Drivers Club, among whose founders was Doctor Dudley Benjafield of the famed Bentley Boys, a colourful group of drivers in the Twenties and early Thirties.

"They lived quite a life in those days by the sound of it," said Brundle. "But for me there is a lot of time ahead in the gym to be absolutely fit for what is a very tough race."

Neil Duncanson

Laid Back TV

"In many ways when he first started, he couldn't quite get his head round us telly blokes because he brought with him the discipline of a racing driver into our world. When I said that we would have a production meeting in the main truck at 11 o'clock, he would be there outside the main truck at one minute to, and couldn't understand why the rag, tag and bobtail mob would meander up and be there by 10 past. He used to get quite miffed about that but in the end, he got his head round it."

Bentley Boy

"Then I went to Bentley in 2001 and really enjoyed that. We very much had to play second fiddle to the Audi team at that point, as they did again in 2002, and then when Audi took a year out they won it in 2003. I was incredibly busy at the Silverstone and the BRDC at the time, being right in the middle of all the big deals. And there were a few things that frustrated me a little bit on the 2001 Bentley programme. There were some things I wanted to do for the following year, and they couldn't happen. But I very much regret now not sticking with that programme.

"When I got out of the Bentley, we were leading. We'd made some good tyre calls, and the car was good. It wouldn't have won but it was a beautiful car. One of the most beautiful racing cars I've ever driven. For me, the long-tailed Le Mans cars are the ultimate racing cars in terms of their beauty. And that was really it for a while; I didn't race professionally for a long time, apart from some fun at Goodwood."

“ Those horribly wide front wings are so ugly, I think they should put brown paper bags over them on the grid. ”

"What a sublime and beautiful racing car the Bentley was." (Sutton Motorsport Images)

Loquacious Wordsmith

"I'm not sure my vocabulary is very good. I sometimes slur my words which people don't often pick up on. It is because I had such a whack on the head, firstly in Monaco in '84 but mainly due to the one in Brazil in '94 where I got hit on the head by Verstappen's Benetton.

"I can write a mean 1000 word column pretty easily but I never perceive myself as a proper journalist. I wrote for the *Sunday Times* for many years and had many nice comments about that. I perceive myself to be a driver who's ended up broadcasting and doing a little bit of journalism. I can string some words together but I won't be using too many clever words. I believe I'm reasonably bright but I think my communication skills came from selling cars and being at the garages. I sold my first car when I was eight and you need to be able to read people, you need to be able to move along quickly and you need to be able to react to what they're saying and paint the picture. Frankly, until Ken Tyrrell stuck me in a Formula 1 car, my life, as far as I could tell, was going to be selling, and running Toyota dealerships in West Norfolk."

"It rained in the early stages and I was able to lead the race but later dramas would put us out of the event." (Sutton Motorsport Images)

Stepping Out

"Murray and I used to walk the tracks together. Tough old boy is Murray. With my dodgy ankle, I'd get about three-quarters of the way round a long circuit, limping, and have to call it a day, and he'd be striding on. He'd be well into his 70s by then. Constitution of an ox. It was just brilliant. He was very easy to work with. He was the leader. I often used to think that, if I walked out the back of the box when he was really going for it, he would never have noticed until after the race!"

"Although the factory team was driven and funded from Bentley HQ in Crewe, the race team was actually based in mid-Norfolk which was handy."

Herbie Blash

Personalities

"I think Martin sounded a little difficult with Bernie to start with but I think Martin is now full of admiration for Bernie and vice versa but it didn't start off very well. Martin obviously likes, as a commentator, not be controversial, but he likes to make a point. He went through a time when Schumacher wouldn't even speak to Martin so he found it fairly difficult in his early days although he was with Murray to start with which was brilliant for him and I'm sure he loved it so much. Now Martin, I would say, is the most respected commentator out there."

" It's a Coulthard in my commentary box! Did you miss the bus or something?"

" If you created a university study to, 'Design the worst possible pit-in and pit-out at a Formula 1 track,' I think this is what they would come up with."

"The Bentley hunkered down at high speed on the legendary Mulsanne Straight." (Sutton Motorsport Images)

Martin Brundle

Off-Track Action

"One *Sunday Times* column about the McLaren spy scandal $100m fine upset Max Mosley and, I suspect, Mr. Ecclestone too. So, Max sued me for libel in a French court, libel being a criminal offence in France. The papers were delivered to my house just before Christmas, 2007. Defending my position involved a great deal of work but, eventually, the case was dropped. It was really all about putting some manners on me and reminding me of the ground rules of F1. It was also a message to other journalists that, if they were prepared to sue *The Sunday Times* and Brundle, then watch out. It's all water under the bridge now."

"One very happy and smug looking Brundle." (Sutton Motorsport Images)

Neil Duncanson

Repartee

"He's very quick-witted, very sharp. My favourite line was from the grid at Monaco when Michael Douglas was banging on about his new movie and Martin was feigning vague interest in it, and Michael said that he was in this movie with Kiefer Sutherland and Eva Longoria and Martin looked at him and didn't understand who Eva Longoria was. Michael said to him, 'Oh, you must have Desperate Housewives in the UK' and Martin said, 'Yes, thousands of them.'"

"Trying to put the rain back into the sky under the famous Dunlup Bridge." (Sutton Motorsport Images)

If you pass go, collect a grid position.

"The moody phase towards dusk as the Bentley presses on." (Sutton Motorsport Images)

❝ **The valves have had a chat with the pistons.** ❞

Neil Duncanson

Explaining Stuff

"His insight into the sport, his way of delivering quite complex technical data in a way in which the ordinary people at home could understand, was quite breathtaking. At Spa, it was teeming down with rain and I went on to him on the talk-back, and I asked him to give us an idea of what it's like as a driver in this. I'm looking at the pictures and all I can see is a red light flashing on the back of the car. He then described how, in many races in the rain, all he could judge the corners on was the sound of the car in front of him because he couldn't see anything. Then he said, 'We've all driven on the motorway and we've gone past big juggernauts in the rain – imagine doing that without windscreen wipers at 200mph.' And the whole crew went, 'Ooohh'. He has quite a rare talent."

"A most famous and prestigious name on my overalls, and in 2013 I still fit them." (Abigail Humphries)

Martin Brundle on ...

Jacques Villeneuve

"Complicated. Fast. deserved his world championship. Get on much better with him now than I did. He didn't used to like me because he hated the media, and it amuses me now to see him being a TV pundit. He saw me as media; he didn't see me as an ex-driver. We were having dinner in Tokyo one night, and I went along with DC, and I could see Jacques's face, 'Oh no, he's brought the journo with him.' I was David Coulthard's manager at the time. So, we get talking over the starters and Jacques turns to me and said, 'So what's your best crash?' and I said, 'Right, so where shall we start?' So I went through my crashes, and we got on like a house on fire because, for Jacques, it's a point of honour to have had a massive accident. He did at Spa in the BAR. He was so determined to go flat through Eau Rouge, even if he crashed. He did crash, of course. Rolled the thing into a ball. Now, as an ex-racing driver, I like his honesty and his clarity of thought. I wish I could be as punchy as that. I can't, because I've got to see these people all day, every day and talk to them on the grid and all that. If I didn't have to deliver lots of other television, I'd like to be nearly as outspoken as Jacques!"

Mark Blundell

One Standard

"Martin likes to make sure that everyone around him is up to the levels that he operates at so he is quite influential in where he wants to be and who he has around him. He's a professional guy with high standards."

"With Murray Walker and James Allen, I believe I am just making a joke about the awards dinner food, to a great cheer, but not everybody was impressed." (James Allen)

"The Brundell Brothers working together again, this time on a track guide for ITV." (Andrew Parr)

" The times tumble like a fruit machine. "

" Back in those days he couldn't drive a nail into a piece of wood. "

Murray Walker

Perfect Pairing

"Martin was the best person I ever had in the commentary box with me, and I've had a lot of people: James Hunt, Graham Hill, Barry Sheene, all sorts of people. But Martin and I worked extremely well together because Martin let me get on with the commentary and did what he was supposed to do which was add to my commentary in terms of having been a racing driver and knowing what he was about. I was the enthusiast and he was the expert."

" This is a dangerous sport – it says so on the back of the tickets. "

Ross Brawn

One Repeatable Story

"I remember one occasion that I can repeat. We were travelling back from a race. I was in my Ferrari days, but I often used to travel back to the UK to grab a day or two after a race before I went back to Italy. We were travelling back and we all got bumped into First Class which was very nice, but which didn't delight the occupants of First Class who included Ron Dennis. Myself, Martin, Mark, Mario Illien and maybe one or two others, then had an all-night party in First Class and cleared them out of almost every form of alcohol they had on the plane! So it was a very entertaining evening. Great camaraderie – at least among the people who were drinking!"

"Preparing for the grid walk in Suzuka with Kevin Chapman. Back then, the cameraman had to be tethered to a transmitter." (Andrew Parr)

❝ Mark, anything you can tell us to make us look intelligent down the pub tonight or at work tomorrow morning?❞

Mark Blundell

Fools Out

"To be fair, 99% of the time, most people in the TV side of things would actually come through me to get to him, because they would sooner I asked him something than them having to ask. He's only a little guy in terms of stature but he has a big presence. Some people might have been a bit awestruck. Martin could be quite direct at times, he doesn't suffer fools. I come from the other side of the fence and I have no qualms about telling him where it's at. And vice versa. That's why we get on so well."

"It is always good to understand how you are being framed in the shot." (Andrew Parr)

Goodwood Ferrari 250 GTO

"Nick Mason's Ferrari 250 GT0: one of the most sublime things I've ever driven. I'll never forget leaving the assembly area to go out for my first ever drive in a 250 GT0, left-hand-drive. You go through that gearbox, that V12 sounds glorious, turn through Madgwick, and they were just finishing a fly-through with the Spitfires, so I've just gone through the first corner, with the revs up, clickety-clacking through the gearbox, and a World War II fighter plane flies through my field of vision as they finish that display. And I'm thinking, 'It will never get any better than that!' Your first ever corner in a 250 GT0 and there's a Spitfire flying through your windscreen! Fantastic!"

"A briefing with Steve Aldous, of F1 ITV, whilst partaking of McLaren hospitality." (Andrew Parr)

> ❝ He's on a three-stop strategy today. It's Heathrow, Dubai and Kuala Lumpur. ❞

"Trackside with Gerard Lane and Kevin Brown - that's where I learn most." (Andrew Parr)

James Allen

Surges

"If you look at the viewing figures after ITV took over, you could see that there would be a spike when people expected the grid walk to be on. Another spike would be at the start and then it might tail off a little bit, particularly during the years when Schumacher was winning everything - obviously people would go off and mow the lawn and then come back for lap 30 and see how it was going. Usually the peak audience was just before the end of the race."

"I hope I tucked my shirt in before interviewing Mr. Ecclestone." (Andrew Parr)

Mark Blundell

Quick Wit

"Humour, I would say, is his biggest asset. He is super quick, super sharp. And while there would be someone trying to think of something to deliver, he's got it out, delivered it and set the scene for the next wave."

Martin Brundle

One-Liners

"I use humour in my commentary as much as I reasonably can. I think humour is a great communication tool; people remember one-liners. Formula 1 is a very complicated sport and very fast moving of course and it helps if you can put it in a bite size, understandable, humorous form. I think humour is very valuable but it's very easy to go too far and just ridicule things, and you're not trying to do that. You're just trying to entertain and inform, as Murray would say."

"By the end of 2013, I had attended over 500 F1 races."

"British Grand Prix track guide with, believe it or not, Mark Blundell in the sidecar." (Andrew Parr)

"Doing a piece to camera with Mark Blundell - we never stop laughing."
(Andrew Parr)

❝ **He looked at me as though I'm trying to sell him double-glazing or something.** ❞

James Allen

Timing Is Everything

"The thing about Martin is, he's always had great timing in his broadcasting career. I don't think necessarily he had great timing in his racing career, but in his broadcasting career his timing has always been spot on. So that was the right moment to get involved with ITV, because it was a new thing, you know, we were going to do Formula 1 in a very different way from how the BBC had done it: significant resources, significant people, dedicated programmes - not part of Grandstand or anything like that. We were going to take the helmet off the sport; that's what we were going to do. And who better to be your guide through all of that from a driver's eye point of view, than Martin Brundle who still thought like a racing driver because in his mind he still was a racing driver."

"The F1 ITV team, anchored by Jim Rosenthal." (Sutton Motorsport Images)

Louise Goodman

Cutting Edge

"He's not just bright, he's sharp – there's a difference."

"I never miss an opportunity to jump back in a Formula 1 car. In fact, I go to a lot of trouble to create opportunities."
(Andrew Parr)

❝ Ran out of space, ran out of grip, and finally ran out of talent. ❞

Mark Blundell

Why So Good?

"For the same reason that he's a good racing driver: he puts the work in. As much as he might not want people to think that there's a lot going on, there is a huge amount going on. He does his research, does his due diligence. He makes sure he's got the facts right. He's an intelligent guy. He has a huge network, a good contact base and uses them at the right time and he sources information he requires. He's held in high esteem, he's articulate, comes across very well. People can relate to him. I don't think there's anybody else in our business of motorsport currently that could hold a candle to him. I'm biased but, in the role that he has, I don't think there's anyone that could match him."

BRITISH VIDEO ASSOCIATION
Gold Retail Performance Award
for Universal Pictures presented to
Martin Brundle
to mark sales in excess of £500,000
for **MARTIN BRUNDLE'S "SUPER CARS"**
DVD & VHS
2003

Louise Goodman

One-Upmanship

"I remember when Martin first started working in the TV side of things. Suddenly, if you were doing television work, it meant you weren't a racing driver any more, and I know a lot of drivers struggled with that concept. I think Martin embraced a new adventure, but he still had that racing driver psychology of not wanting another racing driver to get one over on him. So I can remember specifically him going to interview Michael Schumacher and I thought, 'Well, I'll go in and listen in on that one because it will be quite interesting.' So Martin got there and got everything set up; no sign of Michael. Martin said, 'Well I'm not sitting here waiting around for him.' So Martin left and then Michael came down out of the motorhome. I think Martin probably commented that, 'He was probably sitting in his motorhome watching me waiting'. So Martin disappeared off and then, of course, Michael came down. No sign of Martin. 'Well, let me know when Martin's back.' So neither one wanted to be seen to be subservient is how most of us would look at it. That's a racing driver's psyche, isn't it?"

"An interesting comparison - the Ferrari and Benetton about a decade apart, both owned by my friend Paul Osborne."
(Andrew Parr)

James Allen

I've Got A Plan

"I remember one grid walk at Silverstone. Damon was about seventh on the grid and Martin goes up to him and said, on air, 'Right, it's OK Damon, I've got it all worked out. You get round the inside of Fisichella, you come up the right hand side of Wurtz, then you nail such-and-such into the Copse, down the Hanger Straight, duh-duh-duh-duh, nail Hakkinen into Stowe and then you should be in the lead by the end of the first lap.' And Damon said, 'Do you fancy swapping overalls and you can go and do it for me!'"

"The F1 ITV team looking sharp." (ITV Sport)

"It is always good to interact with the fans at the Autosport Show." (Sutton Motorsport Images)

" You've got to take a view of the whole GP weekend and remember that it's Sunday afternoon when the prizes are handed out. "

Ross Brawn

Relations With Michael

"I think the difficulty for Michael is that when you're part of the team, there's kind of a bond. So he and Martin worked together, they were part of the team. I think obviously in Martin's professional [broadcasting] career, he had to take a more objective view of how he thought drivers were behaving, and how he thought drivers were performing. I think Michael was sometimes sensitive to the fact that he felt, having been part of the team with Martin, that it might have perhaps given him some special privileges, which I think Martin, in his role as commentator, didn't necessarily agree with. And Martin was pretty objective about occasions during Michael's career and that caused a touch of friction. I think towards the end they got on very well, in the latter part of Michael's career. Michael mellowed somewhat and saw things from a slightly different perspective and was much less sensitive to criticism than he was earlier in his career, so didn't take it quite so personally. And I think Michael and Martin actually ended up with a very good relationship."

"Win Percy was one of my first driving heroes and we remain friends to this day." (Philip Porter)

"Trackside at Imola waiting for the opportunity to do a track guide with my blood brother Blundell." (Andrew Parr)

Win Percy

Helping An Old Friend

"Martin's one of the really nice guys that I've met in life and in motorsport. When I was first disabled [in 2003], he was then on the board of the BRDC. He was trying to do his own things as well but he handled all the post for me through the BRDC and he found the solicitors for me. He did everything for me. He's been a genuine friend and I've known him since he was a young boy. I respected his dad in the same way."

Martin Brundle

A Dominant Team Role Paid Dividends

"Michael was plain fast; Mika was just doing his own thing. Those guys had got a psychological advantage because they were so good. I think I did the same in sports car racing because, whenever I went to Le Mans, I was lead driver so I got to develop the car, I got more time in the car. The car was developed around me. I did all the tyre development, so I was the one on the new tyres, I was the one they put out to qualify. And you end up with this huge position of authority and advantage, not because you've been cunning, but because you've just built that around you. Now others who've been through my Jaguar days will say, 'Ah well, Brundle was Walkinshaw's favoured son and he got everything.' Well, Walkinshaw was one tough man and there's one reason why I got the stuff, and that was because I was getting the job done. It was the same at Toyota - I was lead driver. It was the same at Bentley: I ended up in 2001 doing most of the development for that. You get in and deliver, as did the likes of Senna and Schumacher in F1."

Royal Air Force Aerobatic Team
The Red Arrows
3rd June 2005

"I love flying and I have been lucky enough to go up in a number of fighter jets, not least with the Red Arrows."

Alma Brundle

Shy Boy

"The teachers phoned me up one day from school. 'Mrs Brundle I'm so worried about Martin.' And of course I said, 'Why?' And he said, 'He doesn't mix with anybody. He'll stand up near the wall on his own and eat his lunch and then he won't join in.' So they had a problem with trying to get him to mix in with the children at school. And now when I see him I just can't believe it: now, here he is talking to the world."

Sutton Motorsport Images

Martin Brundle

Regent Street

"One of the most extraordinary things I've ever done in a Formula 1 car was the event in Regent Street when we drove the cars up there. Half a million people turned up, they reckon. I've never seen anything like it. The whole thing nearly got called off because there were too many people; the crowd was nearly out of control. I'll never forget coming round the corner of Liberty's and having to squeeze the F1 Jaguar past a policeman's boots as he was leaning in, trying to stop the crowd falling onto the track. There'd have been a riot if they'd called it off. I met people afterwards as we were leaving and also people wrote to me, they even sent me soundtracks. There were people who never got close enough to actually see a Formula 1 car, only hear it, but they still loved it."

❝ **Welcome to Nightmare on Pit Straight.** ❞

"Interviewing DC before he came over to work with us in TV." (Andrew Parr)

Ross Brawn

Wide Angle Lens

"I think Martin's strength is he's been able to look at it from the right perspective. Not just the perspective of a racing driver. Because racing drivers do live in a goldfish bowl in a way. Their perspective is - they put on their helmet and all they see is what's out the slot at the front. Where Martin has succeeded, in my view, is he's kept a much broader perspective than that. He's been able to bring the racing driver's view, and all that experience he has as a racing driver comes through, but he's been able to step back and put a better perspective on everything that's going on. He has not carried any prejudices through into his new career from his old career, and that's sometimes an issue with racing drivers that become commentators. I think the way Martin is able to present what is sometimes a very complex topic is very entertaining. He's one of the world champions of commentary."

"Of all the things I have done and achieved, the grid walk has become my trademark." (Sutton Motorsport Images)

"The grid walk is the only time I get nervous doing television, because it's such a challenge." (Sutton Motorsport Images)

Maurice Hamilton

The Ghost Of Drivers Past

"I'm not surprised he's been brilliant because over the years it's been my pleasure to do quite a bit of work with him. I ghosted a column for him in *Autosport*, when he was a commentator working with Murray, and I would come from the BBC Radio 5 Live commentary box, wait for him to come out, stick a tape [recorder] under his nose, make him talk about the race and then I would ghost his column.

"We did a book together and I have to say, I've ghosted work for many, many drivers over the years: I've done columns, going way back, for Jody Scheckter and John Watson and books with Eddie Irvine, Damon Hill, Eddie Jordan, Linford Christie... Of all the people, Martin is the easiest to work with if you're ghosting something. Normally, you need to sit down and re-write it in their voice. With Martin I could just take it as he said it and put it down: I didn't have to do anything with it. It just sped on. When we did the book together, you could literally put it on the page verbatim, more or less. You'd move it around a little bit but not a lot. With some you had to completely reconstruct it and write it again in their voice. But he would just be eloquent and to the point. So, when he became a successful commentator, it didn't surprise me at all."

❝ Raikkonen wrestling the wheel like he was having a fight with an octopus. ❞

Brundle junior follows in father's footsteps

> **" It makes you about as welcome as a toothache if you run over your own mechanics. "**

"I have very much enjoyed watching Alex develop as a racing driver, even if it's been worrying and expensive."

"Brundle drives a Super Aguri Honda, but only for TV." (Sutton Motorsport Images)

James Allen

All Seeing, All Hearing

"I remember one of the guys from Mercedes came up to us, and he'd watched one of our broadcasts, and he said, 'I hadn't realised you worked like that; you're actually calling it as it's happening. The German TV is always reactive to what happens. You guys are like, with the curve as it's actually going through.' And that's because of Martin's speed of thought as much as anything else. He had this amazing ability to spot things, to see tyres going off, to see drivers making a mistake, to hear things, like an engine that was slightly going off or a missed gear. He could hear if a car was missing fifth gear or sixth gear. Amazing person."

"I received an honorary degree from the University of East Anglia, a doctorate no less. I wind up my children by asking them why it took them three years to get a degree when it only took me an afternoon to get a doctorate."

"I scooped a few RTS awards for myself too."

Martin Brundle

Boring Challenge

"We went through some years when Schumacher dominated. We had seasons when you knew it'd be a Ferrari, and you knew it'd be Schumacher. And I have to say, if you can make that exciting, you can do anything. And that was when Murray was particularly brilliant – in those boring years. I think the last boring season we had was 2004 which Schumacher dominated."

❝ Cars do not go forwards very well when they're up in the air. ❞

"We were pretty pleased to win those BAFTAs." (James Allen)

James Allen

Speed Drug

"The commentary is pure improvisation, and that's exciting and stimulating. And if you were a racing driver and you've been used to putting your life on the line, and the adrenaline of 190 miles an hour and all the rest of it, the only thing in TV on this side of the fence that compares with that is the adrenaline of doing a live broadcast, and particularly races like that last one in Brazil in 2008 when you were hanging on by the skin of your teeth to the narrative of what was going on, who was where, what the story was.

"Hamilton needed to finish fifth to win the Championship. Where is he now? Who's in front of him? What tyres are they on? Oh my God, the Toyotas are still on the slick tyres...and it's starting to rain... If Hamilton can catch Glock, he can be the World Champion still... Massa's won the race... There's Glock... Hamilton's passed him, final corner... Oh my God, he's going to win the World Championship...

"A lot of people got that very wrong, commentating on it for different networks, and it was very, very easy to get that wrong. Moments like that are what you do the job for. That is stimulating, reading your way through what is already a fairly opaque sport and safely navigating your way through some very choppy waters. It doesn't come close, I'm sure he would say, to the thrill of driving a Formula 1 car to the limit but, if that isn't available to you any more, then the next best thing is what he's done for the last 17 years."

Louise Goodman

Tedium Of Travelling

"I suppose it helps when you're up at the sharp end of the plane. Martin's always been very good at organising that. He was always quite good at cadging lifts with people in private jets too. He and Mark [Blundell] were like a naughty, mischievous pair of boys, with, I have to say, Mark as the ringleader but Martin trotting along behind with a big smile on his face."

❝ Two weeks ago we had a wet track in Monaco; today we've got a disposable one, it seems. I hate the Mothercare nature of the car park run-off areas. ❞

Lightweight E At Goodwood

"What little racing I do is as a hobby and for the fun and enjoyment of it. Martin's good to share a car with in that respect; he's good to work with. They've been very enjoyable weekends with him at Goodwood. Drives the car very well, of course. He is very happy to fit in with whatever we want to do – who takes the start – we more-or-less toss a coin – there's no preciousness there.

"We were possibly on for a win in '08 but had a silly problem with the pit stop. I started the race that year and, from about lap three, I could feel something rattling around in the footwell – couldn't see it. There was concern that it could, potentially, get stuck behind the throttle pedal or the brake pedal or something. So I carried on driving. I guess that's the owner's prerogative – you weigh up the risks. I certainly wasn't prepared to let Martin get in it and potentially put him at risk. At the pit stop, I said to the guys, 'There's something in the footwell. You need to get it out before Martin goes out.' In fact, it was a broken clutch stop, which they found, but it delayed the pit stop by quite some time and probably cost us the race."

"The early days of sharing a racing car with Alex, which would lead to us driving together at Le Mans."

"In one day at Silverstone, I drove six cars representing the six decades of F1. This is a Tec-Mec Maserati 250F from the '50s."

James Allen

Recognition

"Talk about being recognised with awards - obviously he completely smashed it in broadcasting terms. He won the Royal Television Society Award, God knows how many times. We as a group won quite a few RTS awards for the programmes. He won personally several times and then he and I, and the team, were very proud to win three consecutive BAFTAs in '07, '08 and '09. For the last one, the judges made it very clear in their citation that it was because of the commentary on the Hamilton World Championship on the last lap in a very confusing situation. He personally established a brand on TV through those years, doing something very different and quickly became as good a pundit as there was on broadcasting in the UK on sport."

Martin Brundle

The Awards

"Four team BAFTAS and seven Royal Television Society Awards. Great kudos. But I was very bemused, I was only doing TV because I couldn't race in F1 any more and now I was more highly regarded and rewarded as a commentator. Now I realise, of course, just how lucky I was to join ITVF1, who really moved the F1 coverage forward in a very comprehensive way."

"Driving a Lotus 49 was also part of the six decade feature."

"I raced against Alex in Formula Palmer Audi at Spa. The kids showed little respect."

THE E-type

E-type Club

issue Forty Eight

the monthly magazine of The E-type Club **November 2008**

in this issue

Nearly there: Series II trimming | E-types gather in Ventura, California

" **Yet another opportunity to remind myself that I'm only half as smart as I think I am.** "

Rubens Barrichello

Keep The Day Job

"The one thing that I can say about MB is that he is a very bad singer - ha ha ha - as I discovered with the karaoke in Japan..."

Neil Duncanson

Key Ingredient

"For us, Martin was one of the key reasons ITV F1 became such a success and over the course of our 12 years doing F1 for ITV, we were nominated for BAFTAs eight times and we won it the last three years in a row. He was a big part of that. He was a joy to work with, a complete professional."

Maurice Hamilton

Being Nice Guy Pays Off

"Martin has got huge respect from my colleagues and had huge respect when he was a driver because he was just a good regular guy, always approachable, always good to talk to, you'd always get a good quote from him, he understood where you were coming from, he had no airs or graces and he hasn't changed, I'm very happy to say, in all the time I've known him. He's just a delight to work with."

Grid Walks – Good TV Or A Nuisance?

"I think they're very good and I've always tried to accommodate him for a few moments of pre-race chat. Direct, straight to the point and he makes it look easy. He's one of the best in the world at this, given the tense environment on the grid."

"Interviewing my old team mate, Sir Stirling Moss." (Sutton Motorsport Images)

❝ To imagine coming up to corners at over 200 miles an hour, get in your bath, lay right back and look across at the taps – that's the view a driver's got. ❞

Martin Brundle on …

Lewis Hamilton

"I don't know if he's faster than Senna or not, but I'm pretty sure he's currently the fastest driver on the track and I've been mooching around the side of F1 tracks for a long time now. Takes too many risks, gets involved in too many incidents he shouldn't be involved in, but he's addressed that recently. He needs a bit more Alain Prost in him really. I think he needs to pay more attention to the end goal, but his speed and control is sensational. Lewis is flamboyant in a car, just the way he changes gear, even though they're micro-switches on the end of a paddle, he's just flamboyant. And when Lewis comes into view the car's alive somehow. He dances the car and I love to watch him. He should have been at least a double World Champion by 2012. His victory at Silverstone in 2008, in the pouring rain when he lapped everybody was one of the best victories I've seen since I've been commentating."

"I enjoyed my days at ITV, despite the adverts. I was sad when it ended." (Andrew Parr)

Martin Brundle

ITV Bail Out

"In 2007, I remember being in Perth, between races, when I got a call from Mark Sharman, the head of ITV Sport. He said, 'We're leaving F1.' I said, 'That's bad news, presumably at the end of the contract?' which was about two years away. And he replied, 'No, at the end of this season.'

"In Kuala Lumpur we had to walk into the pits and do our job for the weekend, when *we* were the story. Sharman flew out to see us, because a lot of my colleagues were understandably thinking, 'We'll be unemployed. What are we going to do now? How are we going to pay our mortgages?' And we got this call to arms, saying, 'The right way to handle this is just to put out the best 12 programmes you've ever created.'

"'Right, we get that. So, you're legging it at season end but meanwhile we've got to put out some great programmes?' I think we all pretty much knew we'd be moving on with whatever was coming next. That was a really difficult year for everybody."

Mark Webber

Why So Good?

"It's his ability to be as passionate about the sport now as he was when he was inside the 'boxing ring,' so to speak, and to explain in layman's term what can be a very complex sport. That's brilliant for the enthusiast. Equally, for the more educated observer, Martin has the ability to pick up some valuable and important facts that are taking place in a race."

Martin Brundle

Racing Was Apprenticeship!

"Turns out that my racing career was a fact-finding mission for my TV career! And in a way the TV career's gone better than the racing you could say. Although, if I look in my trophy cabinet, the BAFTAs and the RTSs don't quite cut it with the Formula 1 trophies, the Le Mans winner's trophy, or the World Championship medal."

❝ It's not good to do the fastest lap right near the end of the race. The team haul you in to say, 'Why weren't you going that fast earlier in the Grand Prix?' ❞

Business & BRDC

Having made his first car sale at the age of eight, one could reason that Martin's business career started while he was, literally, still in short trousers. Though he spent much time in the workshop getting his hands dirty and himself very greasy, he also had an eye for the commercial side. Eschewing university for the local technical college, so he could pursue his motorsport, he gained some useful training on a business course. With his father, who was a great character, playing the role of the old-fashioned wheeler-dealer, the business needed someone to understand the more modern concepts of management accounts and controls. Martin's mother had played a crucial role behind the scenes but now their elder son took more and more of the reins, in spite of his tender years.

He turned the business around and, when he became an F1 driver, his brother Robin had reached the age where he could take over the growing empire and keep up the good work. Being especially close, they kept in touch, often daily, wherever Martin was in the world.

Martin has always had a head for business and, although he had several people to assist him in managing his F1 career, he often handled negotiations himself. Thus this was ideal experience for when his good friend, David Coulthard, asked him to be his manager. He did a fine job for DC.

He was also persuaded by another friend, his F1 partner-in-crime Mark Blundell, to set up a company to look after young drivers, which they appropriately named 2MB Sports Management.

In parallel with his many and varied activities, including his flourishing broadcasting career, Martin, who had been a director of the British Racing Drivers' Club for several years, became that august body's Chairman. They were turbulent times with the BRDC fighting to retain the British Grand Prix at Silverstone. Universally acclaimed for his time-consuming role in this thankless task, Martin helped to ensure the BRDC would end up with a long-term GP contract and a world-class facility at the home of British motor racing. This was Martin's way of quietly putting something back into the sport that had given him so much.

"The garage forecourt at Tottenhill. We didn't sell rally cars but you'd never know it from this photograph."

Alma Brundle

A Natural

"Martin went into the business with his dad when he left college. He brought the garage round. The garage was slipping a little bit at that particular time, but then Martin took the reins and got it sorted, brought it back to life. He was very good at doing things like that. Martin could quickly work out, 'Are we going to make a profit on this or not? If we're not, then leave it alone.' - more than his dad could."

Helen Dickson

In The Genes

"Dad was always a very good entrepreneur – he had lots of ideas. Some of them worked, some didn't. But he always gave them a try. My mother and father have always done things before everyone else did – they had a holiday in Japan to visit Kyoto. The idea that people from Norfolk went to Japan was unheard of. We had the first dishwasher – my father always wanted to have the first of everything – microwave, colour TV. My dad was always a go-getter, which we have all inherited really. Martin's business sense is just as good, if not better, as he had the education and did Business Studies at college whereas my father just did it by instinct."

Martin Brundle

Built By Mum & Dad

"Dad had been the old-style car dealer: you had your bank notes in your back pocket, your used-car lot and you knew exactly how you were doing. He didn't need any monthly management accounts, he didn't need anything. There were no such things as MOTs and warranties and all that sort of thing. Trading in the '60s was pure trading, and he loved it, and he was very good at it. People loved him and he was just a born salesman. Wherever he went, he would sell cars. Not because he was chewing people's ears; he just had a gift for selling, my dad.

"Dad was the dealer, but Mum had got her feet on the ground – the power behind the business, no doubt about that. I think if Mum hadn't have been around in those early days, the business would have gone off the rails. Dad was out there so busy selling, he would never have had time to actually run the business as such. And Mum was the solid foundation.

"Then he got a Datsun [Nissan] dealership, which would have been 1971. He wanted British Leyland but they wanted huge amounts of money in advance. Next I remember being with him at the Motor Show at Earl's Court and we were looking around the Toyotas, and he became one of the first Toyota dealers in the country, which was 1973."

"We were very proud of our new Toyota dealership, built from scratch in the late '80s."

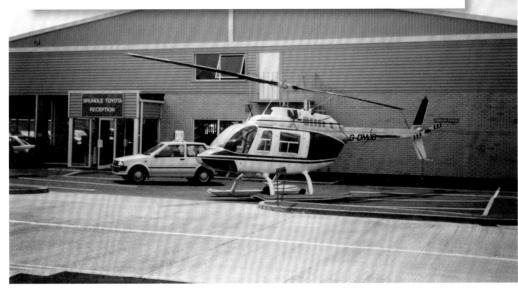

"I was able to drop in to the launch evening. Hopefully, they closed that window before I left."

Martin Brundle

The Reality

"We were doing very well, but cashflow was always an issue. There would be three transporter loads of Toyotas turn up, and a tanker load of Texaco fuel and your heart would sink because you'd think, 'That means in three days' time, when those cheques or direct debits hit the bank account, it's going to be a nightmare.' You had to get the cars turned around. You sold a lot of petrol in those days on account, so the cashflow was a nightmare. I'd spend half the week running around collecting up money for the business basically, arriving at Midland Bank, as it was then, in the centre of King's Lynn on the Tuesday marketplace, with a cheque to pay in at 3.29pm, just before they closed. On really dire days we would swap cheques with the finance company because that bought us three days while they cleared. We never ever bounced a cheque in that business – I've never bounced a cheque in my life - but it was touch and go sometimes. Dad had a driving school, a truck, and an insurance business. Then a mushroom farm. He was a serial entrepreneur and he spread himself a bit thin. His skill was selling cars. I left college at 17 with some fundamental basics in law, economics, accounting, statistics. So I just started applying some of that to the business and quite quickly dad was ready to hand all that over to me. He wanted me to do that, and the staff. The staff were having a riot, really. Some of them were moonlighting. It was a nightmare business and I realised that I didn't want to spend half my week sorting a cash flow crisis."

Martin Brundle

Satisfaction Of Selling

"Dad was still very much around but he was happy for us to do the admin and all the stuff he hated doing. Some years he sold more new Fords than the local Ford dealer. People came to him because they liked doing business with him. He was in the Chamber of Trade, he was in Rotary Club, he was immersed in the local area and he was the go-to man to buy whatever you needed, because people trusted him, and they knew he'd deliver.

"I still get a lot of satisfaction out of selling something to somebody that they need, that's good value, and most importantly that you've made a profit out of. But not just for the sake of making a profit – they've got to be happy, because they've got to come back again. I remember my Dad saying many, many times, 'It takes 20 years to build a good reputation, and one bad deal to lose it.' And I remember he preached that to us, and he was absolutely right. Especially in a rural environment like Norfolk."

Liz Brundle

Succession

"Originally, when we left college, Martin used to run the garage while Robin was still at school, and then by the time Robin came along to run the garage Martin was at a high level of racing. They always worked very closely together as brothers."

Martin Brundle

Travelling Salesman

"I'd speak to Robin every day wherever I was in the world. 'What have we sold? What did we make on that? What are we doing on this?' and that was good. I enjoyed it, and I didn't find it a distraction. I remember Mika Hakkinen once saying to me, 'I never could understand whether you were a racing driver or a businessman.' I can understand his point, but actually I found it very relaxing, very satisfying to hear how the company was doing. You've got to remember, I pretty much lived at the garage through all my young life. And every school holiday I'd be serving petrol or selling and fixing cars."

"TVRs were great cars provided they kept running and didn't leak water." (Sutton Motorsport Images)

"Selling cars was in my blood. I always needed a deal, just as I do today." (Sutton Motorsport Images)

Robin Brundle

Other Priorities

"Marty took the helm with mother and father until he was about 24. When I was 21, we agreed to buy mother and father's shares from them so Marty and I were 50/50 shareholders. But, at that point, his career had taken off and he was into F1. He wasn't really around that much. If he wasn't racing, he'd be working in the race factory with the engineers, doing sponsorship or PR media. We never crossed over."

Robin Brundle

Business Partners

"Marty added so much as he was travelling the world and could bring a global perspective to our national and regional business. He was mixing with the principals of large OEM [original equipment manufacturers] global motor companies so he could see which brands were likely to develop, which ones might struggle going forward and that helped in many ways in the business. He has a very good business brain, a strategic thinker."

B·R·U·N·D·L·E

WITH
COMPLIMENTS

"I chose this design for my stationery, depicting the hand signal to start an F1 engine."

Robin Brundle

Balanced

"He's always been grounded which has made it very easy for the family not to be envious or jealous. We're not that way anyway. But he's never once rubbed in his wealth or status. That's a very important attribute that he has."

"By now Robin was in charge of the businesses and I would drop by to see if we were making any money."

Martin Brundle

Time To Move On

"We'd been Toyota dealers for 35 years. One day a middle manager came down and told us we were terminated because they had a new regional strategy. There was a new thing in the retail world called 'block exemption' – it was a big EU initiative. And so the manufacturers then centralised: like a hub and spokes - big company with satellite dealerships. So we lost Toyota and that was when I started getting a bit fed-up. The manufacturers were drip-feeding you just enough money to survive and sometimes we'd turn over £30m. We had a number of car dealerships, 125 staff, and yet I'd make more in a month doing after-dinner speeches than the garages could. And it just struck me as a remarkably silly business and we decided to sell up in 2007, which I think was very good timing."

"David Coulthard would become an important part of my business life when I managed his career for 11 years." (Painting by Alan Fearnley)

"MELBOURNE VICTORY"

Martin Brundle

DC's Manager But Also Unbiased Critic

"There were one or two provisos. The biggest one for me, being on TV, was commentating - I'm commentating on my client. I realised there was a conflict of interest so I said to him, and this led to DC poking me in the chest on a couple of occasions, 'OK, I'll do that but the deal is if you mess up in a race, I'm going to be saying so. I'm not going to pull any punches.' DC agreed that was fine so long as if I was wrong I'd put it right. That was a given. And actually I think I overdid that. I tried to be too correct about that from time to time, and inevitably DC would get a bit of feedback. I know how sensitive it was with my family when I was a driver. I'm almost completely immune to this situation now. You can say a thousand positive things about a driver or a team, but say one negative thing and... But you never get a word of thanks. Nico Rosberg thanked me once for saying something nice about him. I said, 'Oh, what was that?' And he said, 'I don't know. my Mum told me to thank you.' So even that wasn't really a vote of thanks! That's how it works so get on with it."

"I later joined forces with Mark Blundell to manage young drivers." (Sutton Motorsport Images)

Martin Brundle

Another Job

"I'd to an extent managed myself through a lot of my own career. After Senna's death in May '94, the GPDA [Grand Prix Drivers' Association] met in Monaco which I'd put together with Michael and Gerhard. Then, because I'd done the agenda, and been talking to Michael at length about it, they said, 'Right, you can be Chairman.' So, we re-fired it up with three directors and we all put some money in. It was quite important at the time because it was turmoil with all the accidents.

"DC liked how I handled the next couple of years of that. Towards the end of '97, he asked me if I would manage him. We talked about it at length. On a plane to Tokyo, I agreed a deal to manage his F1 contracts and commercial racing aspects."

David Coulthard

Inside Knowledge

"The main part of the relationship was when he stopped in F1. I identified that I wanted to work with someone from a managerial point of view that knew the paddock, knew the people and our relationship developed to another level from there."

Martin Brundle

Difficult Start

"My very first race as a manager was Melbourne 1998, when DC was forced to yield the victory to Mika Hakkinen. The team said that they'd given Mika some incorrect information on the radio, but if you're not sure what your radio says, you stay out – you don't come in. He came in. I think this instruction to yield, which I still believe to have been unfair, understandably seriously psychologically affected David. It was incredibly negative for him. And so the day after, I'm having a massive shouting match with Ron Dennis. This is my first ever race as a manager and we were both incredibly unhappy with what had happened. It got off on a pretty difficult footing, to say the least. The deal was that Hakkinen would yield the race back to David and it never happened. I managed to get David paid a significant bonus as if he had won that race, and later on in the year to get him paid as if he'd won the World Championship. So I very much did my job in that respect."

Martin Brundle

Good Deal, Good Deal

"Early in 2001, Mika told Ron he was retiring. And Ron obviously wanted to get David tied down. We didn't know Mika was retiring, but it explains why I was able to do a spectacularly good deal. I once tossed a coin with Ron to settle a deal for DC that was an amount of money greater than he paid me as his driver for the whole of 1994! But the reality is you're simply selling your driver's speed, skill and marketability, although there's no list price but all sorts of other 'goodies' you can include, which is the clever part. Ron has the best strategic negotiating brain I have ever encountered."

David Coulthard

Manager And Friend

"I recognised the talent in Martin before he had looked after any driver other than himself and I paid him a salary to do a job. That relationship worked successfully for the remainder of my career and we continue to spend a lot of time together. I believe we talk openly about business opportunities and things that are out there. We've always been swimming in the same business ponds but ticking different boxes in many ways because of the decade or so between us in age, and different opportunities and experiences. Martin, for me, absolutely ticks the box of being professional, whether in motor racing, in broadcasting or in business. You ask him to do something and it is done on time, on budget, with all the due diligence you would expect. That is the perfect business associate and friend because you know exactly what to expect at the time. That's a great, great quality."

"David and I made a strong business partnership as we had different skill sets." (Sutton Motorsport Images)

Martin Brundle

Post-McLaren

"At the end of 2004 McLaren didn't renew David's contract and we were looking at what to do next. Was he going to join another lesser F1 team or retire? Was he going to go to Indycar? First of all, Jaguar were talking to him. Niki [Lauda] had been pressing me like crazy for a couple of years to sign David for Jaguar. 'It is going to be great at Jaguar,' he said. So, I initially replied, 'Look, Niki, my guy's in his early 30s. I want jam today, not jam tomorrow. McLaren gives us jam today.' 'You've got to get him out of there. Ron will finish him.' Typical Niki sort of thing. And I'm replying, 'No, Niki, I'm not interested.'

"Inevitably, what they next do is get hold of your client, and go, 'Hey, David, Brundle's screwing it all up for you.' Luckily David was mature enough to come and talk to me about it. Post McLaren I remember sitting in DC's apartment in Monaco for a whole day once, doing the pros and cons of joining Red Bull which the Jaguar team had just become. We've got David Coulthard stepping out of a McLaren, Jaguar had been a mess and it was being taken over by a drinks company. What should we do? I like to sit and make a long list of pros and cons. Well, the cons at that time looked significantly bigger than the pros. Then we both agreed - very much led by DC, I have to say - 'Let's just do it and see what happens.' The rest is history. DC became a Red Bull driver. Red Bull became much more serious and credible - not in the beginning, but three or four years in - than anyone had ever imagined. Unfortunately, by the time they really got it together, David had retired, but it must never be underestimated what a key role he played in assembling significant ingredients in a team which would come to dominate."

Martin Brundle

BRDC Board

"John Fitzpatrick came to me in '96 and asked if I would join the Board. I think it was another one of those things that helped ease me out of Formula 1 actually as it sent a signal out that I was considering things outside F1. I was a bit surprised to be asked because I had always been seen as a Walkinshaw man and there'd been a coup and they'd booted Walkinshaw off the BRDC Board. Tom had tried to execute a business plan which, frankly, was totally inappropriate. They were quite exciting times but it was initially more about trying to decide which red wine should be on the menu than business. The relatively cheap F1 contract ensured an annual profit. So, it was meeting in the morning, nice lunch and go home. To fast forward, my last board meetings in 2003, when I was Chairman, lasted nine hours with sandwiches on the go and fire-fighting all sorts of dramas."

"Would you buy a driver off these two men?" (Sutton Motorsport Images)

Mark Blundell

A New Business

"Martin was Chairman of the BRDC and I was on the Board and we sat on the remuneration committee for funding young drivers. We decided to set up a management company to see if we could look after other young drivers. Martin already had experience of management with DC, and that's where it came from. Martin was more in the background and I fronted it. We built it over a three-year period and at that point I got to the stage where I wanted to move into other areas of sport and Martin had got to the grand old age of 50 and decided that he wanted to focus on his TV career and Alex's career. So I purchased his shares and went on to grow it a little more. But the founders are still buddies and have their names over the door: the 2MBs – a bit cheesy but everyone knows it."

"With young chargers, Mike Conway and Will Stevens, along with PJ Rashidi from Alpinestars." (Sutton Motorsport Images)

Martin Brundle

Work Mates

"It was really Mark running the business out of his offices. I did it because Mark's probably my closest friend through all of this and he was saying, 'Let's do this together.' And I came up with the name 2MB. But if I'm honest, my heart wasn't in it because I was getting busier and busier on the TV, I had DC's business, had my own son coming along and the BRDC years. I just got to a point where I had to get things out of my life, because it was just manic. I would be sitting there doing long hours every day sorting out piles of legal contracts, big deals and issues. And I realised all I was doing was worrying about everyone else's problems, whether it was the lads in the management company, whether it was DC or Silverstone. As soon as DC stopped racing, I cut him a deal with the BBC. I also helped him negotiate a deal with Red Bull, Mercedes, and many others - it was my leaving present to DC because I thoroughly enjoyed representing him and I learned a lot from him.

"I ought to have been more ruthless because I should still be earning something out of all of those contracts, but that's not the relationship we had. I'm delighted that we have become even stronger friends after that commercial relationship, which doesn't often happen.

"I just wanted to get rid of everything basically. The garages probably got caught up in that. I just got to the point where it was, 'No, it's not right. I've had enough of this. This is not life as I want to lead it.' So I just basically cut loose on everything. I decided to help my son Alex's motorsport career and focus my managerial skills on myself."

The British Racing Drivers' Club
BULLETIN

Volume 17 No 2   March/April 1996

Sir Jackie Stewart

President & Chairman

"Our time together grew as the years passed, particularly in the BRDC when he was Chairman and I was President. That was when I got to know him much, much better. And Ken [Tyrrell] was a good supporter of his. It was Ken that pushed me into becoming President, as Ken was then President, and he said, 'I want Martin to be Chairman,' and I said, 'That sounds fine to me.' And it was only then that I got to know Martin very well. We did a lot together at the BRDC."

Martin Brundle

Off & On Grand Prix

"Then Bernie sold Brands Hatch the F1 contract. We knew that they hadn't got enough land area to run a Grand Prix. So they'd got a Grand Prix and no venue, and we'd got a venue but no Grand Prix. And it's all going off the rails, getting messy and fractured. We had 800 members all wanting to run the Club, all with different ideas, and it started getting very smelly and personal. I was talking to Denys Rohan, who was the Chief Exec, and we came up with the idea of creating a small group to go and attack this situation, because the whole future of Silverstone was in peril now. We were soaking up a lot of cash, the Grand Prix contract had gone and we needed to invest in the circuit. I went to the GP at Magny Cours that evening and asked Frank Williams and Ron Dennis if they'd help. So then we had this four-man Working Group empowered by the Board to find a solution, and then we started to make some ground. And Ron was absolutely brilliant: from his tactical mind, I learned a huge amount through that time.

"All of a sudden it's not about choosing wines; it's about heavy, heavy business. We helped torpedo the Brands Hatch planning - it was never going to work there anyway. At this point Nicola Foulston, who owned Brands and other circuits at that specific moment, started a road show visiting all the BRDC members to convince them to sell their 'share' in Silverstone. Along with others I had very strong views that members are lucky guardians of Silverstone, not owners. Meanwhile Nicola had sold to an American conglomerate who'd bought the tracks and now they had to do a deal with us. That involved leasing everything at Silverstone. It was a quarter of a billion dollar deal and hugely lucrative for us with no downside risk. We had all of the safety nets in place, we kept all of the facilities for the members and we got a £40m Master Plan fund to do up the place. Some £27m of the money was spent on car parks and the dual carriageway. So when I drive into Silverstone now, and I see all those impressive tarmac car parks and dual carriageways, I have a great sense of satisfaction because I was fundamentally part of making those happen, along with keeping the British GP alive."

"It was a lot of blood, sweat and tears at the BRDC but I learned a great deal and am totally satisfied with what I achieved."

NEW BRDC DIRECTOR

Martin Brundle has been co-opted on to the BRDC Board after the retirement of Peter Gaydon who, as reported in the last Bulletin, has taken up the full time position as BRDC Race Director.

Martin is the first active Grand Prix driver to join the Board for many years and as the most experienced current Formula One driver will be of valuable assistance in advising on circuit and safety matters.

In accordance with the Articles of Association of the Club, Martin will stand down and offer himself for re-election at the AGM.

Martin Brundle

Exit Plans

"Some time later, Interpublic, the organisation behind all this wanted out, and Bernie cut a deal with them to exit the British GP contract, such that they didn't have to pay the last £13 million of the Master Plan. The new pit and paddock complex was going to be created in 2003 and the diggers were literally ticking over, ready to go, and it never happened, much to my chagrin. It still annoys me to this day. There would have been new pits and paddock where the old pits were, not where the new ones are now. But they wanted out. So then we had to unravel it and we ended up with it all back. The safety nets I had so carefully crafted in the original lease deal meant we got our business back in highly-improved condition along with a significant exit cheque. And we had a new Grand Prix contract.

"So it was fractious; it was vitriolic; it was unfriendly in the extreme in some respects; fascinating, educational and rewarding for me. It cost me a lot of money because, while I was busy with Silverstone business four days a week, I wasn't doing other things and I was turning down PR jobs. It cost me personally at least a million pounds of lost revenue. But I got to the end of it and, when I look back at those nine years on the Board, three years as Chairman, I'm massively satisfied with what we achieved at that time. It particularly helped when Jackie became BRDC President in the early stages of the whole process."

"Half my life is spent holding a microphone, and the other is being interviewed." (BRDC)

On The Right Track

"He's done good stuff for the BRDC, definitely. He was one of the movers when we really needed somebody there and he was there in a very influential period."

Barrie Williams

Down To Earth

"Martin was always approachable and he has a memory - he doesn't forget his past, he doesn't forget his old chums. I was a BRDC main board director for 15 years and I think Martin was the best Chairman we ever had. You could ring him up; you could talk to him. He always seemed to have a logical answer to everything without upsetting anybody. He was terribly conversant with everything, always seemed to be able to say the right thing at the right time and there was always common sense in whatever he said."

Liz Brundle

Unsung Hero

"Martin's never one for seeking out praise for himself. He'd rather be, 'I've done it, and I know I've done it, and I've done it for me and for other people. I don't need to be given all the praise.' But sometimes it's necessary, because otherwise people don't know what you've done. Yes, he did a lot at Silverstone, hours and hours, and it cost him a lot of money, which he didn't mind. He was prepared to do it and he's put his bit in. He felt he wanted to give something back, which was good. But I don't think people know much about it."

Murray Walker

Critical Role

"Martin always says, 'I'm a car dealer, Murray. I'm a car dealer.' And he's used to dealing with people; he gets on with people very well. So, when he was a driver, part of his stock in trade which made him as successful as he has been, was his ability to get on with people. And his ability to do a deal. Something that a lot of people don't know, or forget, is that Martin was Chairman of the British Racing Drivers' Club. Now Martin is never, ever looking for things to do - he's a very busy bloke, he's got a very full diary, he's extremely active, but he took on the job of Chairman of the BRDC, which at the time was not split down the middle - it was split in every direction you can possibly imagine.

"Bernie is the man who cracks the whip regarding where the British Grand Prix is held. Jackie Stewart, who did not get on well with Bernie Ecclestone, and Martin succeeded in keeping the BRDC afloat, repairing at least some of the divisions, and doing a lot to enable Silverstone still to have the British Grand Prix. Now I'm not saying that Martin did it all, but I don't think that the BRDC would be what it is now, and I suspect that Silverstone might not have the British Grand Prix, but for Martin Brundle. And that's a very, very important consideration, and a very big feather in his cap."

"Cutting the ribbon on new roads, car parks and other facilities at Silverstone. A simple ending to a hugely complex task." (Sutton Motorsport Images)

"The F1 drivers came along to witness Murray receiving his BRDC Gold Medal." (BRDC)

Martin Whitmarsh

Deserves Greater Recognition

"Martin's commitment to the sport is very clear. He's not someone about whom you would naturally use the adjective 'passionate', as he doesn't exhibit it in a Latin style, but he's clearly passionate about it. As to his stint for the BRDC, he's smart enough and experienced enough to know that those sorts of roles are giving something back and, if you do it with an expectation of gratitude, you're likely to be very disappointed. He certainly didn't get the gratitude nor does anyone. I am a member of BRDC but, by observation, those people involved over the last 20 years have given so much time and energy and effort, and it largely goes unappreciated by the majority of people in the sport."

Derek Warwick

Respect

"There was a mutual respect between us that was pretty special. When I was going to make the decision whether to be President, one of the first people I called was Martin. I knew that he'd served his time very well on the board. He's somebody that was hard-working, focused, very intelligent and had a great ability in putting his views across at the same time as listening to others."

"In 2012, Alex and I received the Woolf Barnato Trophy for our Silverstone and Le Mans exploits." (BRDC)

Johnny Herbert

The Right Experience

"It's always good when you've got ex-racing drivers involved and Martin was one of the more modern drivers who was there. And he has the business background with the car dealerships and the BRDC is a business to keep Silverstone there. It's been up and down over the years, with Bernie, but at that point he had a fairly good relationship with him. The input was very good and Martin was very good for the BRDC."

Sir Jackie Stewart

Challenges

"Very positive. Martin is a very straight-thinker and a good thinker and he can see outside the box. Some people can be quite clever but stay within the box, and then not really develop. The Club Martin's developed very well which is, of course, proven by his commentary skills. The Club was just developing away from [being] a totally members' club to something that had to handle the finances of hosting a Grand Prix with the new high cost that that represented. We both struggled to see how that could be affordable for a private members' club. We are still, probably, the only private business in the world that hosts and finds the money to have a Grand Prix. So these were difficult times. Martin left before I did but he did his stint there and he did it well. I was very happy to have him with me."

BBC & Sky
2009 ...

In late 2008 another bombshell exploded. ITV lost the F1 coverage and it returned to the BBC. The new broom did not wish to retain James Allen but effectively had no choice but to engage M. Brundle. Not only was he supremely good at his job, but the BBC would have caused a massive public outcry had they not done so.

Jonathan Legard took on the main commentary role for 2009 and 2010. The duo worked well and, as pundits, DC joined EJ (Eddie Jordan). Ted Kravitz and Lee McKenzie were in the pit lane and paddock, and Jake Humphrey excelled in the main presenter role.

After two years, Legard moved back to radio and Martin found himself as the lead commentator with DC in the box alongside him. As with everything he takes on, Brundle did a superb job and the two old friends worked well together. But nothing lasts and the powers that be at the BBC decided that a good way of saving money was to hand F1 to their rivals at Sky. Sky could not believe their luck and embraced the opportunity wholeheartedly. Of course, first and foremost, they wanted the man who had taken over from Murray Walker as the voice of Formula One.

However, Martin had a dilemma. Sky is only available on subscription as opposed to the BBC being free-to-air. By leaving the BBC, who were going to continue to show half of the GPs live and edited highlights for the remainder, he would be out of reach to some of his loyal fans. On the other hand, Sky were going to create a dedicated F1 channel with far more scope and greater airtime. How could the voice of F1 not be part of all this? It was, in the end, a no-brainer but Martin suffered some hurtful publicity nonetheless.

Sky raised the bar considerably and were clearly dedicated to offering the best possible F1 coverage. Martin continued to be an integral part of that, informing and explaining, amusing and entertaining in his very own style.

"Jenson is one of my go-to guys on the grid - he has always been so generous." (Sutton Motorsport Images)

Martin Brundle

British Broadcasting Corporation

"So then I joined the BBC. It was nice that they wanted me. On my way down to do the deal at the BBC with Niall Sloane, I got run into and almost knocked off my motorbike by a woman steaming out of a T-junction. The BBC took the template of ITVF1 and added some further value to it, all without the adverts, of course. I found it a slightly strange environment to be honest, but I have great respect for the BBC for the quality and breadth of the programming that they put out.

"DC and I had had a bit of a heavy night out and then sat in the first production meeting feeling a bit secondhand. Somebody senior said, 'We're going to get this done, despite everything.' And David and I looked at each other, thinking, 'Did he say what I think he just said? Niall, along with Mark Wilkin, put a strong team together, positioning Jake Humphrey as a very impressive new anchor man, and putting Eddie Jordan, Ted Kravitz and Lee McKenzie in the mix too. But before we ever had our first meeting, Niall moved to become head of ITV Sport. So, the man who put us together was no longer there, which was a pity."

David Coulthard

A New Role

"I worked with him with the BBC and he helped me a great deal. And I think he is naturally gifted when it comes to all that. I don't know how he compares to other broadcasters and I'm not sure that you can really do any comparison across sports and all that sort of thing, it's just the fact that he knows F1 motor racing intimately, he is an enthusiast and he's got a nice way with words. Bring all that together and I think it works well for the viewers."

Martin Brundle

Nationalised Industry

"Where the BBC are very clever is using their multi-media platforms, TV and radio, their website, and the news channels. Sky do the same thing too. They used their on screen 'talent' well and they created the red button programme for after the race. But I struggled to fully engage with the management at the BBC, which is unusual in my career."

"Fernando is not always keen to talk on the grid but well worth waiting for."
(Sutton Motorsport Images)

"The BBC introduced the Forum concept which was very popular. We could chat at length with the likes of Hakkinen and Villeneuve."
(Sutton Motorsport Images)

Keith Sutton

Friend Drops In

"When we were both approaching the big 5-0, I wanted to celebrate and I had a big party in June, in a marquee on the lawn at home. I invited Martin but he said he was very busy at the Grand Prix with all the TV stuff. However, he came to me later on and said that he would love to come, was there anywhere to land the helicopter? That was fantastic; you can imagine my kids and all their mates seeing Martin Brundle land in his helicopter. I live five miles from the track [Silverstone]. He enjoyed himself so much that he stayed the night and then, the next morning, flew back to Silverstone. It takes about one minute by helicopter."

Martin Whitmarsh

Walk On The Wild Side

"I probably shouldn't advertise the fact but the only races I'll ever watch are the ones that we've won – there have been a few of those. But what I'd say is that Martin has all the professionalism, all that discipline in his process, but the grid walk is a break from that and Martin is able to bring quick-witted irreverence to that. Is it a nuisance or is it good TV? I've seen enough to know that Martin stars more in that role than probably he does from the commentary box where he has a much more professional, anodyne style. He comes alive when he does the grid walk. It has, for a number of years, been one of the star features of the coverage of Grands Prix on British television."

Liz Brundle

Husband and Father

"Martin is a great husband to me, and father to Charlie and Alex. Despite being so busy with his racing, commentating and other business commitments, he has always been there for us. He was often away when the children were young but still tried to arrange his life to go to school events, etc., to support them. Since they have been older, he has guided them very well in their pursuits whether work-related or otherwise, giving them advice but also letting them find their own way. He is a gifted person with a great sense of humour. I am very lucky to have him."

"More BBC Forum chat with Jake, DC and Eddie. It could seem a very long day by the end of this show." (Andrew Parr)

"Shared a Lamborghini at Hockenheim with a very young Alex, netting two fourth places."

Robin Brundle

Demeanour

"He can be as serious as you like and he's very politically correct as well, but he can be the life and soul of the party – in a nice way."

James Allen

Relative Values

"He and I have talked a lot about family and children. I've got two boys of my own and I certainly took some cues from him on the way he conducted himself with his children. He's a really very, very good father and I think that shows another side to his character. He's still very close to his brother; he takes great care of his mother. That whole family thing is a big part of why he's such a grounded individual. A very, very good family is just such an important thing in life."

"This A35 is a hoot to drive at Goodwood. The only problem is you sit on the floor and it is not easy to see out of."

Martin Brundle

Murray's Advice

"I said, 'Give me one piece of advice, Murray' when I was becoming lead commentator at the BBC. He said, 'Remember you're there to entertain,' and he's absolutely right. And I'd add 'inform' to that as well."

❝ It's all turned to custard for D'Ambrosio. Thank goodness I got that one out of the way! ❞

Ross Brawn

Mutual Trust

"Sometimes I seek his opinion on things that he could use in his professional career that would breach our trust, but Martin's completely trustworthy. And I've never had any doubt that if I want Martin's opinion - because I still value his opinion on situations professionally within racing - then I know it's between him and me. It's a very important thing for me to know I can trust Martin in that way."

❝ We're in lap 28 of 70 of this race that should be finished by ... Wednesday at this rate. ❞

Martin Brundle

Lead Role

"I liked my expert witness role as co-commentator, my bite-sized pieces of information as if I was behind the wheel. At the time BBC decided they were going to make a change from Jonathan [Legard], but they were undecided as to what they wanted to do. I said to DC one morning, 'If I was to move over to lead comm, would you come up into the commentary box?' He said, 'Yes, I'll try that.' We did a rehearsal in a tiny little room at TV Centre, and it went really well. So they decided to go that way. And I was very happy with it. I won't say I found it quite as naturally easy. If you suddenly said to me, 'There's a race in five minutes, get in the commentary box and talk for two hours,' I could do that, but I had to work harder at being lead comm, especially as I was still doing the grid walk and many other technical features."

"I also took time out of TV work to race against legends such as Johnny Herbert, Derek Bell and Mark Blundell."
(Volkswagen)

Martin Brundle

Light Relief

"I'll never forget taking a quick leak on the way up to the commentary box in Monaco, having come off the grid walk, and they're counting down in my ears. I'm still in the toilet, and I was hearing a 30-second countdown to going live on air. The toilet's right near the commentary box, and I walked in, cans on, pick up the microphone and say, 'Good afternoon everybody, welcome to Monaco,' and it was pretty crazy to say the least. But I did enjoy it and the experience helps my overall TV skills. Then we had the now slightly legendary Canadian Grand Prix. The race was four hours and four minutes with, I think, two and a bit hours of red flag. And DC and I filled for an hour and a half of that and we get a lot of plaudits. And overall, I really enjoyed it. I enjoyed working with DC up there - we had a laugh. We just had fun basically."

Martin Brundle on ...

Jenson Button

"I just love watching him drive. I think he's an artist at the wheel: just the sublime way he controls the pedals and the steering wheel, but it then limits him a little bit, because if the car's not quite right ... he's not so good at driving around problems. He's got a feel for the grip in wet/dry conditions and a confidence - he's got a finesse and a touch that's just pretty special. Obviously when he had a very strong car, he won the Championship. I still think there's another championship in him."

"I just can't kick the racing bug. This is Daytona 24 2011, sharing with Blundell, Zak Brown and Mark Patterson." (Sutton Motorsport Images)

"The Mike Shank car ran perfectly and we finished fourth." (Sutton Motorsport Images)

David Coulthard

Commentating Together

"For me, working with Martin in the commentary box felt right – it felt like I was talking to a buddy about motor racing. The only thing that was alien about that whole process is that you are not having a conversation with your mate down the pub but maybe to somebody who has turned on the TV, expecting to see Dancing on Ice. They see an F1 car and say, 'OK, let's find out what this F1 is'. So you're there to try and educate the new people. You're not there to tell the expert that that's a Ferrari and Fernando Alonso is really fast. But for someone who has never watched F1 before, you need to tell them that that is a Ferrari and Fernando Alonso is regarded as one of the fastest and they have a things called KERS - you say a lot of things as if you were talking to your children, in a fathering, educational way which can appear condescending to the expert fans, of which there are many out there. But you're there to facilitate to the masses, not the minorities. I have absolute trust in Martin and I think we had some good banter between us because we felt comfortable in each other's presence."

"The first victory together for Alex and me, in Radicals at Ascari in Spain. Alex needs to work on his Champagne technique." (Oliver Read)

Murray Walker

Lead Commentator

"I didn't think Martin was as good at commentary as he is at the grid walk and the track stuff that he does with other drivers, and the pundit-in-the-box role, and nor did Martin. It's not just me saying that. When Jonathan Legard lost the commentary job, I understand there was a lot of talk about who was going to take his place and Martin probably volunteered to have a go and got accepted, but he's told me that he didn't feel as comfortable doing commentary as he did doing the other things. Which is not to say that he wasn't doing it very well."

"I am very pensive under the floodlights of Daytona." (Sutton Motorsport Images)

> **If you turned in there like that in the cars of a few years ago, you'd go straight to hospital.**

Martin Brundle

BBC Bombshell

"Then we had a bombshell. I got a call at midnight on the Thursday night of the Hungarian Grand Prix, 2011: 'We're going to announce in the morning that we're stepping out of Formula 1 at the end of the year in terms of covering all the races live.'"

Martin Brundle

BBC Bail Out

"I was really angry, too angry actually. So we had this 8am meeting at the circuit in Hungary, to be told that the BBC had cut a deal with Sky. It was very painful. As a team we were doing a good job – the ratings were stratospheric and it just had a good feeling about it. Everybody in vision, all the creative talent behind the scenes, everything was just working out a treat. And somebody had lobbed a hand grenade into the middle of it, while we were at a race track, without any heads-up.

"Not for the first time we all wander over the old metal bridge into the paddock, and we are the story again. And we didn't know what to say as we had no real understanding of what was going on. I went to see Bernie, once I'd calmed down a little, to gain further understanding. He had continually sent people into BBCF1. I remember Niki Lauda coming in one day and some other guys from Austrian and German TV, saying, 'Bernie's told us to come and see what you do, because he tells us the BBC are so much better than everybody else.' And this would have been right up to the time when it got the heave-ho. Eventually I said, 'So what do you want me to do then, Bernie?' At the end of the day, he's the circus-master. Most winters I go and have a lunch with Bernie. I wouldn't pretend I'm close to him at all - we just like to talk F1, and F1 television. He hesitated. Then he said, 'You should go to Sky,' which I thought was interesting."

"At 52 years old, I was nervous about my fitness for Daytona but it was no problem." (Sutton Motorsport Images)

Martin Brundle

Decision Time

"I learned a lot at the BBC and I liked aspects of what they do. I thought long and hard for months before deciding to join Sky. That was probably the most difficult time of my professional career. I've only really ever had support - if I was having a tough time in motorsport I'd clear off and do sports cars and my mates in the media would politely ignore me. Or if I had a good time, they'd pump me up. And the fans had followed me as a racing driver, followed me through the Jaguar years. I had a very good following building around the world as a commentator. I'd walk through any airport, any street, and people would come up and say, 'Can I shake your hand? I love what you do.' All of a sudden, when I joined Sky, it turned quite brutal with a small element, on things like Twitter, websites and blogs.

"It was a very uncomfortable three or four months that winter [2011/2012] when I took the decision because it was inevitably painted that I was earning a huge amount more money, which was absolutely wrong. I was earning more money but it wasn't anything like what I was reading in the press. So you get painted as being greedy, and, 'Oh, you just leave, you forget your fans, and you just walk away from us to line your pockets. How much money do you need?' I expected a bit of this, but not with the vitriol that was coming through. Some very unpleasant things. But that's all completely and utterly faded away now. It's gone because I made the point that, if there was going to be a dedicated Formula 1 channel on TV in Great Britain, I wanted to be on it. That's what I do. That's my speciality; that's what I do best. And I liked what Sky were promising me; I liked the way they were going to go about it. And I had to stand back and face the facts about where the media is heading in the future. And I immediately gelled with the top guys at Sky. It's been one of the best decisions of my career."

"It is always fun to talk to Flavio. I have forgiven him for firing me!" (Sutton Motorsport Images)

Adrian Newey

Revived For Revival

"I remember the Goodwood Revival Ball on the Saturday night. It is always a bit of a conundrum for a driver who is competing on the Sunday – you want to let your hair down and enjoy yourself but you know you can't be up too late and you don't want to be having too many drinks. Martin arrived, saying, 'I am going to be professional, and disciplined,' and so on and so forth. At one o'clock in the morning, he was still going..! And enjoying the evening. So, it was good to see he can let his hair down."

Martin Brundle on …

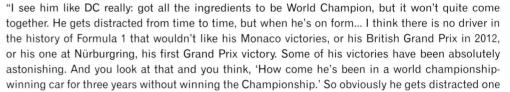

Mark Webber

"I see him like DC really: got all the ingredients to be World Champion, but it won't quite come together. He gets distracted from time to time, but when he's on form... I think there is no driver in the history of Formula 1 that wouldn't like his Monaco victories, or his British Grand Prix in 2012, or his one at Nürburgring, his first Grand Prix victory. Some of his victories have been absolutely astonishing. And you look at that and you think, 'How come he's been in a world championship-winning car for three years without winning the Championship.' So obviously he gets distracted one way or another mentally, but when he's on form I think he's as good as anybody, absolutely anybody."

David Coulthard

Sense Of Humour

"I've helped with that. He was boring when I first knew him!"

"This is a classic BBC F1 shot: Eddie's wild shirt and the three of us wondering exactly what he is going to say next." (Sutton Motorsport Images)

Martin Turner

We Want The Best

"When we rather surprisingly, and it was a surprise, got the offer of the rights for Formula 1, it did come out of the blue. It wasn't something we'd been chasing. The BBC approached us because they wanted to make some savings. The first thing we thought about, of course, once I'd been given the job to front up our coverage, was, 'Who's your front-of-house, who's your talent,' whether it be commentary or presentation. Now clearly in sport there are very few iconic commentators but the ones there are, are really held in very, very high esteem: Dan Maskell, Brian Moore, David Coleman... Sometimes they're lead commentators; sometimes they're experts.

"Now Martin was the pre-eminent voice and personality in sports broadcasting, certainly in terms of Formula 1, but a major figure in broadcasting over the last 15 years. So it was a no-brainer really: you go for the best. He was, and is, the best and so we were delighted that he said yes to us. He was our first target and our biggest target, and it was almost like we couldn't have started without him. He was the first person I spoke to and the one I put the most effort into."

Martin Brundle

Blue Sky Thinking

"It all began to get very difficult at BBC, because the hand grenade had gone into the middle of it, and some of the production people were heading off. Nobody knew where they stood really. It was a little bit of 'everybody for themselves' at that point. So your team spirit that you'd built up over three years – out of the window. Then I got talking to Barney Francis and Martin Turner at Sky, and they began to tell me the things they were going to do, and how they were going to do it, and I just found it a breath of fresh air. They talked straightforwardly. They were empowered to do a deal and they talked my language – they were business people. And TV people. And it was like, 'Here's the deal, here's the situation, here's how we're going to do it. Here's what we think the challenges are, here's the solutions. We've got this idea, we've got that idea. We want you to front it for us. We will promote you, we will support you.'

"They made me a raft of offers and promises, all of which they've fulfilled, and it is not often you can say that in life. It still took me a long time to make the decision. I'd be at home talking to Liz about it, I'd talk to my family, I talked to some journalists. We always have a media dinner – well, a couple of nights actually – in Monza, Hotel de la Ville, two or three mates and I'm like, 'Right guys, I'm going to tell you some things that are off the record. I'll tell you in confidence, here's the situation, what do you think I should do?' I spoke to Theo Paphitis, I spoke to Chris Evans. I spoke to a number of people who were in the TV business that I trusted, and who were in the F1 business that I trusted, including of course Murray Walker. And I took the decision to go to Sky. And I'm very pleased I did."

> **❝ Looks like somebody had an Airfix kit for Christmas and lost the instructions. ❞**

Martin Turner

Expert Again

"When he came to join us at Sky, I was clear that whilst I respected him greatly as a lead commentator, I wanted him to come and join us as the expert, and as the front man, that is the face of our coverage. I said, 'Look, this means going back to what you were doing before, but the reason is, if you're a lead commentator, you're just not going to have the energy also to be an expert, to rush out of the commentary booth and come down to us and be an expert. In vision, you'll be absolutely shattered. So I felt that, and I also felt that there was more room for him to express himself as the expert commentator, even though it's a partnership and a conversation. I felt that there was a lot more opportunity for him as an expert. I wanted to create a new partnership and working with David Croft, I felt, was the way we would do that. I thought they would get on particularly well. When they came in and did their first practice commentary with us, it was like they'd never been apart, but they'd never commentated together before. Normally, commentary teams take a long time to build, to form a partnership. The fact that he could do both roles, lead commentator and expert so successfully, is virtually unprecedented."

"Gearing up for yet another stint at the Daytona 24 Hours." (Sutton Motorsport Images)

"Another victory with Alex, this time in Radicals at Brands Hatch." (Oliver Read)

" Those kerbs are so high they're going to have snow on them in the winter. "

"I have been on the podium at Goodwood in both of these magnificent cars - Adrian Newey's Lightweight E-type and Nick Mason's 250 GTO." (Philip Porter)

Adrenaline Junkies

"Sportsmen, after they give up their sport, have a unique characteristic and that's insight. Now insight's all very well, but the key element is being able to translate that to an audience, to be able to speak to an audience and not only put them in the driver's seat, in this case, but be able to explain the emotions, the challenges to some extent, and make the viewer or listener feel like he understands. Insight is an oft-used term and some people feel that anyone who has been a sportsman can offer that insight. They have it, but whether they can communicate it is a different matter. That's something that Martin does in spades, and what he does particularly well is he conveys not only his interest in driving and his interest in drivers, but an interest in the public as well. It's all very well doing it for yourself or doing it for your peers, but he's got a real interest in getting that across.

"From my own experience, when I haven't understood something and I've asked him about it, he hasn't raised his eyes to the heavens to say, 'Oh God, why don't you understand what I'm talking about?' He's really keen to tell me what it is and to share that. And that passion to share your own experiences is something I've seen in a lot of great sportsmen who have gone into the media – they want to share the buzz and in some way get the public to enjoy it more. I think in our environment, and I think that's one of the major reasons we see certain sportsmen go into TV and media, but particularly television is, it's one of the few mediums that replicates their life. It's not sport: they're not racing round the track and risking their lives, but they are on air, they are live, there is that buzz that's it's about to start, and when the lights go out and the race starts, that's when they start and many of the things that happen on track and happen in sport, are happening in commentary - they're living…"

"A last piece of advice from Murray before thrashing the life out of this £25m car." (Philip Porter)

"The first thing that strikes you when you race a 250 GTO is that you are the crash structure." (Philip Porter)

David Croft

TV Networking

"We formed a partnership, a good partnership, very quickly. We seem to be on each other's wavelength. He has boundless energy and enthusiasm for what we do and, though he is about 10 years older than me, he sometimes has more energy than me, especially when doing a grid walk. I think that is one of the best bits of TV that you'll ever get to watch. It's just one man very much at home in his environment.

"Who do you know who could stand on a grid in Monaco and go to talk to whoever, and then get harangued by Jools Holland and Eric Clapton because he wasn't talking to them! There's not many people on this planet who would get hassle off Eric Clapton because he's talking to somebody else. I think it's funny how people do respond. You look at Jenson Button's interviews with Martin when they start tweaking each other's nipples and stuff - on TV. That's 10 minutes before JB is going to step into a car and go and win a Grand Prix. That's a brilliant bit of TV."

❝ Button's been as sharp as a sushi knife all year with overtaking. ❞

Jools Holland

Sheer Music

"What I really like is the clear and concise way he expresses himself. He has this vast breadth of knowledge. As we say in the music business, 'Some people have the shirt and some have the knowledge.' I know myself, just from doing track days, the enormity of his achievements, not just in Grand Prix racing but also at Le Mans. He has this great wealth of knowledge and experience and yet the genius of it is the way he puts it over to the public with great lightness."

Mark Hales
Martin Brundle

Martin Turner

Avoiding Fences

"Is it challenging? I think any live television is challenging because you don't get a second chance. Everything you say is taken as a commentator, and when you're in vision likewise, you're asked a question you're expected to be pithy, funny, erudite and most of all to have an opinion. I think that's one of the things he does very well, and it's often said that the worst experts are the ones that sit on the fence and that's the great thing about Martin. He will always consider his point, but he's very rarely to be found on the fence."

David Croft

Pub Chatter

"As the season [2012] went on, there was more interplay between the pair of us and more relaxed gag-cracking and joking around a little bit. You need that warmth coming through. When the lights go out, we're so focused on what's going on. It's great; I love it. We get paid to stand, as mates, and talk to people, every other Sunday during the season. I get the feeling that if we weren't doing that, we'd probably go down the pub and stand at the end of the bar and do exactly the same thing."

"With our own F1 channel, it's a huge amount of work at Sky F1 but it's very rewarding that we still have time to have great fun amongst friends." (Sky Sports)

David Croft

Hard Luck

"The thing about Martin as well is that we should never forget that, as good a broadcaster as he is, he was a bloody good driver as well. It's big shame that people think he's more successful as a broadcaster than he was as a driver. He could have beaten Senna in the British F3 Championship and should have done and, had he been a bit more ruthless, would have done. If he had taken Senna out like Prost and Senna used to do to each other, he would have been the Champion. That's the mark of the man, Martin is very hard and determined, knows what he wants and knows how to go and get it. But he's not the sort of person to trample on you in the process. If he doesn't respect you, that's because you're not living up to how he thinks the job should be done but if you do live up to how he thinks the job should be done, or put that effort in, he will always respect that. And I don't think he'd ever go over the line and crap on people from a great height because that's not the man he is – he's actually quite a softie at heart, but he wouldn't want you to know that."

❝ It's only lap seven and I'm out of breath already! ❞

"I may look unhappy but I'm without doubt planning my opening lines for the grid walk." (Sutton Motorsport Images)

Martin Brundle on ...

Fernando Alonso

"For me, the most complete driver on the track today. Admire his determination, admire his positive mental attitude, his never-say-die approach to it. And how he carries the car, how he so badly craves the podium. I love to watch him in a car. He's fast, he's got everything. A driver's driver."

"Our anchor man, Simon Lazenby, has quickly taken to Formula 1. I once did the anchor role for ITV in Fuji but never again." (Sutton Motorsport Images)

James Allen

Solid Roots

"There are people, and I won't name any names, but there are people in Formula 1 who famously have completely, deliberately forgotten their origins and forgotten their background and where they come from. And they just focus on the money and the power and the glamour and that sort of stuff. But he's definitely not one of them."

"Thankfully Christian Horner is always a willing participant despite being out-numbered as we are all eager to ask the next question." (Sutton Motorsport Images)

Adrian Newey

Uploading, Downloading

"We share information in both directions and have off-the-record chats that we just respect are confidential. As far as I know, in all cases, it has remained so."

Robin Brundle

What Not Good At?

"He's not a great cook and he's not very good at rounders. When we get together in the summertime, with our daughters and wives, one of the games we'll play is rounders and he's really not very good because he nearly lost his feet and his ability to run is not good. So he's rubbish at rounders. I'm still fairly mobile and active so there's usually a queue of people wanting to be on my team rather than his team. We play snooker every couple of years and are probably equally rubbish at it."

Martin Brundle

The Risks In Perspective

"I've kind of got the view, and it might be a bit blasé, especially as I've got a son who races, but the last death we had in F1 was Ayrton Senna [in '94]. And how many people die riding at a point-to-point? Or get a broken neck in rugby scrum? Or die in some kind of aviation? On a bicycle? Yes, motor sport is dangerous, and yes it does hurt when you hit things hard, but I've always had the view that people die down the pit, or on an oil rig, and they still do, and they don't get paid millions and applauded all the way round the world. Not that a lot of drivers get paid millions these days."

Martin Brundle

For The Defence

"Actually, I'm famous for my BBQ steak. They travel for miles around for my birthday BBQ! But it's true about the rounders."

Nigel Roebuck

Quote Unquote

"I think Martin has evolved into a brilliant sports commentator. I think he's a superb analyst. I always thought James Hunt was. I think Martin gets it just right. We have a ritual: we always have lunch just before Christmas and talk through the year past and I always write the piece up and he always rings me afterwards and says, 'God, did I really say that?' 'Yes, you know damn well you did.' 'Actually, I should be more like that in my commentary. I read your piece every year and think, "Why don't I say things like that more often?" I think he is quite outspoken sometimes - maybe not as much as James, but perhaps nobody ever will be!"

Louise Goodman

In Creases

"I don't mean this to sound patronizing, but he's always struck me as being a boy from Norfolk who's still excited at the way his life has developed. He's never lost that thrill, that appreciation. He was a lot more the boy from Norfolk when I first knew him. I remember having a debate in the office about who was going to tell Martin that he really shouldn't be ironing creases into his jeans any more – it really wasn't a good look. EJ [Eddie Jordan] was saying, 'Well, you've got to fookin' tell him, you're the press officer.' And I was saying, 'No! You're a man! I can't discuss Martin's clothing with him. You're the one who's into the clothes, you tell him that you don't like the jeans that he's wearing.' To say he is now a 'sophisticated man of the world' sounds a bit trite, but he's maintained that appreciation of the fact that he's a very lucky bloke and he's seen a lot more than he possibly ever thought he would do when he was a 10-year-old growing up in Norfolk. He hasn't become cynical."

"Sky have created many interesting ways to tell the F1 story and engage the fans." (Sky Sports)

❝ It takes a special effort to get into that gravel trap. ❞

Liz Brundle

Left - "I am pretty sure I have the best job in the world." (Andrew Parr)

Ability To Describe In Simple Terms

"It's funny really because he can sometimes be quite frustrating to talk to at home! He doesn't always listen properly or finish a sentence because his mind is distracted by something else. The children and I often say we only end up with half the story, and he replies, 'Yes, but I get awards for being able to explain things to people, so it must be you!' And we think, 'No, it's not! It's you!'"

Martin Turner

Ever The Competitor

"I remember when we were doing the 'buzz game', which is a hand-to-eye co-ordination competition which involves taking a circle around the track and not touching the sides, he immediately, unbeknownst to anyone, turned the machine off, proceeded to whizz all the way around the track without setting off any buzzers only to be caught just before the end by one of our presenters saying, 'Oy, you've turned it off!' He responded, 'No-one said we couldn't turn it off!' He quite seriously wanted to win, so he was prepared to use any means to win."

"One of the absolute highlights of my racing career has been sharing a Le Mans car with my son Alex." (Nissan)

Martin Turner

As A Colleague

"I would imagine like many Formula 1 drivers: very picky, wants to get down to the detail, wants to get everything right, wants to extract every tenth... To stretch the analogy to breaking point, he wants to wring every tenth out of this particular motor car. From a personal level, he wants to make sure that he comes across as well as he can. He's a perfectionist, but he's a real team player. He wants us all to do our best; he's a great sharer of information; he's not a hoarder. Sometimes you find with experts, they don't want to share because they want the knowledge to themselves so that they look the cleverest. But he's very generous in that regard. He knows that he probably has a hotline to a darn sight more behind-the-scenes info than most of the rest of us, and he's very generous with sharing that, and [that's] vital for our journalistic presentation team, rather than our experts like Hill and Herbert."

Dave Redding

Keeping In Touch

"He's kept his eye in racing himself but also because he's well-liked. I talk to him regularly as do other people so he gets an update on the hot topics, on how the tyres are performing this year – not on-the-record interviews but a chat over a coffee that helps him piece the puzzle together. If he gets three or four of us saying the same thing, he'll use it as a credible thing to say about tyres, development parts, or strategy for the weekend, or whatever. He's kept in contact, he's a friendly and amenable guy and people trust him. It's testament to him because he's kept in contact. If people say, 'Don't mention this', then he won't."

❝ I'm in danger of having to talk to the tarmac to get a decent interview out of anyone. ❞

"Father-son moments don't get much better than this. I was pleasantly surprised how much speed I still had."
(Nissan)

"With this impromptu ducking, it wrecked my iPhone and £15,000 worth of broadcasting equipment." (Sutton Motorsport Images)

Nigel Roebuck

One Hundred Per Cent

"The great irony for me is that, as Martin says, for the last 10 or 12 years of his life, he has been stopped more times in the street that when he was a mere Grand Prix driver. I think Martin is one of those people who will confront a situation he's in and just say – right, I'm going to make the best of it. There are plenty of drivers who have done a bit of commentary when they've stopped driving and given the impression that really it's a bit beneath them and that they don't really want to be doing it but Martin, having taken the decision to do it, absolutely embraced it. If you talk to Niki [Lauda] about Martin as a commentator, he will say that there's no-one like him, in any country. Considering Niki has been doing that job himself for German TV for so long – Martin is just a very easy bloke to admire."

> ❝ Been there, done that, crashed the car. ❞

Sir Stirling Moss

An Admirer

"Never afraid to push in - very important really. I think, because of that, he is respected by other reporters as well. He's cut himself a really good niche. We watch Sky."

Martin Turner

The Superstar!

"In general, the feedback has been great across the channel and as our major star and our major front man, he gets a lot of the credit for that. I think it was obviously a major factor in why a lot of people turn to us to watch Formula 1 and he was our biggest signing. He's like the Ronaldo of Formula 1 broadcasting; in fact he's like the Ronaldo of sports broadcasting."

"Comparing notes before going into battle at Le Mans." (Nissan)

Martin Brundle

Man & Boy

"Sharing a car with my son at Le Mans was one of the highlights of my driving career. As always, Liz and Charlie played an important supporting role through a tough week. Handing the car over to Alex in the middle of the night and sending him off at 220mph was both rewarding and alarming to say the least. I was emotional when I crossed the line at the finish. He was only 21 but he drove beautifully, day and night, wet and dry."

"I can't remember what made us laugh so much but overall it was a very happy experience."
(Nissan)

❝ The stopwatch never lies. ❞

Alex Brundle

Driving Together At Le Mans

"Fantastic! We didn't get the result that we wanted, and we're very competitive like that. We wanted to deliver. But we talked about it afterwards of course. We both felt like we performed the best we could, and gave our utmost. Mechanical failures caught us out in the end but we got the car to the finish. The experience is something that I'm trying to build on, obviously, with my current racing ambitions and conquests."

Martin Brundle on ...

Sebastian Vettel

"Old head on young shoulders. I'm pretty convinced the peak is between 28 and 34. And if anything that's lengthening because of mental and physical preparation, and the fact the cars are so much safer now. You don't get broken bits, so you don't start carrying lots of injuries. I think that's the crossover point between youth and experience. He's 25 [2013] and got three World Championships under his belt - I think he'll just get better and better in terms of his race-craft, his qualifying, his car setting up, how to get the best out of a team and all that. I sincerely hope that he's a multiple champion with not too many dark sides although, in the end, we love a flawed champion however much people moan."

Martin Brundle

Goodwood Lightweight E

"Adrian Newey's E-type is glorious: we had a comedy pit-stop in 2008, otherwise we should have won it the first time I drove it. Then I drove it again 2012. Adrian spun off and then drove brilliantly and frankly I just had to bring it home after that. We pretty much dominated that race."

"Winning a paddock quiz with a man who has become very used to winning." (Sutton Motorsport Images)

“ How he didn't slam that in the barriers is ... pure luck, I would imagine. ”

"Life can be tough making TV for F1." (Chris Lobina)

Adrian Newey

Goodwood Victory

"To win the TT Celebration race at the Goodwood Revival meeting with him in 2012 was really good. I managed to make a bit of a hash of the first lap but was roughly back to where we needed to be by the time of the pit stop. From there, it was a relatively straightforward race."

"Adrian Newey is a brilliant designer and a thoroughly good man. It was a pleasure to win at Goodwood with him."

"I think I am warming up my shoulders before, literally, putting the Austin A35 on." (Philip Porter)

❝ If he didn't have a crash helmet on, he'd be scratching his head. ❞

Murray Walker

Great Father

"There's another aspect of Martin that I have always admired and respected, and that's Martin Brundle as a father and a husband. Because he has always had an extremely active life, an extremely demanding life, but he's brought up a fine son in Alex, and I don't think Martin will have pressured his son to go motor racing. I imagine Alex is doing it of his own volition because, like me, he wants to be like his father. And Martin is going about it all in exactly the right way and he's not being a pushy dad like so many that I've seen in motorsport where the child doesn't really want to do it and the father is trying to live through the son, something that he wanted to be. Well Martin has been that someone, and Alex is getting all the right sort of opportunities and Martin is able to help open doors for him. It's going to be down to Alex in the end because it's down to the chap behind the steering wheel with his foot on the accelerator in the end analysis, but Alex is lucky to have a chap like Martin as his father."

Alex Brundle

Why Racing?

"Very much because I want to. In fact, I pushed him into it. In the early phases, I very much drove it. I was nine when I began karting and your parents have to be as dedicated as you, there's absolutely no doubt about that. And as I've grown, I've become more and more passionate, and understood that it's a lifestyle and that it is something that I want to do to define my life, rather than just a hobby alongside school or whatever. This came from the experiences that I'd had myself through my childhood years and then, as I've become older, it's grown into passion for the sport."

Liz Brundle

Hearing The Passion

"I love to see Martin's face when he's driving a racing car. He did a Ferrari piece last year and in his voice you can hear how much he loves it. I so enjoy watching him. We went out to Jerez together last year [2012] where he was making a tyre feature for television with Pirelli. He was going to drive some laps on different tyres and in different conditions. At the end of filming he said 'Oh, have I got to get out now? Can I do a few more laps?' When he climbs out he's so full of it, and that's what comes across on the TV – his passion for driving. People latch on to it and absorb his enthusiasm."

Lord March

Revival Star

"It has been great having Martin driving at the Revival and he has put in some fantastic performances in all sorts of cars. He is always near the front and is one of the most thrilling and exciting drivers to watch. His ability to pick up any car and ring its neck is extraordinary."

"Rae Davis owns the baby Austin - he is quite a character." (Philip Porter)

Sir Jackie Stewart

Commentating Skills

"He's very analytical in his observations. He verbalises those very well and makes it easily understandable not just for the aficionado petrolhead or anorak but the uncles and aunts who are more mature and maybe aren't core motor racing fans. I think Martin's commentary has developed very well where he brings humour into it as well. I think the combination of he and David Coulthard was very good. I remember working the odd time with Murray Walker and even the odd time with Raymond Baxter. These things are necessary for you to see how other people work and Martin has seen all of that and listened well and paid attention and today he does it with great skill."

❝ Tragically, it tells you that the car is every bit as important as the driver, which we try to hide from time to time! ❞

"My Sky co-commentator David Croft took me for a night out at the darts. That was a whole new experience."
(David Croft)

Martin Brundle

Like Father, Like Daughter

"Charlie has had to put up with me being away a great deal as she grew up and sitting around at a race track with a lot of focus on her brother. Her solution was to pick up a pit board and a stop watch and be one of his biggest supporters while building a great career for herself in car design, plus numerous other activities and challenges. She takes too much on!"

"A montage I commissioned when I thought I had finished racing. Thankfully, numerous Le Mans cars and suchlike are missing." (Painting by N. Newnham)

Mike Greasley

Too Cerebral

"A very talented chap. Probably too much of a thinker for a racing driver if that makes sense."

James Allen

The Prof

"If you look at the boys from that era, they were the last generation of drivers who actually got hurt in Formula 1 cars. And it's never to be forgotten just how bloody dangerous it was because those turbo cars he was driving in the '80s were very dangerous. It was good that he - not that there was any doubt that he would - came to Prof Watkins's Memorial Service. His was absolutely the generation that, when they woke up from an accident, they weren't sure if the first face they would see would be God or Sid. And Sid did a great deal to change the lot of racing drivers and those guys were at the forefront of that, and it was disappointing that, as far as I could see, Martin was the only one of his generation that turned up."

Sir Stirling Moss

Why So Good?

"I think because he has the courage to go and ask people questions. He'll fight to get a mic in with other people. He's very knowledgeable about things that the public wouldn't necessarily know about – the tyres and so on. He certainly learned a lot in his racing career and he does a tremendous job."

"The grid has now become packed with media imitating our grid walk but we still find a gap somewhere."
(Sutton Motorsport Images)

Murray Walker

The Patriot

"So many Formula 1 drivers float off to Monaco or somewhere like that where it's tax-free. Martin, like Graham Hill, is a decent, honest Englishman and is proud of it, and is prepared to pay the taxes and continue to live where he's always lived, in King's Lynn, and I take my hat off to him for that."

Alex Brundle

Family Pride

"The whole family are very proud of him. And [I am] increasingly proud and respectful as I grow older and I understand more the challenges of trying to achieve what he managed to achieve in his time and the competition that he faced. As always, when you're looking at something from the outside, it appears easier. A comment that my girlfriend made to me the other day: 'Why don't you just drive faster?' springs to mind. You never truly understand the fraught struggle of trying to perform as a professional racing driver until you've really tried to achieve it."

❝ It's a long way down to Turn One – over the hills and far away – but it's very exciting when you get there. ❞

"I've known Eddie Jordan for 30 years and we've had a few ups and downs in that time."
(Andrew Parr)

The Raceaholic!

"Martin is one of those rare breeds or talents which is able to cross categories – sports cars, F1, touring cars... He has at various points raced all of them to a competitive, successful level. I think it's a fairly rare breed of racing driver that is able to multi-task like that – others are specialists in each particular discipline. Martin today, at 50 something, would still talk as if... you give him a Red Bull, he would go and have a good go at it. My personality is that I'm 42, I wasn't quick enough at 38 when I stopped and I ain't getting any quicker as I get older. The last thing I would ever pretend or presume is that I could go out on the race-track today and be competitive. I believe Martin would give it a go. He's such a committed racer. Give him an opportunity and he would take it."

Jonathan Palmer

Special Relationship

"Our friendship has even survived our sons Jolyon and Alex racing against each other in three championships that MSV [Motor Sport Vision] was involved in - T Cars, FPA and F2! Ultimately, after knowing each other for 30 years, we both have a great deal of respect for each other and what we've achieved professionally. We're also very close friends who trust each other totally. And that's a very special quality."

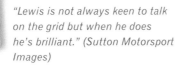

"Lewis is not always keen to talk on the grid but when he does he's brilliant." (Sutton Motorsport Images)

Martin Brundle

One Wise Man

"I don't do anything in my F1 television life, if it's a key decision, without first speaking to Murray. Like the Sky move, for example, which I was tormenting myself over for about three months. And Murray was one of the key people to - not talk me into - but recommend going to Sky. He's just a very solid man."

"I am, and always will be, a complete petrolhead." (Abigail Humphries)

Mark Webber

Not Bad For A Pom

"Martin has always been a pretty level-headed sort of guy and has never got above his station. In terms of English commentary about our sport which is ever changing, he's arguably one of the very best we've had. He was massively underrated as a F1 driver; he should have had race wins but never found himself in the right car at the right time."

Henry Pearman

Martin & E-type Jaguars

"In 2003, I helped Martin with the acquisition of his original Mosport Jaguar XJR-6 but it was not until there was the opportunity to acquire this car from him that we finally made 'proper' contact, and I was blown away at just how approachable and friendly he is. He said he had followed my company Eagle for a long time and told me of his exploits as a schoolboy, driving the E-types around the family's garage premises in Norfolk after school. I suggested he drop by when he had time. He did just that in 2009, just ahead of the start of the GP season, purely for a social visit, but left as the new owner of a lovely, low mileage red V12 E-type roadster.

"He very kindly attended Salon Privé for us that same year, for the public début of the first Eagle Speedster and we then took part together in the E-type 50th anniversary run to Geneva, with Martin and Liz in their V12.

"Martin has always loved the E-type Coupé and it was an honour to supply him with a fully-restored example. I delivered it to Silverstone where he was sharing driving in the WEC race with son Alex. The plan was then for Martin to drive from Norfolk to Spa for the GP and then on to Monza for the next round, all with Liz. He was initially concerned at such a long first trip for a freshly-restored car, but I assured him it would be fine and he enjoyed a fantastic trouble-free trip, even taking an Alpine scenic detour en route."

"Nearly half a century after being dropped off at school in an E-type, I am the proud owner of an Eagle 4.2 Coupe."
(Abigail Humphries)

Derek Warwick

Top Class

"Although Martin didn't win a Grand Prix, I still put him up there amongst the best of British racing drivers and the world's racing drivers. It's just that he didn't have the opportunities."

Ross Brawn

The Compleat Commentator

"It's frustrating to me that Martin never enjoyed more success at Formula 1 because I think he deserved it and I think he should certainly have won a race, and it would have been lovely for him to have that under his belt. But, since then, he's more than made up for that and it's great to see him with such a successful career outside the car. And I think he's a very complete person: good family life, but also happy to enjoy himself with the boys. And I think one of the secrets of his success with the commentary side is that everybody in Formula 1 respects him, and is comfortable with him. He's able to get a picture. I can't think of anyone in Formula 1 who has any issue with Martin. He's been able to achieve that, but still be pretty forceful in his opinion of what's going on out on the track. So it's kind of Murray-ish in a way, but in a different area. Murray was a sort of supercharged enthusiast; Martin for me is a very well-informed and experienced specialist. But also brings enthusiasm and entertainment to the commentary."

"We are always looking for new ways to do a track guide. This time it is with Paul di Resta and cycling legend Sir Chris Hoy." (Sutton Motorsport Images)

" All that dry ice looks like a dodgy nightclub, doesn't it? "

"Even F1 stars who don't come on the grid are not safe from my microphone, like Ferrari team principal Stefano Domenicali." (Sutton Motorsport Images)

Rubens Barrichello

Knowledge And Passion

"I rate MB as a commentator very highly … in fact I love to watch the races with his voice. He knows what he is talking about. Plus he has emotion when he talks which makes us spectators feel very close to him."

Sir Jackie Stewart

Well Rounded

"His social skills are very good. He mixes with people well, whatever level in life they are, and that's important. That's why I think he's been successful in television. People wouldn't see that skill as being so very important but it is. He's enjoyed by a great variety of folks and that's always a good indicator. He's been able to mix comfortably with all walks of life."

Sir Stirling Moss

Appreciation

"We all owe him a tremendous debt of gratitude for what he's doing now – he does it bloody well."

Philip Porter

Jenson Button

The Last Word

"Martin not being on the grid would just feel odd now - you always know you're going to see him, usually nudging out one of the crews from overseas! He's been there and done it, so knows what we're going through before a race so has a great way of just getting what he, and the viewers back home, want to hear but never interfering with our preparation."

"This was one of my tougher assignments: handling the podium in Malaysia in 2013, after the famous Red Bull multi-21 team orders saga. In fact, none of the three drivers were happy to be up there for differing reasons." (Sutton Motorsport Images)

Murray Walker

Top Bloke

"I have the greatest admiration and respect for Martin - as a person and as a professional at whatever he decides he's going to turn his hand to. He is an extremely nice person; it was always a joy to work with him. He's just altogether a top bloke, as far as I'm concerned."

Martin Brundle

Do You Consider Driving An Art?

"Yes, I do. I think you're dancing with the car, you're at one with this machine, and when you get it right, it's very satisfying. Which is why I love driving the current F1 cars because they're so utterly good at what they do. They're so brilliant in that they're just like an extension of your mind and your body. You spend all your life trying to make a racing car perfect and then you jump in a current F1 car and it feels perfect. It's not, of course, when you put it absolutely on the limit."